# Shakespea[re]
# The Director's Cut

Michael Bogdanov is a theatre director of international repute. He has directed Shakespeare in many of the world's leading theatres and with major theatre companies including the Royal Shakespeare Company. He was Associate Director of the Royal National Theatre for eight years and he co-founded the English Shakespeare Company in 1986 with actor Michael Pennington. He was also Chief Executive of the Deutsches Schauspielhaus (National Theatre) in Hamburg, 1989–1992. He has won numerous awards at home and abroad including the Society of West End Theatres (SWET) Best Director for his production of *The Taming of the Shrew* (RSC) and the Laurence Olivier Award for Best Director for his seven-play history cycle *The Wars of the Roses* (ESC). He lives in Cardiff and Hamburg.

Capercaillie Books

# Shakespeare
# The Director's Cut

essays on Shakespeare's plays

Michael Bogdanov

Capercaillie Books

CAPERCAILLIE BOOKS LIMITED

The essays on *Hamlet, Romeo and Juliet, The Tempest, The Merchant of Venice, The Winter's Tale, The Taming of The Shrew, Macbeth*, and *King Lear* were first published by Capercaillie Books Limited in 2003. The essays on the Histories were first published by Capercaillie Books Limited in 2005.

This revised edition with four new essays is published by Capercaillie Books Limited, Registered Office, 1 Rutland Court, Edinburgh EH3 8EY in 2013.

© Michael Bogdanov

The moral rights of the author have been asserted.

Printed by Antony Rowe, Chippenham

Set in Galliard by 3btype.com, Edinburgh

A catalogue record of this book is available from the British Library

ISBN 978-1-909305-31-1

To Bill Wallis, Chris Dyer
and Michael Pennington
with whom I explored many of these ideas.

# Contents

# Tragedies
and
Comedies

# Introduction

I have a particularly strong affection for Leicester. It is the city where I first made a breakthrough in my thinking on Shakespeare. First with a lavish production of *Romeo and Juliet* at the newly opened Haymarket Theatre, and then at the Phoenix Theatre with what we called the '£94 Hamlet' – that sum being all we had to spend on the physical elements of the production. Scaffolding and wear your own clothes.

That production I did of *Romeo and Juliet* in 1974 had Jonathan Kent as Romeo, Alan Rickman as Paris, Mary Rutherford as Juliet and Bill Wallis as Mercutio. It was, for me, a seminal experience. In rehearsal the story had been coming over hard, clear and very exciting. Adrian Vaux had designed a very interesting modern steel structure for the set, and the costumes were uncompromisingly Renaissance.

When the production moved from the rehearsal room and arrived on to the stage, somehow the clarity and the hardness, the linear quality of the story, had gone. What was more, audiences weren't responding either to the production or the play. At the last moment, after the very final preview, I cut the whole of the end scene, where the Friar recaps the story for the benefit of Escalus and, after the death of Juliet, I switched to a press conference around the unveiling of the two gold statues that Capulet and Montague erect to the memory of each other's child.

Rock music built to a crescendo during a blackout and, when the lights came up, the entire company was assembled in modern dress in front of Romeo and Juliet, now dressed in gold cloaks and masks standing on the erstwhile tomb. Musak played. 'Fly Me to the Moon' . . . Escalus, the Duke, read the prologue as an epilogue from a cue card, as if inaugurating an unveiling ceremony. 'I hereby name this ship' . . . The main protagonists were photographed in front of the statues, shaking hands, the Nurse holding up a rope ladder, Escalus attempting to bring about the familial reconciliation with a three-way hand clasp. Jimmy Carter's smile of the time as he handed over the presidency to Reagan.

The transformation had an extraordinary effect. People in the audience shouted, people walked out, people cheered, people bravoed, people booed, and I thought 'For three hours they have been bored out of their minds and suddenly something has challenged them. A moment of real theatre.' It was an anarchic stroke and it turned the whole evening around in a most remarkable way. More importantly, it served to emphasise that I was going up the wrong path in attempting to ape what I thought was a traditional way of performing Shakespeare. There are many directors in many parts of the globe who are able to tell a Shakespeare story with tremendous power and clarity without having to go to the lengths that I have described, but that is how I discovered a way to tell the stories. By removing the barriers that exist between the language and the audience, by allowing them to identify with the characters clearly, by associating the events with contemporary politics, I allowed the plays to breathe. (I received more letters of complaint from apoplectic Colonels for my production of *The Taming of the Shrew* at the RSC than I ever did for *The Romans in Britain*).

The battle for modern dress has long been won. There were famous Barry Jackson and Tyrone Guthrie productions in the 1920s and 30s. In fact a critic recently applauded an Elizabethan dress production as a refreshing change. The argument has moved on to gender bending. All male – cos that's how Will did it; all female – cos that strikes a blow for equality; and role reversal – a white Patrick Stewart playing Othello in Washington with an all-black cast. I have no problem with any of this; theatre is the suspension of disbelief. But if, as in the case of all-male Shakespeare, it is in the name of experiencing the plays as they would have been performed in 1600, then I have a huge quarrel. It is impossible for us to receive the plays in any other form than a twenty-first-century appreciation of what is in front of us. All-male Shakespeare is just not our bag. So the only question that has to be answered is whether the plays themselves make sense textually, politically. . . . Claudius is still Claudius, Bolingbroke is still Bolingbroke, and Katherine is still the victim of a male wish-fulfilment dream of revenge, no matter what gender or mode of dress. No post-Burton/Taylor chauvinist romp will suffice, even when all parts are female.

*Hamlet* in 1975 was my first of five essays into the politics of the play. On the evidence of the gravediggers, Hamlet is thirty. Gertrude says he is 'fat and scant of breath'. The role was played for me in Leicester by the small, amply rotund figure of Bill Wallis. The play – and Hamlet's problem – opened up in a completely different way from that of the tall, thin, pale, haggard, meditative young prince of popular and traditional view. It posed a lot of awkward questions that the text had to answer. And it taught me an important lesson. That directing a Shakespeare play is like reading a detective story, piecing the clues together one by one, never taking anything for granted, ignoring received opinion – the narrative is of paramount importance. Also it taught me to look for those hidden moments, easily overlooked, that told the real story, moments that Stephan Greenblatt calls 'Invisible Bullets' (*Political Shakespeare,* ed. Jonathan Dolimore and Alan Sinfield, MUP, 1985). Was this the way to open up Shakespeare for a new generation of unengaged kids?

How do we deal with the plays in the twenty-first century in an increasingly multicultural society? And anyway has there ever been a time when these islands were not multicultural? I suspect that the courtyards of Elizabethan England teemed with 'masterless men', the tongues of a hundred regions grappling with the sound of a language comprised of the scraps and leftovers of a dozen other languages. Hard enough today for some people to distinguish Cork from Glasgow, Liverpool from Birmingham, Newcastle from Cardiff, Belfast from Bethnal. London then was the polyglottal stop-over for regional run-aways, a bubbling linguistic British brew, the pot full of the still succulent sounds of French, Latin, Goedelic, Brythonic, Norwegian, Saxon, Platt-Deutsch, Hoch Deutsch, Middle-High Deutsch, fresh words entering the language (in a variety of spellings: Mr Shakesshaft, Shagsboar, Shakespear with or without an 'e') at a faster rate possibly than at any other time until the post-war American cultural invasion of Mr McDonald and the white-hot technological revolution. This hybrid, as yet unstandardised, form of communication where a society conversed in strange alien sibilants, dentals and palatals, eyes often bright with misunderstanding, formed the basis of a new language captured in the raw by Shakespeare and others and moulded into a mosaic of multi-faceted storytelling. And this language carried a public health warning. It could kill. It was dangerous, a verbal contract sometimes taken out on one writer by another. Imprisonment was risked to attack public figures, the subjects of thinly veiled allegories set in Thebes, Athens, Verona, Venice.

My love of this and any language is a passion inherited from my father. In pre-revolutionary Russia before the turn of the twentieth century even, in the world in which my father grew up, the word was power. The balladeers, the pamphleteers, the poets, the novelists, the playwrights – those who could read and write held the key to the future. In a world of such devastating illiteracy, they were the truth. They were the word.

My father spoke English with consummate grammatical perfection, as only someone for whom it is not a native language can. And he had the vocabulary to match. Were he alive today he would be shocked to realise how many words that he used in everyday speech have already disappeared or are under threat. But this is the point, language must evolve. The battle for the survival of English in America is already on. An inexorable wave of Spanish is slowly flooding up the North American continent as the Mexicans take back by stealth what was taken from them by force. Los Angeles is already seventy-five per cent Spanish-speaking. What will the map look like in a hundred years' time? Already there is legislation against Spanish in some states, the first sign of a beleaguered minority about to dig in and fight a reactive battle against the force of time. What price Shakespeare in fifty to a hundred years? With hundreds of words dropping yearly out of use, what will be left of our understanding of his plays in centuries to come if we do not adopt a more radical attitude to these changes? Beowulf and Chaucer in translation – why not Shakespeare if it opens up the plays to the vast untapped energies of popular debate?

# Introduction

I was put off Shakespeare at school. We spent the whole of one term studying just one of Hamlet's soliloquies – 'How all occasions do inform against me.' We knew every comma, caesura, the etymology and derivation of every word backwards. Not a whiff of theatre in sight. Our English master was a Pickwickian character who read us chunks of Chaucer in what he informed us was the original accent – how did he know? It pained me to find that thirty years later my son was being taught in exactly the same way.

I didn't come back to Shakespeare until I was thirty myself. I had been eleven years in Ireland – Trinity College Dublin followed by a career in revue, musicals, variety, the folk scene and latterly a three-year stint as a TV Producer/Director with RTE (Radio Tefetis Eireann). I wished to return to theatre and realised that I would have to tackle the Shakespeare question. I went as an Assistant Director to where (I thought) they knew more about Shakespeare than anywhere else in the world – The Royal Shakespeare Company. I was the oldest assistant they had ever had. I soon realised that my political view of theatre and education, coupled with my experience at the sharper end of entertainment, was at odds with the dominant ideology there and left some eighteen months later to put my ideas into practice.

The intervening years have seen nearly sixty productions – some good, some bad, some ugly. Some plays I have directed four or five times in various parts of the globe – *Richard III, Hamlet, Romeo and Juliet, Macbeth* – each production an attempt to improve on the previous one and solve outstanding problems. (*The Tempest* I have directed five times but never get more than half right. The trouble is it's never the same half. I shall be doing it again.) Others – *Julius Caesar, Measure for Measure, The Taming of the Shrew, Timon of Athens* – I have done only once, achieving, I think, as much as I am able. As a director if you get it seventy-five per cent right you are world class. The English Shakespeare Company's *The Wars of the Roses* was some twenty-four hours of Shakespeare. Working on the seventy-five per cent basis, six hours were naff. That's two whole plays! (Opinions were divided as to which two.)

These essays do not attempt to analyse any of the productions. Indeed I do not even make reference to them. They are rather an attempt to set out the thinking that has informed my work over the years and in two cases, *King Lear* and *Othello*, I have yet to attempt to scale the mountain. Enjoy. Or not, as the case may be.

**Michael Bogdanov,**
**September 2003 and April 2013**

# Hamlet

a northern European power struggle

*Hamlet* is the play that is buried most deeply in the English nation's consciousness. It is arguably the most famous play in the world, the most popular, the most quoted, the play that has given the English-speaking peoples a sizeable chunk of their vocabulary: 'to be or not to be', 'sweets for my sweet', ''tis brief as woman's love', 'something rotten in the state of Denmark', 'the rest is silence', and so on. It is seen variously as a play about the individual versus the state, freedom of choice, good and evil. It is a play of great soaring power and beauty in its language and at the same time a philosophical and theological debate about the meaning of existence.

It is also a play about a northern European power struggle. For no matter whether Hamlet is a homosexual misogynist, an Oedipal ditherer or a noble nutter, he is caught up in the mechanism of a great wheel that rolls inexorably over the Danish soil. Hamlet is the cog that comes loose in that great wheel and sends the Claudius steamroller careering downhill to crush them both at the feet of the conquering Norwegian army. And the straight fight between Hamlet and Claudius, the outsider versus the forces of the 'massy wheel', as Rosencrantz says, is the climax of a thrilling political story that often remains buried in a dungheap of psychological self-indulgence. In other words, familiarity with this language and the fact that *Hamlet* is one of the principal sources of cultural nourishment that drip feed the conservatism of educationalists and politicians alike, have helped to disguise the fact that it is one of the most powerful political plays of all time.

*Hamlet*, for the director, is a great whodunit. The art of detection lies in unravelling the mystery, following the clues, building up the evidence, deducing the story. On the surface, that story does not change: a series of events defines the parameters, whatever the year, whatever the century. To alter or omit some of these events is to redefine the story and therefore to alter the play that Shakespeare supposedly wrote. This is perfectly permissible, even desirable in the tradition of theatre as a living entity, something that grows organically, springing from the spirit of the time – indeed, the very way that Shakespeare arrived at his version of the story.

Ay, there's the rub, or 'the point', as Quarto One would have it. Will the real text of *Hamlet* please stand up? Quarto One consists of some 2,200 lines compared with Quarto Two's 3,800 – almost double – and is generally termed 'bad'. Bad and good: qualitative judgements implying a right and a wrong, for and against, inside and outside the law, acceptable and unacceptable.

Much post-war thinking has been influenced by the Laurence Olivier film of *Hamlet*, which, coincidentally, also contained some two thousand lines. But with a crucial difference. The Olivier film managed to omit not only Fortinbras, but also Rosencrantz and Guildenstern, thus emphasising the disembodied quality of Hamlet's introspection. In other words, Olivier crucially changed the story of the play, as have recent productions by Matthew Warchus and Peter Brook, following in Olivier's footsteps and reducing the play to some two hours in length. They are therefore guilty of as much editorial corruption as those pirates accused, by generations of commentators, of corrupting Quarto One.

Fascinatingly, the objective storyline from Quarto One to Quarto Two through to the Folio presentation of 1623 has not altered. However, it is axiomatic that, whatever version is used, there are always many inconsistencies, not least of time, accidents of memory, improvisations by actors, insertions by commentators and 'tidying up' by editors. And, of course, there is that catch-all old argument that Shakespeare was not interested in detail, a convenient way of ignoring the collaborative process by which the performance was arrived at. But dramatically, for the practitioner, a loose end cannot be ignored as a matter of convenience because it does not fit in with a particular theory. It has to be tied up and bound tightly into the story.

Our tradition over the last century has been one of naturalistic detail. Audiences today demand a kind of logic. It is not a question of patting our heads and rubbing our theatrical tummies at the same time. An audience identifies with a piece of theatre at the point where it is performed. It does not say to itself 'that's what happened four hundred years ago'. If, for one moment, and one moment only, a point of contact and identification is made in the present, then the play immediately becomes a play of our time. That is why Shakespeare has been called the greatest living dramatist, and *Hamlet* the most enduring piece of *contemporary* theatre.

Bertolt Brecht's view of the play, written just after the Second World War in his *Short Organum for the Theatre* is as follows:

> . . . the theatre should always be mindful of the needs of its time. Let us take, as an example, the old play of *Hamlet*. I believe that in the view of the bloody and gloomy times in which I am writing this, in view of the criminal ruling classes and general despair of reason, the story of this play may be read thus: it is a time of war. Hamlet's father, the King of Denmark, had, in a victorious war of plunder, killed the King of Norway. While the latter's son, Fortinbras, is preparing himself for a new war, the King of Denmark is also killed by his brother. The brothers of the dead kings, having become kings themselves, conclude peace with each other. Norwegian troops, on their way to a war of plunder against Poland, have been permitted to cross the Danish territory. Just at this time, the war-like Father's ghost asks young Hamlet to revenge the crime committed on himself. After some hesitation as to whether he should add one bloody deed to another, Hamlet – willing even to go into exile – meets at the seashore young Fortinbras and his troops on their way to Poland. Following his example, he turns back and, in a scene of barbaric slaughter, kills his uncle, his mother and himself, leaving Denmark to the Norwegians. Thus we observe how, in these circumstances, the young man, already somewhat stout, badly misuses his knowledge acquired at Wittenberg University. This knowledge gets in the way when it comes to resolving the conflicts of the feudal world. His reason is impractical when faced

**with irrational reality. He falls, a tragic victim to the discrepancy between his reasoning and his action.**

'The theatre should always be mindful of the needs of its time.' Plays go in and out of focus, different aspects are suddenly highlighted by contemporary events, shifts in global balance of power throw new light on old characters. Some years ago, *Hamlet* was the perfect Watergate play – bugs, tails, eavesdropping. (Q: What is the difference, in production terms, between a notebook and a pocket Dictaphone? An abacus and a calculator?) Polonius, grooming his son, Laertes, for potential office, has him tailed in Paris in order to 'by indirections find directions out'. Then, some eighteen years ago, the Captain's explanation of Fortinbras's march on Poland uncannily echoed the Falklands conflict, even down to the number of soldiers deployed and the description of the terrain. Hamlet comes over the hill and sees twenty thousand soldiers marching across the Danish plains. 'Good sir, whose powers are these?' (Incidentally if you were Prince Charles coming over the Sussex Downs and suddenly discovered twenty thousand foreign troops marching across your land, how would you react?)

> CAPTAIN: We go to gain a little patch of ground
> That hath in it no profit but the name.
> To pay five ducats, five, I would not farm it;
> Nor will it yield to Norway or the Pole
> A ranker rate, should it be sold in fee.
> HAMLET: Why, then the Polack will never defend it.
> CAPTAIN: Yes, it is already garrisoned.
> HAMLET: Two thousand souls and twenty thousand ducats
> Will not debate the question of this straw.
> This is th'imposthume of much wealth and peace,
> That inward breaks, and shows no cause without
> Why the man dies.

> (Act IV, Scene iv)

Suddenly the resonances of this scene were immediate, the tensions were modern; the impact in the 1980s, electrifying.

HAMLET: Witness this army of such mass and charge,
Exposing what is mortal and unsure
To all that fortune, death, and danger dare,
Even for an eggshell. Rightly to be great
Is not to stir without great argument,
But greatly to find quarrel in a straw
When honour's at the stake . . .

                  . . . I see
The imminent death of twenty thousand men
That for a fantasy and a trick of fame
Go to their graves like beds, fight for a plot
Whereon the numbers cannot try the cause,
Which is not tomb enough and continent
To hide the slain?

(Act IV, Scene iv)

Twenty thousand men, the exact number of the British Falklands task force, going to die for a patch of ground that isn't even big enough to bury the number of dead. What better description of that extraordinary last jingoistic fling of British imperialism?

Brecht, then, sees the story as a northern European power struggle. He omits, until the very end of his scenario, all the psychological and emotional complexity of the characters and relates only the events. Who on the basis of that analysis of the story would dare leave Fortinbras out of the play? The story would be destroyed, the political implication non-existent, the character of Claudius emasculated. Laurence Olivier *et al*. have a lot to answer for. What story were they telling?

Is Brecht's version similarly biased, in as much as he leaves out other parts of the story to put a greater emphasis on his interpretation? And there's the rub. When facts are omitted to reshape the story to the particular interpretation, it becomes a new play.

*Hamlet* is still often read in terms of sick psychology. Either Hamlet has a paralysing fixation on his mother, or it is, to quote Olivier's film, 'the tragedy of a man who could not make up his mind'. The intellectual constitutionally incapable of acting. Or, to paraphrase Hegel, the noble art of revenge embraced by Greek tradgedy founders on the mundane rock of Christianity.

\* \* \*

Let us look at the opening scenario, the wellspring from which the main action flows. Denmark is preparing for war, twenty-four hours a day, seven days a week, a round-the-clock arms race.

MARCELLUS:       . . . tell me that he knows,
Why this same strict and most observant watch
So nightly toils the subject of the land,
And why such daily cast of brazen cannon
And foreign mart for implements of war,
Why such impress of shipwrights, whose sore task
Does not divide the Sunday from the week.
What might be toward that this sweaty haste
Doth make the night joint-labourer with the day?

One can almost hear and see the roar of the blast furnaces, the Tornadoes, Exocets and Cruise Missiles rolling off the assembly lines, the troop ships being loaded, the cranes swinging the Shermans onto the quayside.

HORATIO:       . . . And this, I take it,
Is the main motive of our preparations,
The source of this our watch, and the chief head
Of this posthaste and romage in the land.

(Act I, Scene i)

Where is this heady atmosphere of war preparation, this 'posthaste and romage' ever reflected in performance? In Kozintov's Russian film version perhaps. Yet it is crucial for our understanding of both the events that unfold and particularly of Claudius's motive for killing Old Hamlet. It is often cut, as in the production by Sir Richard Eyre, former Artistic Director of the Royal National Theatre, at the Royal Court Theatre, with Jonathan Pryce playing Hamlet, some years back. Royal acceptability. This huge essential piece of the jigsaw was missing from the very beginning. Try making sense of the picture after that.

As it happens, there is a case for reversing these speeches of Marcellus and Horatio. Horatio has only just returned from Wittenberg, ostensibly for the funeral of Hamlet's father, though Hamlet darkly hints it was for the marriage of Claudius and Gertrude. Hamlet has been in Elsinore some two months or thereabout. 'But two months dead, nay, not so much, not two!'

However, there is no reason for Horatio to hang around Elsinore for two months. If he *has* been there for two months, why has he not seen Hamlet before this? Of course, he may have gone back to Wittenberg and then returned again, but there is no evidence that he knows Hamlet well enough in Elsinore to drop in and see him as soon as he arrives. It takes a Ghost to do that. It would appear that however well Hamlet knew him in Wittenberg, Horatio probably lives in the equivalent of an Elsinore semi, presumably at college on the equivalent of a Danish Guild Scholarship from the local comp – classmate of Marcellus and Barnardo. The bright boy of the year. Wouldn't dream of dropping in at Buck House under normal circumstances. What doesn't seem to make sense is that an officer of the Guard, Marcellus, does not know why the military preparations are taking place and a student just returned from Wittenberg does. Further, Horatio says: 'The whisper goes so.' The soldiers would also have heard that 'whisper'. Hence the questions come better from the student just returned, mystified by the preparations, and it is the officer who is on the spot who gives the replies; and although later some editors give speeches to Horatio in Act IV, Scene i, there is no evidence that Claudius and Gertrude have any knowledge of Horatio. Not like those two nice boys from school, who came to tea once. What were their names? Rosamund and Gallimar? Send them a telegram, perhaps they can help.

So when do all these events take place that Horatio/Marcellus is describing? Thirty years ago. Source? The Gravediggers (this evidence is crucial on several counts). So what has Old Hamlet been doing for thirty years? It would appear, resting on his laurels, for now the forces are massing on the borders again, younger contenders (Norwegians, Polacks) eager for revenge, hungry to repossess lands they think is rightfully theirs.

> . . . Now, sir, young Fortinbras
> **Of unimproved mettle hot and full,**

Hath in the skirts of Norway here and there
Sharked up a list of lawless resolutes
For food and diet to some enterprise
That hath a stomach in't; which is no other,
As it doth well appear unto our state,
But to recover of us by strong hand
And terms compulsatory those foresaid lands
So by his father lost.

(Act I, Scene i)

Are young Fortinbras's soldiers 'lawless resolutes'? Have they been 'sharked up in the skirts of Norway' ready for any 'enterprise that hath a stomach in it'? When we see them first, marching across Denmark to Poland, and then returning victorious – (Q: Why do they come back via Elsinore? They didn't go anywhere near it on the way to Poland) – it is clear that they are a highly professional, disciplined fighting machine. There is no evidence for this, merely deduction via the relationship of Fortinbras and the Captain, plus the discipline it takes to force-march across a continent, fight and win a battle on foreign ground, and return again (cf. the Falklands again). Are the comments of Horatio / Marcellus then merely biased patriotic propaganda? If so, they certainly are better in the mouth of Marcellus the soldier.

Thirty years of peace and now the threat of war. Is the following scenario possible?

CLAUDIUS: Put that bottle down brother, the situation is dangerous.

OLD HAMLET: Rubbish, I did it before, I'll do it again.

CLAUDIUS: But that was thirty years ago! Any day now they'll attack and we'll be defending with bows and arrows! We've got to . . .

OLD HAMLET: Just you leave it to me, old boy. Have a drink!

(A custom more honoured in the breach than the observance.)

Claudius could not leave it to his brother. There was not much point in Old Hamlet resting on what were now somewhat tatty military laurels. Denmark could be overrun at any minute. So Claudius killed him and took over. The theme of usurpation is one to which Shakespeare returns again and again in the plays, constantly proving that blood is not thicker than water. Brother kills brother, father betrays son, son kills father, cousin kills cousin. The Histories are a litany of fraternal and paternal slaughter.

To the end of his life the question fascinated him. (See the relationship of Prospero and Antonio in *The Tempest*.) Q: Did Claudius murder Hamlet for the love of Gertrude? Impossible. Nobody murders a king, kills a dictator, assassinates a president, and takes over the running of the country merely for love. Who wants all those problems of war, taxation, unemployment? Power must be wanted. Love of Gertrude there may have been, it is true, but there were other ways of sustaining love without giving himself the banging headache of running a country already in trouble. If you take over a country you take over all the problems that go with it. And Claudius is not negligent. He assumes the responsibility for the consequences of his action immediately, and sets the country on a war footing. He instantly dispatches two ambassadors, Voltimand and Cornelius, to Norway to tell them to cut it out:

> . . . to suppress
> **His further gait herein, in that the levies,**
> **The lists, and full proportions are all made**
> **Out of his subject.**

> (Act I, Scene ii)

Power, and the nature of power, the use and abuse of it, usurpation, the territorial imperative, these are the themes.

\* \* \*

Let us then examine the proposition that Hamlet should have been king. That he would have 'proved most royal, had he been put on'. This expectancy and rose of the fair state.

Thirty years. Hamlet is thirty.

**HAMLET: How long hast thou been grave-maker?**

**CLOWN: Of all the days i'th'year I came to't that day that our last King Hamlet overcame Fortinbras.**

**HAMLET: How long is that since?**

**CLOWN: Cannot you tell that? Every fool can tell that. It was that very day that young Hamlet was born – he that is mad, and sent into England . . . I have been sexton here, man and boy, thirty years.**

(Act V, Scene i)

An auspicious double event, a cause for great national celebration – the defeat of the Norwegians and the birth of a future king, a red-letter day known by the whole population and presumably celebrated nationwide. Not only that, the day the Gravedigger landed his job! No fallible memory this. And if that were not enough, the Gravedigger throws in another bit of proof – deduction this time.

**HAMLET: How long will a man lie i'th'earth ere he rot?**

**CLOWN: . . . Here's a skull now hath lien you i'th'earth three-and-twenty years.**

**HAMLET: Whose was it?**

**CLOWN: . . . This same skull, sir, was, sir, Yorick's skull, the King's jester.**

**HAMLET: . . . I knew him, Horatio . . . He hath bore me on his back a thousand times . . . Here hung those lips that I have kissed I know not how oft. Where be your gibes now? Your gambols, your songs, your flashes of merriment that were wont to set the table on a roar?**

(Act V, Scene i)

Twenty-three years in the earth. Carried Hamlet on his back a thousand times. Hamlet remembers his jokes and his antics. He knew him. It does not seem probable that he only knew him for, let us say, one year, from the age of two and a half to three and a half, thus putting Hamlet's age at, say, twenty-six. His memory is longer, deeper and fuller than that. The acquaintance is obviously a sustained one and Hamlet's command of language sufficiently developed to appreciate his wit. Yorick died when Hamlet was seven. Hamlet is thirty. So what is he doing at the age of thirty, still kicking around university at Wittenberg? Why wasn't he around to take his share of responsibility while all the problems were building up for his father at home? Drinking too much, probably, talking rather than doing, and getting fat.

The legacy of the thin, gaunt, pale young prince is a romantic one. The part was written for Sir Richard Burbage at the age of thirty-seven when, from the evidence of portraits, he weighed about seventeen and a half stone. When Gertrude says 'he's fat and scant of breath', she means just that. No pretending that 'fat' means 'sweaty' will do. In all other contexts in Shakespeare, fat means fat. Sir John Falstaff wasn't sweaty, he was fat. So was Sir Toby Belch. Yet the only reference to a fat Hamlet in performance is a caricature by Robert Dighton in 1794 of Stephen Kemble in the part.

> HORATIO: You will lose this wager, my lord.
>
> HAMLET: I do not think so. Since he went into France I have been in continual practice.
>
> (Act V, Scene ii)

Continual practice? For the last three or four months all he has done is run around the palace behaving like a lunatic. No sign of a workout, jogging, the exercise bike. No wonder he's 'scant of breath'. It begins to look as if Brecht was right.

So what is this 'expectancy and rose of the fair state'? Would he have 'proved most royal had be been put on'? (How does Fortinbras know? Did he ever meet him? Is he just saying nice things about the dead?) What evidence do we have that Hamlet is popular with the people, apart from Claudius's paranoia? After all, 'the rabble' shout 'choose we, Laertes shall be king'. Not 'bring back Hamlet'. Hamlet's lack of decision would certainly have landed Denmark in a right old mess.

> QUEEN: I hoped thou shouldst have been my Hamlet's wife.
> I thought thy bride-bed to have decked, sweet maid,
> And not have strewed thy grave.
>
> (Act V, Scene i)

Was this possible? How old was Ophelia? In Shakespeare's day, girls were marriageable at the age of twelve. Juliet was not yet fourteen (just like her mother) when marrying. Miranda was not much older, and she had been on a desert island all her life. At seventeen one was on the shelf. Even if we pitch Ophelia's age at sixteen there is still a fourteen-year age gap between Hamlet and Ophelia. So: what is the thirty-year-old heir to the throne doing messing around with the sixteen-year-old daughter of the Prime Minister? Laertes knows it is dangerous and that it will only end in tears. Polonius likewise. He cannot have a sexual scandal touch him. The liaison is impossible. Royalty must marry royalty. From all sides there is pressure.

> LAERTES:                    . . . But you must fear,
> His greatness weighed, his will is not his own.
> For he himself is subject to his birth.
> He may not, as unvalued persons do,
> Carve for himself. For on his choice depends
> The safety and health of this whole state.
> And therefore must his choice be circumscribed
> Unto the voice and yielding of that body
> Whereof he is the head. Then, if he says he loves you,
> It fits your wisdom so far to believe it
> As he in his particular act and place
> May give his saying deed; which is no further
> Than the main voice of Denmark goes withal.
>
> (Act I, Scene iii)

Hamlet may only marry the King's (and Queen's) choice. He may not 'carve' for himself! It would be a political disaster for Polonius to be involved in a court sex-scandal.

> POLONIUS: I would not, in plain terms, from this time forth
> Have you so slander any moment leisure
> As to give words or talk with the Lord Hamlet.
> Look to't, I charge you.
>
> (Act I, Scene iii)

From the beginning we only see an unhappy girl with a brother and a father laying a very heavy scene upon her. There is no let-up, no escape. Repression and suppression are in the air. Ophelia is used and abused. Polonius dresses her up and sets a trap, using the poor, frightened, defenceless girl as bait, the implication being that Hamlet would try to seduce her and reveal all. Hands up all those who think Hamlet has slept with Ophelia, and why not? With no other person around (none that we can see at any rate) to advise her, to confide in, it is no wonder that Ophelia goes mad. Mentally, she is savagely raped. Hamlet's will not his own? Neither is Ophelia's. Polonius is completely uninterested in the disastrous effect his plot has had on the mind of his daughter. He brusquely brushes off her attempt to talk to him about the traumatic experience she has just undergone:

> POLONIUS:        . . . How now, Ophelia?
> You need not tell us what Lord Hamlet said:
> We heard it all.
>
> (Act III, Scene i)

As to the brother – write to me, he says, 'Let me hear from you'; but there is no evidence that Laertes ever writes to Ophelia. A young girl alone in a male world of high politics. Worse, the handsome young prince (now fat), whom she used to see round the castle when she was small, whom she hero-worshipped (he was a wonderful fencer in those days), who started flirting with her a while back when he noticed one day that the little girl with pigtails and braces on her teeth had suddenly grown up . . . this thirty-year-old prince, once the 'expectancy and rose of the fair state', is behaving in an extraordinary fashion. Her mind cannot cope. Sweets for the sweet? Gertrude hasn't spoken to her for months. Ducks into doorways when she sees her coming. Easy to say now it's too late.

'I hoped thou shouldst have been my Hamlet's wife'? No chance.

The precocious little upstart daughter of the Prime Minister got what was coming to her. Harsh? It's a tough world for a woman. After all, Gertrude has managed to stay at the centre of power, a wife of not one, but two kings. No one wants an ex-queen around the palace. Like Queen Margaret in *Richard III*, once a woman is no longer married to power, it is down the slippery pole. And so much for brotherly love. Laertes did not even know what was happening to his sister.

Similarly, Polonius is right-hand man to not one king, but two. He manages to make the transition and be trusted.

**POLONIUS:** Hath there been such a time – I would fain know that –
That I have positively said ''Tis so',
When it proved otherwise?

**KING:**                    Not that I know.

**POLONIUS:** Take this from this, if this be otherwise.
If circumstances lead me, I will find
Where truth is hid, though it were hid indeed
Within the centre.

(Act II, Scene ii)

There is an inescapable echo here of the Elizabethan CIA – operated so efficiently by Burleigh and Walsingham, the one that did for Mary, Queen of Scots and many others.

No tedious old fool this. Rather a calculating, cunning, conniving politician who keeps tabs on everything and everyone, even putting a tail on his priggish son in Paris. His one mistake? To let personal family feelings interfere with an objective judgement, and then, unable to admit that he is wrong, careering headlong to his death in the relentless pursuit of the proof of his convictions. 'By indirections find directions out.' He found out all right. 'Thou knowest to be busy is some danger.'

\* \* \*

*Hamlet* is one of the great existential plays. Throughout the canon Shakespeare is obsessed with the nature of action, how far short we fall of our own expectations of ourselves, the discrepancy between the thought of action and the act itself.

**HAMLET:** Oh God, I could be bounded in a nutshell and count myself a king of infinite space, were it not that I have bad dreams.

(Act II, Scene ii)

As long as we do not allow the imagination to take over, we are capable of anything. The man who succeeds is that man who says 'this is what I am going to do' and does it. The *Realpolitiker*. The pragmatist. Richard III, fine until his imagination takes over. Antonio, taking over Milan, after years of neglect by his brother, his only contribution in the final twenty minutes of the play to Prospero's attempt to elicit feelings of guilt from him, an objective appraisal of Caliban's financial worth. 'A queer fish and no doubt marketable.' Prospero, for whom everything happens in his head, taking revenge, re-ordering the Universe . . . until he wakes up from his dream.

So often Shakespeare poses a *status quo* against which he pits a protagonist. This protagonist usually smashes him or herself to pieces against the rock of state. The turtle is turned over on its back, before being righted and lumbering off on its reactionary way. What lessons have been learned? The pyramid of power remains intact, the territorial imperative is exercised once again in the name of justice, divine right, necessity of state, and so on. *Hamlet* begins with an act of usurpation by a man of action, and finishes with one.

When we first meet Claudius he is in control. He has killed the king and is himself king. He sets about running Denmark. Military preparations are made. Two ambassadors are dispatched with ultimata. Hamlet is told to stay at home in Elsinore. 'For your intent / In going back to school in Wittenberg / It is most retrograde to our desire' – after all, we can't have the rightful heir to the throne running around a foreign country, brooding on whether he should have been king, enlisting foreign support, returning with an army. 'Be as ourself in Denmark.' The 'massy wheel' is turning: as yet no spoke has been thrust in its mechanism, to bring it to a grinding halt. Gradually the antics of Hamlet begin to prey on Claudius's mind. By the time the ambassadors return he is more interested in news of Hamlet than in the news of Norway. And what a poser 'Old' Norway has set him! Voltimand and Cornelius arrive back waving a piece of paper that ostensibly says 'Peace in our time'. Not only has 'Old' Norway given Fortinbras more money, he has given him more soldiers in return for a promise not to go against Denmark, and, what's more, he has asked Claudius's permission to march across Denmark to fight Poland. What does Claudius do? Say no and risk Norway's anger? Say yes and have twenty thousand foreign troops on his soil? No wonder he is 'like a man to double business bound' and 'stands in pause' where he shall 'first begin and both neglects' (Act III, Scene iii).

Deal with Hamlet – or with Fortinbras? Claudius fiddles, Denmark burns, and Fortinbras ends up annexing Denmark as he annexed Poland, the usurper at the gates (so that's why he came back via Elsinore!).

> **FORTINBRAS: I have some rights of memory in this kingdom,**
> **Which now to claim my vantage doth invite me.**
>
> (Act V, Scene ii)

What rights? Oh yes, Hamlet did say something about that. 'I prophesy the election lights on Fortinbras.'

> **HORATIO: Of that I shall have also cause to speak,**
> **And from his mouth whose voice will draw on more.**

Too late, Horatio. It would not have made a jot of difference if Hamlet had 'prophesied' or not. Fortinbras is going to rule Denmark. He accomplishes it without bloodshed. That had been done for him. He will rule until the Danes decide they do not want a foreigner as their leader, then another act of deposition will follow, bloody or otherwise. The lesson of history is never learned. And just in case there is some public unrest, we'll make a show of Hamlet, place him high above stage.

> **HORATIO: But let this same be presently performed,**
> **Even while men's minds are wild, lest more mischance**
> **On plots and errors happen.**
>
> (Act V, Scene ii)

Pacify the people, the world loves a good state funeral.

* * *

To opt in or to opt out. What does Hamlet do? If he kills Claudius he will be king. Does he want to be? What sort of king would he be? A Caligula-type king? Would his humanitarian and egalitarian feelings have taken over? The levelling of beggars and kings? Certainly the arts might have flourished. Or would his ruthlessness have come to the fore? Viz., his callous treatment of Rosencrantz and Guildenstern, sending those two unfortunate nonentities gratuitously to their deaths, not near his conscience. Only at this stage, far too late, is his indecision over. He realises finally the value of taking responsibility for one's actions.

**HAMLET: If it be now, 'tis not to come. If it be not to come, it will be now. If it be not now, yet it will come. The readiness is all.**

                                                    **(Act V, Scene ii)**

Too late. In his death, far from avenging his father's murder, he only succeeds in bringing about what, thirty years earlier, his father had fought to avoid: Norway conquering Denmark. 'Thus conscience doth make cowards of us all.'

Action. Inaction. The final shoot-out between Hamlet and Claudius is inevitable. They begin poles apart but, as with the sound of marching feet coming closer to the gates of Elsinore, so Claudius and Hamlet come inexorably together.

**HAMLET:                    . . . O, 'tis most sweet**
**When in one line two crafts directly meet.**

                                                    **(Act III, Scene iv)**

Indecision brings chaos, the winner is he who decides – and does it. The readiness is all. Existential.

                              \* \* \*

**FORTINBRAS:              . . . such a sight as this**
**Becomes the field, but here shows much amiss.**

                                                    **(Act V, Scene ii)**

Hamlet, mad for love? Mad in craft? Immaterial. His real / feigned madness destroys everything he comes in contact with, turns the world upside down. Polonius, mad to prove his theory. Ophelia, mad with grief, isolation, rejection. Laertes, mad for revenge. Claudius, conceiving a mad, convoluted plot with Laertes, involving poisoned bottles and foils. If ever a plan was bound to go wrong. . . . By now the whole world is mad. Getrude drinking herself to an early grave; order restored by Fortinbras, a foreigner, taking over a country of which he has no need and on which he has no claim. 'I will rule with the olive and the sword,' says Alcibides in *Timon of Athens*. The trouble is – how much olive, how much sword? When will the purge start?

As with all detective stories there are many suspects and a number of culprits. As to who the real villain is – Claudius, Old Hamlet, Young Hamlet, Fortinbras, or the Ghost – it depends on how you interpret the story.

Oh yes, the Oedipus theme is pretty interesting too. And the one of what life is all about.

# Romeo and Juliet

a marriage of inconvenience
and social irresponsibility

Any production of *Romeo and Juliet* must begin with an analysis of the social responsibility for the deaths of the two young people. The acceptance on the part of much critical thinking that the two lovers had to die in order to (a) reconcile their parents' hatred, and (b) show society the way forward, begs the question as to whether the deaths might have been avoided in the first place, and prompts a debate about such measures that could and should have been taken to stop the feuding in Verona's streets.

In other words – was the tragedy man-made? Did it stem from choices and decisions, taken at certain critical moments, by consenting adults, that were wrong or at best unthinking, governed by self-interest, muddled do-gooding, or whatever? Society is a past master at stable-door bolting, whether the shrill cries of outraged indignation are directed towards oil-spilling tankers, rail crashes, underground station fires, or famine. But whatever the size or nature of the disaster, the root cause is always human error, and, more often, human greed. And we know that when that first outcry of public indignation dies down, apathy and self-interest will reassert themselves and a new variant of the old catastrophe will reoccur. In the wake of public protest, legislation is sometimes rushed through in an outward display of governmental action, seemingly to prevent a repeat of a particular disaster. But where commercial interest is involved, these measures are usually half-hearted, half-baked and in effect an avoidance of political and social responsibility, with no long-term benefit.

Historically, orthodox criticism has enveloped the deaths of Romeo and Juliet in a romantic aura. Romeo swigs from a little bottle marked 'Poison' and the audience suspends its disbelief. What would be the reaction if Romeo stabbed a needle into his arm? This romantic interpretation stems from the very first words of the Prologue – a prolific source of misinterpretation. As with so many opening scenes, Shakespeare sets up a proposition that cries out to be challenged or a condition that is immediately contradicted by events:

Two households, both alike in dignity
In fair Verona, where we lay our scene,
From ancient grudge break to new mutiny,
Where civil blood makes civil hands unclean.
From forth the fatal loins of these two foes
A pair of star-crossed lovers take their life;
Whose misadventured piteous overthrows
Doth with their death bury their parents' strife.
The fearful passage of their death-marked love
And the continuance of their parents' rage,
Which, but their children's end, naught could remove,
Is now the two hours' traffic of our stage;
The which if you with patient ears attend,
What here shall miss, our toil shall seek to mend.

(Prologue)

'Two households both alike in dignity': on examination, this proves not to be an accurate description of the two families, or rather the two heads of the families, Capulet and Montague. The language of Montague is cultured, elegant, conciliatory, well, how would you describe it? – dignified.

MONTAGUE: Many a morning hath he there been seen,
With tears augmenting the fresh morning's dew,
Adding to clouds more clouds with his deep sighs.
But all so soon as the all-cheering sun
Should in the farthest East begin to draw
The shady curtains from Aurora's bed,
Away from light steals home my heavy son

And private in his chamber pens himself,
Shuts up his windows, locks fair daylight out,
And makes himself an artificial night.
Black and portentous must this humour prove
Unless good counsel may the cause remove.

(Act I, Scene i)

His speech shows an anxious concern for the welfare of his son and is couched in quietly lyrical language. And that's about it as far as Montague is concerned. We don't really hear any more of him. But Capulet?

CAPULET: God's bread! It makes me mad.
Day, night; hour, tide, time; work, play;
Alone, in company; still my care hath been
To have her matched. And having now provided
A gentleman of noble parentage,
Of fair demesnes, youthful, and nobly trained,
Stuffed, as they say, with honourable parts,
Proportioned as one's thought would wish a man –
And then to have a wretched puling fool,
A whining mammet, in her fortune's tender,
To answer 'I'll not wed, I cannot love;
I am too young, I pray you, pardon me'!
But, an you will not wed, I'll pardon you!
Graze where you will, you shall not house with me.
Look to't, think on't. I do not use to jest.
Thursday is near. Lay hand on heart. Advise.
An you be mine, I'll give you to my friend.
An you be not, hang, beg, starve, die in the streets,
For, by my soul, I'll ne'er acknowledge thee,
Nor what is mine shall never do thee good.
Trust to't. Bethink you. I'll not be forsworn.

(Act III, Scene v)

Not a lot of dignity there. Rather, the 'call a spade a spade' language of a middle-class businessman ruling his daughter with a rod of iron, blunt, hard, brutal, lacking any finesse. One-syllable words stabbing out, like his fingers, into the 'frail bark' of his daughter's mind and body. The contrast between Montague and Capulet could not be greater. Both alike in dignity? Not a bit, one dignified, yes, the other not. (All right – so dignity sometimes means social standing.)

'From ancient grudge break to new mutiny.' We never discover what this grudge is; the reasons for the feud are buried somewhere in the dark abysm of time. 'Three civil brawls make civil hands unclean', but why? How? What is it about? Merely the senseless repetitive Pavlovian hatred of one group for another without any foundation – not even religion, that traditional haven of hatred. Reasons forgotten. Merely a Montague so hit him. I was going into Lombard Street Studio in Dublin one day, a rehearsal space belonging to Trinity College. Two kids were passing by. One said to the other, peering in at the window, 'Only English bastards go in there.' I had to stop myself protesting, 'I'm not English, honest. Russian and Welsh.' Pavlovian hatred.

'A pair of star-crossed lovers.' References to fate and destiny abound, principally from Romeo: '. . . he that hath the steerage of my course, direct my sail'; 'O, I am fortune's fool'; 'I defy you stars.' It is true that the deaths of Romeo and Juliet are caused by forces outside of their control. But these forces, these circumstances and events in which the pair find themselves caught up, are entirely man-made, and their deaths the result of a complete abdication on the part of society of all social responsibility. Their mistake, made because of youth and immaturity, was to place their trust in an adult world of competence. The choices and decisions that were taken on the part of those people they trusted (principally the Nurse and Friar Laurence), and who should have known better, are the real reasons why Romeo and Juliet died.

'Doth bury their parents' strife.' Oh yes? Has society altered? Have the rules changed? Montague and Capulet may be reconciled but what happens when another girl wishes to marry someone who is not the choice of her parents? Must she obey? Or elope, to be captured and punished? The tragedy of Romeo and Juliet will repeat itself again and again unless a society that allows women to be bartered to the highest bidder without choice can be reformed and humanised.

Where does Escalus, the prince, stand in all this? Who has the ultimate responsibility? Is it inevitable that only the deaths of Romeo and Juliet can 'bury their parents' strife'? What other measures could have been taken to stop the senseless feuding? Was Escalus too indulgent? Erecting gold statues won't change anything. Only laws of equality will.

'The two hours' traffic of our stage.' Shakespeare may have intended the play to be only two hours long when he started out to adapt the poem by Brook, the source of the plot, but in order to speak an unexpurgated text in that length of time, it would require a speed-run of the play as pacey as the bullet train from Tokyo to Kyoto.

On closer analysis then, there are questions raised by the Prologue which must be answered. Assumptions are made that are challenged directly by the events of the play, proving, if proof were needed, that to take what Shakespeare wrote at face value is often to miss the subtle social and psychological knife wound inflicted verbally on the body of conservative society.

\* \* \*

Love is in the air – or at least, lust. When we first meet Romeo, he is pining, as it turns out, for Rosaline. But love?

> ROMEO:          . . . She'll not be hit
> With Cupid's arrow. She hath Dian's wit,
> And, in strong proof of chastity well armed,
> From love's weak childish bow she lives unharmed.
> She will not stay the siege of loving terms,
> Nor bide th'encounter of assailing eyes,
> Nor ope her lap to saint-seducing gold.
> O, she is rich in beauty; only poor
> That, when she dies, with beauty dies her store.
>
> (Act I, Scene i)

Romeo has tried everything to get her into bed, but Rosaline is not going to come across. He even offers to pay for it: 'Nor ope her lap to saint-seducing gold.' Do girls in this society do the business for fifty crisp ones? 'Then she hath sworn that she will still live chaste?' asks Benvolio incredulously. Unbelievable.

**ROMEO: She hath; and in that sparing makes huge waste.**

It is quite clear that Romeo is merely suffering from a severe case of sexual deprivation despite all his love-sick poetry. Benvolio knows the answer – gatecrash Capulet's party and grab a piece of the action. It is clear that the norm in this society is that the girls sleep with the boys and not to do so is a mite peculiar. Rosaline, a heterosexual anomaly, is holding out on Romeo and is going to make him suffer for it.

Romeo visits Friar Laurence to tell him of his new-found love for Juliet:

**FRIAR:        . . . then here I hit it right –**
**Our Romeo hath not been in bed tonight.**

**ROMEO: The last is true. The sweeter rest was mine.**

**FRIAR: God pardon sin! Wast thou with Rosaline?**

The Friar immediately jumps to the conclusion that Romeo has cracked it at last. Who? Rosaline? Can't even remember what she looks like. But Juliet – this is for real.

**FRIAR: . . . But come, young waverer, come, go with me.**
**In one respect I'll thy assistant be.**
**For this alliance may so happy prove**
**To turn your households' rancour to pure love.**

**ROMEO: O, let us hence! I stand on sudden haste.**

**FRIAR: Wisely and slow. They stumble that run fast.**

What did he say? Did I hear him aright? He's actually going to marry Romeo and Juliet without a second thought? It's only thirty seconds since he was chiding Romeo for 'doting, not for loving, pupil mine'. Chastising him for forgetting Rosaline so soon:

**And art thou changed? Pronounce this sentence then:**
**Women may fall when there's no strength in men.**

                                                      (Act II, Scene iii)

So that's it then for the Friar – women are sexual vampires. Noble, strong-willed men have to turn them back to the path of righteousness away from the fires of lust and lechery. 'Wisely and slow. They stumble that run fast' – Friar Laurence is running faster than them all, and 'stumbling' has got to be the order of the day. An ironic ending to the scene. In his position of authority, the Friar should have ascertained that there was, in fact, a serious basis for this new love of Romeo's life and offered to negotiate, on behalf of the young people, with the two families. True, it might 'turn their rancour to pure love', but not by marrying them in this hasty, ill-timed, clandestine fashion. Had he stopped to think, he might have known what an uproar it would cause. But the Church in this play is dressed only in a little brief authority. Births, marriages, deaths, confessions or 'shrift'; otherwise it's a herbalist. It is an act of gross irresponsibility on the part of the Friar to marry Romeo and Juliet clandestinely and in such haste, and the tragic events that unfold stem directly from this instantaneous, unthinking decision.

Sex is in the air. For the Nurse, Juliet represents surrogate licentiousness. She titillates and fantasises about Juliet lying on her back with legs in the air, and vicariously relives the pleasures of her youth through the fourteen-year-old body of Juliet (or the not quite fourteen-year-old body). On Lamass Eve, she is eligible. Get the baby factory rolling.

> LADY CAPULET:          . . . By my count,
> I was your mother much upon these years
> That you are now a maid.
>
> (Act I, Scene iii)

So Lady Capulet was married even earlier. By the time she was fourteen, she was a mother, Juliet had already been born. Paris, asking for Juliet's hand, says 'Younger than she are happy mothers made.' Married at twelve, mother at thirteen. And Capulet replies, 'And marr'd too soon are those so early made.' Something strange there, he sounds a bit bitter, maybe his marriage to a twelve-year-old hasn't worked out so well. Lady Capulet is now twenty-eight at best. How old is Capulet? Fifty? Sixty?

> CAPULET: [at the party] . . . you and I are past our dancing days.
> How long is't now since last yourself and I
> Were in a mask?

**COUSIN CAPULET: By'r Lady, thirty years.**

(Act I, Scene v)

There is probably a gap of at least thirty years between Capulet and his wife, and is Juliet the only survivor in a long line of cot deaths?

**Earth hath swallowed all my hopes but she;**
**She's the hopeful lady of my earth.**

(Act I, Scene ii)

There's a lot riding on Juliet. But certainly Capulet doesn't appear to be too happy that he married quite such a young girl himself.

However, sex is in the air. Woo her, gentle Paris, come to my party. Capulet joins in the titillation too:

**At my poor house, look to behold this night**
**Earth-treading stars that make the heaven light.**
**Such comfort as do lusty young men feel**
**When well-apparelled April on the heel**
**Of limping winter treads, even such delight**
**Among fresh female buds shall you this night**
**Inherit at my house.**

(Act I, Scene ii)

And Romeo goes to the party too. Why? Peer pressure? He doesn't have to. 'He that has the steerage of my course . . .' Nobody is steering him – apart from Mercutio and Benvolio. He chooses to go. Wilful. He sees Juliet, grabs a passing servant. Who's that? 'I know not, sir.' (Who is he – outside catering?)

'O, she doth teach the torches to burn bright!' From that decision stems the first real tension strand of the story. The first encounter of Romeo and Juliet linguistically leaps out of time and convention. The wooing sonnet is couched in religious imagery. The moment elevated to a higher plane than that of merely 'examining other beauties'. A deliberate contrast to the sexual quips and innuendo of the levelling language in the previous scenes.

**JULIET: Good pilgrim, you do wrong your hand too much,**
**Which mannerly devotion shows in this.**

For saints have hands that pilgrims' hands do touch,
And palm to palm is holy palmers' kiss.

ROMEO: Have not saints lips, and holy palmers too?

JULIET: Ay, pilgrim, lips that they must use in prayer.

ROMEO: O, then, dear saint, let lips do what hands do!
They pray: grant thou, lest faith turn to despair.

JULIET: Saints do not move, though grant for prayers' sake.

ROMEO: Then move not while my prayer's effect I take.
(*He kisses her*) Thus from my lips, by thine my sin is purged.

JULIET: Then have my lips the sin that they have took.

ROMEO: Sin from my lips? O trespass sweetly urged!
Give me my sin again. (*He kisses her*)

JULIET:               You kiss by th'book.

(Act I, Scene v)

Whichever way you cut it, sonnet or not, blushing pilgrim's hand, holy palmers notwithstanding, within thirty seconds of meeting Juliet, Romeo is kissing her. Ten seconds later, he's kissing her again. All pretty normal really. And don't forget, 'He that can lay hold of her will have the chinks.' Worth a lot of money, that girl. But note the Nurse's terminology: 'Lay hold of her.' Later she will say of Paris: 'There is one who would lay knife aboard. A pirate, plundering and pillaging.'

Sex is in the air. Post-party, Mercutio bawls raucous obscenities into the night, business as usual.

MERCUTIO: . . . I conjure thee by Rosaline's bright eyes,
By her high forehead and her scarlet lip,
By her fine foot, straight leg, and quivering thigh,
And the demesnes that there adjacent lie,
That in thy likeness thou appear to us!

BENVOLIO: An if he hear thee, thou wilt anger him.

MERCUTIO: . . . 'Twould anger him
To raise a spirit in his mistress' circle
Of some strange nature, letting it there stand

     . . . . .

I conjure only but to raise up him.

. . . . .

**O, Romeo, that she were, O, that she were,**
**An open-arse and thou a poppering pear!**

(Act II, Scene i)

Once again there is a deliberate juxtaposition of the obscene language and profanity of Mercutio and the beauty of the language in the balcony scene. How would an Elizabethan audience have responded to these obscenities? What 'business' would the actor playing Mercutio have indulged in? An intriguing problem for the modern director. Be true to instinct (and probably history) and hit it for all it's worth, or submit to the pressure of English hypocritical Puritanism, where the breasts of royalty are splurged all over the front pages and ministers are caught with their trousers down or knickers up, while Shakespeare, that 'upholder of saintly virtue', is censored. No prizes for guessing where I 'stand' (Shakespearean pun – see Nurse).

And what of Mercutio? Asexual, bisexual, homosexual, misogynist? Young, old, thin, fat? Does he leap around like a leprechaun (played like Puck?) or sit around like some fat alcoholic bar-fly weaving magic with words, mercurial of mind rather than body? Quicksilver. The one who talks rather than does. My money's on the overweight drinker at the bar, spinning Celtic yarns into the night. Climb over twelve naked women to get to a bottle of stout. Beady after twelve pints or a couple of bottles of the red; pick a quarrel with a lightbulb.

\* \* \*

The whole of the first part of the play is intent on building up an image of a young, macho society of swaggering swains, parties, street life, sexual promiscuity. A materialistic society based on the false values of fighting and fucking. This society collides head-on with the pure emotion that Romeo and Juliet feel for each other. Already the time is out of joint, they are out of step with the conventions and behaviour of their peer group. Love? Pooh! 'You speak like a green girl.' Think yourself lucky that 'a man of wax' is asking for your hand. Marriage, my girl, is about wealth and position.

Lawrence Stone says:

In the late Middle Ages, the 'nuclear family' of the 'landed elite' was no more than a loose core at the centre of a dense network of lineage and kin relationships. The reason for this is the preoccupation with the preservation, increase and transmission, through inheritance and marriage of the property and status of lineage, of the generations of ancestors stretching back into the remote past. The larger the property and status, and the more ancient the family encamped on its ancestral acres, the more intense was the preoccupation with the lineage, and thus the greater participation of the kin in the formation and daily life of the conjugal family. To understand the moral premises upon which such a society is based, it is necessary to rid ourselves of three modern, western, culture bound, preconceptions.

The first is that there is a clear dichotomy between marriage for interest, meaning money, status or power, and marriage for effect, meaning love, friendship or sexual attraction; and that the first is morally reprehensible. In the sixteenth century, no such distinction existed, and, if it did, effect was of secondary importance to interest, while romantic love and lust were strongly condemned as ephemeral and irrational grounds for marriage. The second modern preconception is that sexual intercourse, unaccompanied by an emotional relationship, is immoral, and that marriage for interest is, therefore, a form of prostitution. The third is, that personal autonomy, the pursuit by the individual of his or her own happiness, is paramount, a claim justified by the theory that it in fact contributes to the well being of the group.

(*The Family, Sex and Marriage in England, 1500–1800*,
London 1977)

To an Elizabethan audience, the tragedy of Romeo and Juliet, like that of Othello, lay not so much in their ill-starred romance, as in the way they brought destruction upon themselves by violating the norms of the society in which they lived. Property and power were the predominant issues, which governed negotiations for marriage, while the greatest fear, in a society so acutely conscious of status and hierarchy, was of alliance with a family of lower estate or degree than one's own.

Lady Capulet describes Paris:

This precious book of love, this unbound lover,
To beautify him only lacks a cover.

(Act I, Scene iii)

Form therefore is all-important, content immaterial. Your marriage has nothing to do with you, it is a family matter. Now be a good girl and stop crying. 'For this drivelling love', says Mercutio, 'is like a great natural that runs lolling up and down to hide his bauble in a hole.' But Romeo has moved on. Hiding his bauble in any old hole is no longer his prime concern.

Why does Mercutio fight Tybalt? It's not his quarrel. Wilful. Irresponsible. It could only end in tears. Why does Romeo fight Tybalt? It is his quarrel, or is it? In that internecine male world of pride and prejudice, the manly virtues have to be displayed, a friend avenged. But it is a choice. Mercutio chooses, and Romeo chooses. Juliet has a husband chosen for her, but also chooses to choose another. The men go along with the peacock laws of vanity. Juliet goes with her instinct, breaking the male law of non-choice. Brave, outspoken, practical, vulnerable, a female beacon of civil liberty in a dark, chauvinist world.

\* \* \*

The contrast in the two lovers is apparent from their very first meeting. Romeo oblivious of the danger around him, his language, like his love, soaring on wings, daring death by twenty swords for one glimpse of his 'bright angel'. Romantic, impractical. Like a puppy. Juliet, concerned with the danger, practical, forthright, to the point. Declaring her love with a simple beauty before Romeo has the chance to. A modern, emancipated miss:

> JULIET: Thou knowest the mask of night is on my face,
> Else would a maiden blush bepaint my cheek
> For that which thou hast heard me speak tonight.
> Fain would I dwell on form – fain, fain deny
> What I have spoke. But farewell compliment!
> Dost thou love me? I know thou wilt say 'aye'.
> And I will take thy word. Yet, if thou swearest,
> Thou mayst prove false. At lovers' perjuries,
> They say, Jove laughs. O gentle Romeo,
> If thou dost love, pronounce it faithfully.
> Or if thou thinkest I am too quickly won,
> I'll frown, and be perverse, and say thee nay,

So thou wilt woo. But else, not for the world.
In truth, fair Montague, I am too fond,
And therefore thou mayst think my 'haviour light.
But trust me, gentleman, I'll prove more true
Than those that have more cunning to be strange.
I should have been more strange, I must confess,
But that thou overheardest, ere I was ware,
My true-love passion. Therefore pardon me,
And not impute this yielding to light love,
Which the dark night hath so discoverèd.

(Act II, Scene ii)

A disarming directness and simplicity. Reversing the order of conventional behaviour. Nice girls don't proposition. They wait to be asked. Nonsense says Will. If you think and feel something, say it. Love isn't about playing games and social niceties. It's about honesty and equality. (Compare Miranda, *The Tempest*.) Juliet, organising the wedding, masterminding the plan, practical, a chip off the old parental block. Romeo bragging, Juliet silencing. Romeo sometimes like a spoilt child. Juliet sometimes like a gently chiding teacher. Humour is absolutely vital. Otherwise the story is a tedious tale of two over-earnest kids. Let them enjoy themselves for goodness' sake. This relationship, this balance, is maintained throughout the play and is reflected in their language. Romeo, impotent in the face of events, is swept along by the actions of others. Juliet, a determined figure of action, forces, wills things to work. Two youngsters attempting to make sense of a senseless world, a world in which they were ahead of their time.

* * *

Who can Romeo and Juliet turn to for help? In the play, it is the Nurse, a surrogate parent, Juliet's confidante, her companion, her adviser, to whom she turns. It seems that Lady Capulet has a tentative relationship with Juliet to say the least. She is probably jealous and too close in years to be much help. What should the Nurse have done? She certainly should not have encouraged the relationship. But this desire to extract vicarious pleasure from the thought (and act) of Juliet losing her virginity, leads her to abandon all sense of her position and her responsibility. After all, it's fun running around with rope ladders in order to climb moonlit walls and act as go-between, pass love notes and trinkets from one to the other. 'I am the drudge, and toil in your delight. / But you shall bear the burden soon at night' (nudge, nudge, wink, wink). She encourages the liaison with disastrous consequences. Juliet has had her fun. Romeo is banished and a husband who is not in the bed may as well be dead.

> I think it best you marry with the County [Paris].
> O, he's a lovely gentleman!
> Romeo's a dishclout to him.

> (Act III, Scene v)

'Is that what you really think?' 'Cross my heart and hope to die.' Total irresponsibility. Juliet is abandoned. The Nurse, having wrung the last drop out of her love, squeezed her emotions dry, tosses Juliet aside like a rag doll. The Nurse has had her fun. Back to the reality of a proper marriage, there's a good girl. Sleep tight.

Friar Laurence, confessor to both children, their spiritual advisor, Romeo's mentor, desperately attempts to cover up his mistake and compounds it even further. He conjures up a fantastical plot, fraught with so many difficulties that it was odds-on to fail. And what is it that he is asking a young girl to do? Take a potion that counterfeits death for forty-two hours and, when she wakes up, she'll be in a vault with the decomposing bodies of her uncles and aunts.

> Take thou this vial . . .
> And this distilling liquor drink thou off;
> When presently through all thy veins shall run
> A cold and drowsy humour. . . .
>           . . . . .
> No warmth, no breath, shall testify thou livest.
> The roses in thy lips and cheeks shall fade
> To wanny ashes, thy eyes' windows fall
> Like death when he shuts up the day of life.
> Each part, deprived of supple government,
> Shall, stiff and stark and cold, appear like death.
> And in this borrowed likeness of shrunk death

> Thou shalt continue two-and-forty hours,
> And then awake as from a pleasant sleep.

> (Act IV, Scene i)

What sort of plan is that? It's crazy. And Juliet does as he suggests with a fortitude which is quite extraordinary.

The Friar, as the one having spiritual responsibility for the well-being of the children, should have known better. The Nurse, having material responsibility for Juliet, should have proceeded with equal caution. Love is not a game. All the events in the play could have been foreseen and averted. People make bad decisions and then use destiny, the fates, the heavens, the stars to excuse them. It is a play about social responsibility and existential choice. There is a social system operating where, unless specific fundamental reforms occur, just such a tragedy is waiting to happen again. This is a mercenary society, grasping, greedy, avaricious, uncaring, and any individual who pits him or herself against it, is doomed.

\* \* \*

The overriding preoccupation of the Montagues and the Capulets is made clear in the aftermath of the tragedy when the two bereaved fathers promise to set up golden statues to each others' children.

> MONTAGUE: . . . I will raise her statue in pure gold,
> That whiles Verona by that name be known,
> There shall no figure at that rate be set
> As that of true and faithful Juliet.
> CAPULET: As rich shall Romeo's by his lady's lie.

> (Act V, Scene iii)

Even now, they choose to express their loss in monetary terms. For the only way they can measure the value of their children is by financial sacrifice. But the children died because Capulet wanted more wealth and was prepared to disinherit Juliet if she refused to marry Paris, a relative of Prince Escalus, and thus move the family closer to the seat of power. Juliet is treated like a chattel by her father, a pawn in a game of power, whose feelings are of minimal interest to him. 'The most you wanted was her advancement', says the Friar, in a rare flash of insight.

In its commitment and extravagance, the passion of Romeo and Juliet stands out against a background of licentiousness, on the one hand, and commercial transaction (the usual preliminary to marriage), on the other. Capulet's speeches to his daughter are violent in their cruelty; he will be obeyed. Love is not part of the marriage bargain; he is pleased that he has found a suitable match:

> **A gentleman of noble parentage,**
> **Of fair demesnes, youthful, and nobly trained,**
> **Stuffed, as they say, with honourable parts.**

> (Act III, Scene v)

And that is the extent of his interest in Juliet's welfare. Contrast the crocodile tears of melodramatic falsehood from the family, on the fake death of Juliet, with the real emotion of both Romeo and Juliet at their respective deaths.

Juliet is abandoned by her mother: 'Do what thou wilt for I have done with thee.' She is deserted by the Nurse: 'I think it best you marry with the County.' And the best the Friar can do is to come up with a cockeyed, crazy plan involving drugs and tombs. Admittedly he is at knife-point for the second time in twenty-four hours as both young people go to him in desperation for some way out of the mess that he has got them into. But there is no way out. His plan depends on too many unknowns, a desperate remedy for a desperate time. Capulet advances the marriage by one day. (It was already too quick, but he couldn't wait any longer to get his grasping, greedy hands on Paris's title.) The Friar's plan is blown. (Critics of the modern-dress school of thought point out that Friar John being locked up in a house of plague and therefore unable to deliver Friar Laurence's letter to Romeo is unbelievable. Friar Laurence would have texted or phoned. *Tant pis*.)

And Romeo meanwhile? He is in Mantua still believing in fates and stars:

> **If I may trust the flattering truth of sleep,**
> **My dreams presage some joyful news at hand.**
> **My bosom's lord sits lightly in his throne,**

And all this day an unaccustomed spirit
Lifts me above the ground with cheerful thoughts.

(Act V, Scene i)

In the next moment, when he receives the news of Juliet's supposed death, there occurs one of those astonishing Shakespearean objective flashes of insight into the way the world wags, his real view of what surrounds him. In buying poison from an Apothecary with which to kill himself, Romeo suddenly steps right outside the character of a wimpish, lovelorn loon, tossed hither and thither like flotsam and jetsam on the tide of man-made idiocy, and delivers a devastating comment on the society in which he finds himself. He pays the Apothecary:

There is thy gold – worse poison to men's souls,
Doing more murder in this loathsome world,
Than these poor compounds that thou mayst not sell.
I sell thee poison. Thou hast sold me none.

(Act V, Scene i)

In this moment, he reveals a social conscience and an acute aware-ness of the motives of greed and avarice that dominate all thinking, a hitherto totally unseen side of the feud, an echo of his opening encounter with Benvolio. It is Shakespeare the egalitarian, the humanist at work. Romeo instinctively and ideologically comprehends the very root-rottenness at the base of not just Escalus's regime, but of all regimes that treat women like cattle at auction and put commerce before humanity. Compare Romeo's speech on gold with one from *Timon of Athens*:

TIMON: Gold? Yellow, glittering, precious gold?

. . . . .

. . . Thus much of this will make
Black white, foul fair, wrong right,
Base noble, old young, coward valiant.

. . .Why, this

Will lug your priests and servants from your sides,
Pluck stout men's pillows from below their heads.
This yellow slave
Will knit and break religions, bless th'accursed,

Make the hoar leprosy adored, place thieves,
And give them title, knee, and approbation,
With senators on the bench. This is it
That makes the wappened widow wed again –
She, whom the spital-house and ulcerous sores
Would cast the gorge at, this embalms and spices
To th'April day again. Come, damned earth,
Thou common whore of mankind, that puts odds
Among the rout of nations, I will make thee
Do thy right nature.

(Act IV, Scene iii)

Marx analysed it thus: money, as much as it possesses the ability to buy and appropriate everything, is the object most worth possessing. Money is the pimp between the desire and the desired, between life and man's means of living.

Shakespeare paints a brilliant picture of the nature of money. He brings out two properties in particular. One, money is the visible divinity, the transformation of all human and natural qualities into their opposites; their universal confusion and the inversion of things. Money brings together impossibilities. Two, money is the universal whore, the universal pimp of men and peoples. The inversion and confusion of all human and natural qualities. The divine power of money lies in its nature as the estranged and alienating specious essence of man which alienates itself by selling itself. It is the alienating capacity of mankind. But what I, as a man, cannot do – i.e. what all my individual powers cannot do, I can do with the help of money. Money therefore transforms each of these essential powers into something which it is not. Into its opposite.

Money is both a pimp and a whore, the real poison in the world.

I am not trying to make out a case for Romeo being an early Marxist (or am I?). But as with so many of the visible and invisible bullets in the plays, here, in this little scene with the Apothecary, in Romeo's statement of gold being the real poisoner, the real murderer in the world, we have the real story of why Romeo and Juliet died. And recognising this reality, the scales drop from Romeo's eyes: 'I defy you stars.' He has reached the existential point arrived at by so many of Shakespeare's protagonists, where the realisation sets in that one's destiny is in one's own hands and in no one else's.

No stars, no heavens, no Fates. 'Tomorrow, and tomorrow, and tomorrow.' 'The readiness is all.' 'We are such stuff as dreams are made on.' 'On, on, if not to heaven, then hand in hand to hell.' Romeo is now a man of action. He will buy poison, go to Verona, prise open the tomb, die with Juliet – decisive at last. No longer 'fortune's fool'. And nobody will get the blame. The Friar is exonerated. Escalus says to him, 'We still have known thee for a holy man.' At least in the Brook poem from which Shakespeare took the original story, Friar Laurence is banished for his part in the tragedy. But no, there are no scapegoats in Verona; everything, as is customary in politics, is smoothed over. Important to present a united front in these matters.

And those gold statues will atone. They cost a lot of money.

# The Tempest

## in the cold light of day –
## exile and dreams of revenge

In *The Tempest* old Shakespearian friends meet for the last time: man of action friend, man of imagination friend, nature versus nurture friend, usurpation friend, theatrical friend, power friend. A man sits in exile in a café in Paris, Prague, Miami, Bogota – and dreams of revenge on those who have booted him out of his kingdom. It is a waking dream, a sleeping dream, a daymare, a nightmare. He wakes up, pays for his coffee, his croissant. Goes off down the street, maybe picks up a cigarette butt, or if you are Imelda, tries on one of a thousand shoes. Nothing has changed, he is still the same, others are still in charge. He is still in exile, the café table his world, his distracted mind his globe.

**O God, I could be bounded in a nutshell and count myself a king of infinite space, were it not that I have bad dreams.**

**(*Hamlet*, Act II, Scene ii )**

I was once standing in a toilet in Neary's bar in Dublin and there was a man standing next to me doing what is necessary. A great, big, broad hunk of a fella in a shabby suit, and he said to me 'I'm the King of Connaught.' 'I beg your pardon?', I said. 'I'm the fuckin' King of Connaught.' (Don't ask me why the King of Connaught spoke with a Dublin accent but he did.) 'And do you know where the King of Munster is?' 'No', I said. 'He lives in a bungalow in Brighton.' So I thought, Well, yes, all right, so the King of Munster lives in a bungalow in Brighton, I suppose that's the fate of contemporary Irish kings who have no hope of ever inheriting the land again. But somewhere in Brighton the King of Munster is still sitting there with his sword and insignia, hoping and pretending that there is life after republicanism.

So exile could be anywhere. It could be a café table, it could be lying in bed, on top of a bus, it could be a desert island. It could be Brighton.

The magic of the island as represented by Ariel and Caliban and the restoring of harmony to a disordered universe by the old wizard himself, have conditioned critical thinking on *The Tempest* for almost four centuries. This thinking, along with the classification of the play as a romance, has successfully served to disguise the fact that *The Tempest* is a vicious play about a wish-fulfilment dream of political revenge. The story is simple.

Prospero, the ex-Duke of Milan, is obsessed with his brother, Antonio, who has usurped his position as Duke, and with those who have aided him, principally an old enemy, Alonso the King of Naples along with his brother Sebastian. It is yet another turn of the old screw that Shakespeare uses in earlier plays: the theme of the usurping brother, of blood not being thicker than water, and so on. But this time it is a political killing rather than a literal one. Usually a brother kills a brother to take over the throne, whether it is Claudius killing Old Hamlet or Richard III killing everybody. Here, Antonio metaphorically 'kills' Prospero by sending him into exile. Everything that happens in the play stems from that one act of usurpation. Prospero then sits in a bungalow in Brighton for twelve years, brooding on revenge. That is the story. Simple.

Napoleon on Elba:

What was left to him? No future, only ultimate death on the island. How could this extraordinary man adapt himself to this position? After activity and glory on such an heroic scale how could he be content to do nothing but wait patiently for death? How impotent, frustrated, and hopeless he must have felt. A magnificent past, an impotent present, a hopeless future. How could he pass the time? He made a definite effort and buried himself in his memories, but how futile these reminiscences of past greatness and glory as contrasted with his present circumstances.

**An ordinary man may have submitted and adapted himself to the situation, but not an extraordinary man such as the Emperor.**

(James Kemble, *Napoleon Immortal*, 1959)

The ambivalent heart of *The Tempest's* fantastical mosaic leads to some of the most bizarre productions of any of Shakespeare's plays and to the widest possible divergences of opinion as to its meaning. And, because it is a play about imagination, it invites that imagination to run riot in such a way that the staging of no two *Tempests* is ever alike. That is both the strength of the play and its weakness. This weakness manifests itself in production as a lack of a coherent political centre, and accordingly many productions resort to peripherals to try and demonstrate what a particular director thinks was going on in Shakespeare's mind at the particular time in his life when the play was written.

Now it is clear that Caliban and Ariel are two quite extraordinary creations that have come to fascinate people through the ages – performers, directors, critics, academics – to the point where the play has been seen to be only about Caliban and Ariel and a bunch of boring lords. They are always called 'boring lords' – and (inadvertently) are often played as such. But the problem with 'those boring lords' (of whom let us not forget Prospero is one) is that they occupy three-quarters of the play. Now, if they are that boring, what is it in the play that is so exciting? You may as well get rid of them (some productions do), and be left with some weird play – about the psyche and psychoanalysis, the id and the ego, the bestiality of man versus the spiritual – that lasts about an hour.

*The Tempest* is supposedly Shakespeare's last play with just a chunk of *Henry VIII* and other collaborations to follow. It is, I suppose, inevitable that his artistic farewell would be interpreted down through the ages as Shakespeare's 'swan song', 'the death of the artist' (one of the most consistent interpretations), and the final lines of the Epilogue as a plea for forgiveness for all that the artist creates. Prospero's staff is seen as the muse: once it is broken, and the muse has deserted the artist, he/she stands alone, a bare forked animal – 'What strength I have's mine own.' Ultimately the fate of the artist to succeed or fail lies in the hands of those people who respond to his or her work. A broken staff is no defence against critical opprobrium. So, it has been seen as Shakespeare retiring to enjoy the autumnal twilight of his life in the golden glow of his orchard in Stratford-upon-Avon, looking back over his life and forgiving those critics who have been less than favourably disposed towards his works. A play of nostalgia and regret, and personal battles with the ego, the spirit, the body, and so on. All these allegorical interpretations hold water up to a point, but only to half-way up the bottle; there is too much air at the top. Yet the clues as to the structure are laid out in a very clear trail right the way through the entire canon of plays from the very moment that Shakespeare first explodes into the round world of the Elizabethan 'O' or oblong.

\* \* \*

The very first clue is in the title itself – *The Tempest*. Just about everybody recognises now, although this is a recent acknowledgement, that the tempest is not simply an elemental storm during which a real boat is shipwrecked. More important, the play is concerned with the tempest of the mind, or of the soul, a deep psychological trauma that is induced through the releasing of the subconscious either by natural means – sleep and dreams – or through some kind of self-induced hallucinatory experience. A brainstorm. Lear, mad on the heath, identifies with the elemental storm, 'the tempest in my mind'. There is a moment in *Richard III* when Richard's imprisoned brother, George, Duke of Clarence, just prior to his murder by Richard's hired hit-men, wakes up and describes his nightmare to his jailer, Brackenbury: 'O then began the tempest to my soul.' That 'tempest to the soul', his nightmare of death by drowning at the hands of his brother, is the starting point of the play, *The Tempest*. But it is now Prospero's soul that is tempestuously in turmoil.

Now sleep and dreams are, in essence, the key words of *The Tempest*. 'Sleep' occurs some thirty-odd times, and 'dream' forty times, and speeches based on waking or sleeping are dotted throughout the play, permeating the atmosphere:

> **We are such stuff**
> **As dreams are made on; and our little life**
> **Is rounded with a sleep.**

(Act IV, Scene i)

We are concerned here with the power of an imagination that is released by dreaming, the power of the mind to conceive of things that, paradoxically, the mind does not even comprehend. It is this boundless infinity of the imagination, a consequence of all our thoughts, our hopes, and aspirations, that Shakespeare analyses. But the power of man to accomplish what he achieves in those dreams is not infinite, it is very finite. Put more simply, it's the discrepancy once again between the thought of action and the act itself.

This tempest of the soul, this dream of Prospero's is the same dream that we all have, for example, when, on being sacked from our job, we go out of the office and think of what we should have said. How we should have cut the boss, the teacher, the tax inspector, down to size, stood up for our rights. In any situation in which we are humiliated by someone more powerful, we experience a well of frustration, of impotence, of injustice, of anger that surges up through our souls and we replay that moment of humiliation over and over again, inventing for ourselves a completely different scenario of what we should have done, of what we should have said, of how we would handle the situation if it were ever to happen again. It does not obscure the fact, however, that we are still standing outside that office door having got the sack, fantasising about how we should have taken over the firm, the country, the universe ourselves. In other words it is that same wish-fulfilment dream of Prospero's to reinstate himself as Duke of Milan that is at the very heart of *The Tempest*.

In our dreams we can all win the Olympic hundred metres in a world record time – do it in our heads. I've just done it. I've just done it again! The actuality of it is that this morning I ran up and down on the spot 140 times and took five minutes to do it (in an effort to get fit – again!). The actuality, of course, is 'bounded in a nutshell'; it is the narrowest channel of thought that corresponds to how we perform.

When the down-trodden underling has to yield to circumstance and to take things lying down, he dreams of himself standing up for his rights and being victorious. He did not realise that he had it in him until he dreamed of himself actually living that role. The very fact of having that dream boosts his self-esteem: he squares his shoulders, is encouraged to have another shot at it, and he comes out successfully. Thus a dream is not merely a wish, it is an encouragement and inspiration. Because it shows a man what he can be, it enables him to become so. The dream is not merely wishful thinking, it is creative and purposive; it does not merely allow us to sleep in the night, it encourages us to action in the day.

(J.A. Hadfield, *Dreams and Nightmares*, 1954, p. 29)

I talk constantly in these essays of the man of action, the *Realpolitiker*, the man who seizes the moment, the man who is capable of extending his capacity along the lines that correspond to what he is capable of conceiving in his mind. Antonio is that man in this play. Antonio is the man of action, Prospero of inaction caught half-way between his responsibilities as a leader of the state and other intellectual pursuits that lead him to be a bad ruler.

This is one of the prime tenets of the piece – that the regime of Prospero was obviously on the slippery slope. The similarity is with the rule of Old Hamlet, or Richard II – the state or country is on the slide, and therefore the need to reinstate firm government, to re-establish the *status quo*, is seen by those surrounding the leaders – a brother and a king, in this instance – as an opportunity to move in and right the tottering regime.

The island that Prospero inhabits in his mind is an island of insularity, but it is also the world, it is also the cosmos. That island, as Jan Kott says in *Shakespeare Our Contemporary* is winter, it is summer, it is spring, it is autumn. It is barren, it is fertile. It is rocks and lunar landscape, it is bowers and flowers. It expands and contracts in our minds according to outlook and attitude. In other words, we are looking at the universality of a problem, but through the personal eyes of a man who at this moment is suffering from the deprivation of his position of authority. Prospero is a Tzar of Russia, the Shah of Persia, a political prisoner, frustrated, angry and bitter, unable to return. The real, true meaning of exile. Banished ('Banishment?' says Romeo – 'Do not say "banishment"!' – 'Be merciful, say "death"'), forever cut off from the culture, the society, the people, the roots that you understand, unable to return to the place of your birth or your culture. That is the situation that Prospero finds himself in.

This then is a dream of wish-fulfilment revenge that might occur in anybody. Merely to apply to the play the theory of the artist in the twilight of his career asking for forgiveness for his work misses the social and political centre of the piece, and relegates the play to the realm of soporific romanticism.

* * *

The story begins with the lives of a bunch of usurpers being placed in the hands of an artisan, a boatswain. 'What care these roarers for the name of king?' This is fundamental. Political order is reversed – all the wealth, power and position of the royal party are as nothing. They are forced to rely on 'hard-handed men' whose trade is the rope and the sail. 'My kingdom for a horse.' Shakespeare the great leveller. Then, at the point when the boat goes down and the lords are about to be killed, what miracle happens? Bang! Not even wet, not even spoiled in any way. Lifted out, dumped on dry land, clothes coloured brighter than bright, as if the whole bunch had been on a 'midnight mushrump' binge. Miraculously, just like that. Just as they're about to drown I go 'bang' and I've saved them. There they are. In my head.

My desire for revenge wants to see them dead, drowned. But the problem with that is I would be left on my own, still without power, without position. So I'll torture them further. Humiliate them – I want them to fall in front of me on their knees and humble themselves, beg my forgiveness and give me back my dukedom. I'm not going to let them drown with the boat, I'm going to drive them through hell and back to make their lives a misery until I'm ready. Prospero accordingly proceeds to make a vicious use of his imagination and terrorise his foes in the guise of Ariel, the agent of his mind, a figure akin to a barbaric instrument of torture, the process of thought operating at the speed of light.

The storm, the brainstorm – the 'tempest to the soul' – calms somewhat and the story begins. We learn who Prospero is, who these boring lords are, and lo and behold they are about as boring as a bunch of rattle-snakes. Prospero, in his head becomes a man of action, the impotence of exile banished. He says what he's going to do and then proceeds to do it. A series of mirror images permeates the play: master and slave, power and weakness. The acquisitive nature of Antonio grabbing the crown is mirrored in the clowns, Trinculo and Stephano, grabbing the trinkets. Right the way from the bottom of the ladder up, everybody is on the make, fighting to be top dog, and whatever rung they reach, they are concerned only with booting those beneath them further down. So with Trinculo and Stephano.

Even before Prospero's deposition by Antonio there is an act of usurpation. Prospero the arid, Prospero the intellectual, Prospero, back in Milan, the academic, subdues Prospero the bestial, the animal, the natural, the instinctive. Post-Antonio yet another act of usurpation; that of the island. Prospero, deposing Caliban, creating him his slave. Caliban, part Prospero's animalism, part symbol of those foreign territories that had been captured and explored by Elizabethan sailors plundering the Indies, discovering strange islands inhabited by wild, primitive peoples and enslaving them; strange animals that are brought back and exhibited in the streets, as Trinculo says, 'for a piece of gold'.

\* \* \*

Prospero in his head conjures up a boat in a storm. On board are all his enemies. More important, it contains his brother Antonio who, in collusion with the King of Naples, has booted him into exile. Not killed this time, just one minuscule humanitarian stage further back. After all he's no danger. And what a story he tells Miranda, his daughter! (Does she exist back in Milan? Or is she too part of his wish-fulfilment?) This 'good old man' renowned for the liberal arts, this aesthete, the leading intellectual of his time (so he says), left the running of the state to his brother.

Consider the following scenario.

**ANTONIO: Prospero, there are three million unemployed, a hundred thousand businesses going bust. The pound has been devalued twenty-five per cent. A quarter of a million people are homeless and all you do is worry about what Wittgenstein really meant!**

**PROSPERO: Don't bother me now, Tony, I am just perfecting a disapp-
earing dove. Have you got a silk handkerchief? (You old sorcerer you!)**

No wonder his brother took over. Prospero? His library was
'dukedom large enough'. And now Antonio has ruled for twelve years.
No one has got rid of him, he was too clever, did a deal with the King
of Naples to leave him alone.

**PROSPERO:**          **Of temporal royalties**
**He thinks me now incapable, . . .**

(me – with reason)

                     **. . . confederates –**
**So dry he was for sway – wi'th'King of Naples**
**To give him annual tribute, do him homage,**
**Subject his coronet to his crown, and bend**
**The dukedom, yet unbowed – alas, poor Milan –**
**To most ignoble stooping.**

     . . . . .

**MIRANDA: Wherefore did they not**
**That hour destroy us?**

**PROSPERO: Well demanded, wench.**
**My tale provokes that question. Dear, they durst not;**
**So dear the love my people bore me;**

(proof, please!)

**A mark so bloody on the business, but**
**With colours fairer painted their foul ends.**
**In few, they hurried us aboard a bark,**
**Bore us some leagues to sea, where they prepared**
**A rotten carcass of a butt, not rigged,**
**Nor tackle, sail, nor mast. The very rats**
**Instinctively have quit it.**

     . . . . .

**MIRANDA:**          **How came we ashore?**

**PROSPERO: By Providence divine.**
**Some food we had, and fresh water, that**

> A noble Neapolitan, Gonzalo,
> Out of his charity, who being then appointed
> Master of this design, did give us, . . .

(So they are not going to starve, and presumably it must have been at least a month's supplies. No point else.)

>                 . . . with
> Rich garments, linens, stuffs, and necessaries
> Which since have steaded much. . . .

(I see, quite a Harvey Nicks full!)

>          . . . So, of his gentleness,
> Knowing I loved my books, he furnished me,
> From mine own library with volumes that
> I prize above my dukedom.

>                (Act I, Scene ii)

Prospero's tale emerges as biased and emotional. And why not? After all, it has taken him twelve years to tell it. This rotten carcass of a boat, this leaky hulk, this rat-quitting bark, suddenly expands, becomes larger and larger, like the fisherman's tale in the adage. The fissures are suddenly caulked up, the bilges are baled, and it finally ends up as something of a three-masted schooner. Food, water, rich garments, linens, stuffs, necessaries, books from his library 'which since have steaded much'. Sounds like he should have applied for an export licence. And do we think that Gonzalo would have risked his life to do all this unauthorised? Prospero thinks so. More probably it was by design, otherwise Antonio might just as well have killed them. And Miranda? What is her memory of all this?

>             'Tis far off,
> And rather like a dream than an assurance
>                . . . Had I not
> Four or five women once that tended me?

>                (Act I, Scene ii)

This worries Prospero. If Miranda recalls this experience, perhaps she remembers the real events of twelve years ago. No. Thank goodness.

He can tell the story his way. But the important thing about Miranda's memory is that her one recollection is of privilege. Nurture has already tainted her. She has inherited a sense of class difference, there can be no fresh start. Despite her innocence her language to Caliban is appalling:

> MIRANDA:　　　　　　　　Abhorrèd slave,
> Which any print of goodness wilt not take,
> Being capable of all ill! I pitied thee,
> Took pains to make thee speak . . .
> 　　　　　　　　. . . when thou didst not, savage,
> Know thine own meaning, but wouldst gabble like
> A thing most brutish, I endowed thy purposes
> With words that made them known. But thy vile race,
> 　　　　. . . had that in't which good natures
> Could not abide to be with. Therefore wast thou
> Deservedly confined into this rock, who hadst
> Deserved more than a prison.
>
> 　　　　　　　　　　　　　　(Act I, Scene ii )

No wonder some editors give the speech to Prospero – too distasteful, otherwise.

Why a daughter? Why not a son? Impossible. His revenge is surrogate. In his dream his daughter will marry the son of the king. This son will himself be king one day. She, herself now queen, will bear a son who will be king. Prospero's revenge will be complete. His grandson will rule Milan and Naples. This is Prospero's goal, the grooming of Miranda. This will be his revenge. But for Miranda, the memory of the first two and a half years is fatal. Her place in a male world of privilege and power is already ordained.

The chess game:

> MIRANDA: Sweet lord, you play me false.
>
> FERDINAND:　　　　　　　　　No, my dearest love,
> I would not for the world.
>
> MIRANDA: Yes, for a score of kingdoms you should wrangle,
> And I would call it fair play.
>
> 　　　　　　　　　　　　　　(Act V, Scene i)

Whatever you do – cheat, lie, brag, corrupt, kill, conquer – I will support you. Prospero has lost her. That game of chess, a metaphor for the power politics of the world, sums it all up. Foot-soldiers are overwhelmed, the castle stormed, the knights and bishops overthrown, the king captured. The queen will call it fair play, whichever way it is accomplished. Ends and means. Miranda has already accepted the corrupting force of the territorial imperative. Everything is legitimate if it is accomplished in the name of power and possession. The Antonios of this world. In that one small nugget of a scene, Miranda legitimises her uncle's behaviour as Prospero admits to himself the inevitability of might over right. It is a frightening moment when Miranda steps out from the cell, looks at the courtiers, Antonio and Sebastian, the thugs, the sharks, the villains, who have done her father down, and says:

> **O brave new world,**
> **That has such people in't!**
>
> (Act V, Scene i)

'Tis new to thee', says Prospero. He knows she is soon to be corrupted. Since he is not able to be part of it himself, it is an irony that Prospero will send Miranda back to Milan to swim in that shark-infested pool. It is a cynical view of the world: if you can't beat them, join them. Miranda, as Ferdinand's queen, will take her place in a formal, corrupt society that only knows how to play by certain rules. If you don't play by those rules, you don't win. Prospero didn't win, but his daughter will. But at least if she can't be king she can be the next best thing, queen, and, maybe, a mother of kings. In Shakespeare's society the only way for women to have power was to be next to the source of power. If you are Gertrude, in *Hamlet*, and you manage to marry two kings, you stay where you have the influence. It is a society where women are bartered to the highest bidder. A harsh world, a hard world. One that sickened Shakespeare. No wonder his plays deal with dreams and change.

\* \* \*

So where does Caliban, that 'debauched' fish, fit into the dream?

Evidence of archaic images is found in our bodies, carrying about with them traces of their archaic ancestry. Our aquatic ancestry, for instance, survives not only in the persistence of gills as the Eustachian tube connecting the mouth with the ear, but also in the fact that in our veins there flows a stream of blood plasma which consists of practically the same constituents, sodium, potassium, and calcium, and nearly all the same proportion, as sea water, which it originally was. As with our bodies, so with our minds – we carry about with us archaic modes of thinking and of behaviour. Have we not all at times been astounded at the bizarre thoughts that occur to our minds, at the shocking desires which sometimes possess us, and at the irrational impulses that sway us against our volition? They come 'out of the blue' of our radical unconscious and are quite alien to our ordinary civilised modes of thinking. It is not surprising that St Augustine thanks God that he was not responsible for his dreams!

(J.A Hadfield, *Dreams and Nightmares*, 1954)

Caliban is that suppressed side of Prospero's sexual nature, the cock that has to be chained, the incestuous feelings of a single man for his daughter, alone together on a desert island for twelve years. Miranda is now fifteen, sleeps alone. Has to, Prospero dare not trust himself.

Hadfield says,

This collective unconscious, says Jung, consists of the 'inherited potentialities of human imagination'. 'It is the all-controlling deposit of ancestral experiences from untold millions of years, the echo of pre-historic world events to which each century adds an infinitesimal small amount of variation and differentiation. These primordial images are the most ancient, universal, and deep thoughts of mankind.' The collective unconscious therefore 'contains not only every beautiful and great thought and feeling of humanity, but also every deed of shame and devilry of which human beings have ever been capable.' The collective unconscious constantly affects our habits and behaviour quite unknown to ourselves, for 'it is a determining constituent of all experiences'.

(Ibid.)

Caliban the cock, Caliban the cannibal, the primitive, has to be subdued, colonised. Caliban the man, no fish – 'legged like a man', 'fins like arms', 'the third man that e'er I sighed for'. Ferdinand, too, has to be chained up like Caliban, his sexual desires (and Miranda's) too strong to be let loose. Show them a masque (this would please the court, particularly King James).

The play, after all, moves towards a wedding, and the most palpable example we see of the magician's powers is the anaesthetised betrothal masque, presided over by Juno, where the lusty Venus and her destructive son Cupid have been banished from the scene. But the performance is also preceded by the most dire warnings against sexuality:

> PROSPERO: . . . If thou dost break her virgin-knot before
> All sanctimonious ceremonies may
> With full and holy rite be ministered,
> No sweet aspersion shall the heavens let fall
> To make this contract grow; but barren hate,
> Sour-eyed disdain and discord shall bestrew
> The union of your bed with weeds so loathly
> That you shall hate it both. Therefore take heed.

Male sexuality this time: all the lust is presumed to be Ferdinand's, whilst Miranda remains Prospero's innocent child. Ferdinand's reassuring reply, an overly emphatic protestation of chastity, includes submerged fantasies of rape and more than a hint that when the lust of the wedding night cools, so will his marital devotion:

> . . . the murkiest den,
> The most opportune place, the strong'st suggestion
> Our worser genius can, shall never melt
> Mine honour into lust, to take away
> The edge of that day's celebration . . .
>
> (Act IV, Scene i)

This is the other side of the assumption that all women at heart are whores: all men at heart are rapists – Caliban, Ferdinand, and of course that means Prospero too.

* * *

*The Tempest* has been subject to these doubts, subversions and reversals not only because part of its subject is colonisation. The play would have been put on the defensive anyway if only because the master–slave relationship of Prospero / Caliban is openly subject to racist interpretation. No amount of noble savage will do.

And Ariel, that malicious needle of darting light – the vicious revenge-exacting agent of Prospero's thought-process (no gentle spiriting here) – is enslaved to Prospero in the same way:

> . . . **I will rend an oak**
> **And peg thee in his knotty entrails, till**
> **Thou hast howled away twelve winters.**

> **(Act I, Scene ii)**

Prospero's mind is trapped in the thought of vengeance, and until that vengeance has been exacted, he cannot relax. His mind is twisted in bitter torment. Only when he has smashed and pummelled his enemies into submission can Ariel be released from that torment, from that 'cleft pine' that he has inhabited for twelve years. Twelve years. The exact time that Prospero has been in exile, his head trapped in the pine and pain of the past. Only when he has purged himself of those feelings can he release his mind from the bonds that bind it. Be free. Move forward. It has taken him twelve years to tell Miranda the story.

The play progresses in a very clear pattern of vengeance for power taken and power to be regained. And there is haste, there is speed. Time is not on Prospero's side. Time is not on your side when, in your dream, you run to catch the train, and, with the train gradually pulling away, you sprint like mad to keep up with it. Sometimes you succeed in jumping on and you breathe a sigh of relief. Sometimes you relax and say 'Too bad, I've missed it', and wake up. The time element of the dream is absolutely crucial – there is haste, there is speed – Prospero's plans have to be accomplished within a certain time-span – what's the time, what's the time? Two o'clock, three o'clock, four o'clock. It must be done by six o'clock.

> **ARIEL: Is there more toil? . . .**
> **Let me remember thee what thou hast promised,**

Which is not yet performed me.

PROSPERO:                    How now, moody?
What is't thou canst demand?

ARIEL:                 My liberty.

PROSPERO: Before the time be out? No more.

Prospero himself wants rid of this pain, this turmoil, but there will be no let-up in the torment until he has purged himself of the hate and frustration, waking in a cold sweat of reality. Before the time be out? Impossible. Trapped in a nightmare of his own making.

'Freedom, highday, highday, freedom.' 'Get a new master, get a new man.' Take these chains from my mind and set me free. By six o'clock. Sebastian and Antonio would murder Alonso – brothers in arms. Trinculo and Stephano would murder Prospero. Wake up! Wake up!

Correspondingly, through this mirror imagery, the time-span of the play may be that of an afternoon performance on a stage, artificially, in front of an audience. That artificiality, that act of creation of a piece of theatre that we see mirrored in the time of the real world, is, yet again, the acceptance that a play is like a dream, that it is not real – that spectators and actors alike are drawn into a relationship with each other suspending disbelief together in a unifying act that is broken and smashed the moment the performance is ended and the audience exits into the street. On that stage, we've fought for crowns and battled with monsters, we've created fantastical images and wrestled for kingdoms, but we go out into the dark of a city night, among the tin cans and the rubbish and the lorries belching out fumes. Out into reality. In other words, nothing has changed; only, for a short period of time, we have suspended ourselves in animation before going back out into the real world.

So it is with Prospero, so it is with the performance – the two things running parallel. Prospero does not have much time, he has the length of the dream in which to accomplish everything. But when Prospero, having gone through this exorcism, finally goes back into the real world, he will be the same old Prospero who was booted out of Milan. The same old man sitting on the park bench. The same old Russian waiter in exile. The same old heir to the Romanian throne fighting with somebody in a garret in New York over who is next in line to take over. He's me, still doing my 140 running-on-the-spot jogging exercises. He's the King of Munster in his bungalow in Brighton.

\* \* \*

And so to the final scene. Why didn't Prospero finish off Antonio, Sebastian and Alonso while he had the chance? He was too soft. That is why he will never return to Milan and regain his dukedom. If he did, Antonio would take it all over again. He, Antonio, had no need to kill Prospero. He knew that Prospero was too ineffectual to be able to combat him.

> MIRANDA:          Wherefore did they not
> That hour destroy us?
> PROSPERO:          . . . Dear, they durst not.
>
>                          (Act I, Scene ii)

Durst not? That man? What a joke. Prospero has a need to kill Antonio, but he doesn't – he forgives him. Wrong. As the dream starts to fade, as morning approaches, as his mind starts to clear, so the effort of the night is banished and the desire for total revenge fades.

> PROSPERO:          . . . The charm dissolves apace.
> And as the morning steals upon the night,
> Melting the darkness, so their rising senses
> Begin to chase the ignorant fumes that mantle
> Their clearer reason.
>
>                          (Act V, Scene i)

And throughout the final scene, during these waking moments, as the mind swims up into consciousness to take in the ugly industrial wasteland of a world that is there instead of the desert island, so Prospero's strength ebbs too. From being at first bewildered and disbelieving, he finds the arrogance of the court reasserting itself. As 'miracle' succeeds 'miracle', so the revelations become commonplace. It is like attempting to keep up with modern technology. Wonders will cease. Prospero doubts himself. They doubt him. Dressed in his everyday clothes he is no longer a magician. His staff is broken, his strength is his own, which is most faint. And, as this insubstantial pageant fades leaving not a wrack behind, so he is left at his café table, on his bench, in his bed.

And Antonio? No begging forgiveness for him. 'Ha ha, brother', says Prospero, 'Bet you're sorry now.' Not a bit of it. Antonio says nothing in the last scene except to comment on the commercial viability of exploiting Caliban.

> SEBASTIAN:   Ha, ha!
> **What things are these, my lord Antonio?**
> **Will money buy 'em?**
>
> ANTONIO:              Very like. One of them
> **Is a plain fish, and no doubt marketable.**
>
> (Act V, Scene i)

The nature of Antonio has not changed one iota. He is still the synthesis of *Realpolitik*, of Machiavelli, as Prospero has known very well all along. In that one (a plain fish and no doubt marketable) line, as so often is the case in the final scenes of Shakespeare's plays, a bullet is fired with a ferocity that shatters all illusion. No play about forgiveness this. The fundamental clash is between the man of action and the man of imagination. The polarity of the canon itself. As long as we believe in a system of acquisition and exploitation, the Antonios will always triumph over the Prosperos. Let W.H. Auden have the last word from *The Sea and the Mirror*:

> As all the pigs have turned back into men
> And the sky is auspicious and the sea
> Calm as a clock, we can all go home again.
>
> Yes, it undoubtedly looks as if we
> Could take life as easily now as tales
> Write ever-after: not only are the
>
> Two heads silhouetted against the sails
> – And kissing, of course – well built, but the lean
> Fool is quite a person, the fingernails
>
> Of the dear old butler for once quite clean,
> And the royal passengers quite as good
> As rustics, perhaps better, for they mean

What they say, without, as a rustic would,
Casting reflections on the courtly crew.
Yes, Brother Prospero, your grouping could

Not be more effective: given a few
Incomplete objects and a nice warm day,
What a lot a little music can do.

Dotted about the deck they doze or play,
Your loyal subjects all, grateful enough
To know their place and believe what you say.

Antonio, sweet brother, has to laugh.
How easy you have made it to refuse
Peace to your greatness! Break your wand in half,

The fragments will join; burn your books or lose
Them in the sea, they will soon reappear
Not even damaged: as long as I choose

To wear my fashion, whatever you wear
Is a magic robe; while I stand outside
Your circle, the will to charm is still there.

As I exist so shall you be denied,
Forced to remain our melancholy mentor,
The grown-up man, the adult in his pride,

Never have time to curl up at the centre
Time turns on when completely reconciled,
Never become and therefore never enter
The green occluded pasture as a child.

> *Your all is partial, Prospero;*
> *My will is all my own:*
> *Your need to love shall never know*
> *Me: I am I, Antonio,*
> *By choice myself alone.*

(*Selected Poems* by W.H. Auden, Faber & Faber, 1979)

So that, then, is *The Tempest*. Scenic splendour, allegory, what you will, the various pieces of the jigsaw must fit together. Written in the sparest of language, each gem an intricate and delicate facet of a jeweller's mosaic, it is a revenge dream of enormous political potency. It is once more the perennial struggle for power, the gulf that exists between thought and action that we see in *Hamlet*, that we see in *Richard III*, that we see in *Timon*, that we see in Shakespeare's plays played out on a stage all over the world. Man fighting man for greed and gain, for who is to have the ultimate say in government. Fighting for the crock of gold that lies at the top of the pyramid of power. Jan Kott's grand mechanism, the escalator shuttling the contenders up to the top until they reach out and topple off the edge. And at the same time there is another system to be comprehended, another way of ruling; that life cannot always be this perennial struggle to put the boot in the faces of those who are weakest. That somewhere there is a system – maybe it is that of Gonzalo – the commonwealth system, based on Montaigne and his theories of fertility and abundance and shared organic growth. No machines, no science, although this is a commune with a king (Gonzalo's mind does not stretch as far as a Marxist redistribution of power and wealth). Here, the final imaginative leap has not been made. But maybe it is a world where those who toil, where those who use their hands and not their minds are the real kings of the universe – 'The master, the swabber, the boatswain, and I, / The gunner and his mate.' What use is ambition and morality if 'Imperious Caesar, dead and turned to clay, / Might stop a hole to keep the wind away' (*Hamlet*, Act V, Scene i)?

Ambition. We could all end up as a piece of clay stuck in a hole in a wall to stop the wind coming through. Buried in *The Tempest*, once again, is that strange, not even subconscious feeling from Shakespeare that something else must be there to put in the place of this extra-ordinary avaricious existence and brutalising system of government. 'My ending is despair.'

# A Midsummer
# Night's Dream

we are such stuff . . .

In 1971, during my 18 months as Assistant Director at the Royal
Shakespeare Company, my time happened to coincide with one of the
seminal productions of the second half of the twentieth century – Peter
Brook's *A Midsummer Night's Dream*. Not only was I Assistant, I was
responsible for taking replacement rehearsals for the New York
Broadway run and for two years I was his Associate for the world tour.
It scarred me for life. For forty years I refused all offers to direct the play.

I finally tackled it in the strangest of ways.

There is a dialect of North Germany called Platt Deutsch. A lot of its
vocabulary has much in common with old (and current) English, a living
testament to our Anglo-Saxon linguistic connection. Platt was (is)
spoken in the rural areas and in the ports across northern Germany and
as with so many dialects and minority languages is on the wane, spoken
mainly by an older generation, although some authorities in Nieder-
Sachsen, Schleswig Holstein and Hamburg are now teaching it in junior
schools. It is much more musical than Hochdeutsch, the German
equivalent of English RP, having none of the guttural harshness of its
parent body. North it mutates into Danish, east into Dutch.

There are a few theatres dedicated to keeping the language culturally alive – a small theatre in Rostock, an amateur one in Oldenburg: the Staatstheater in Schwerin in old East Germany which has a number of productions each year in its repertoire. The theatre in Bremen closed recently but an amateur group continues to perform intermittently. By far the most important is the Ohnsorg Theater in Hamburg.

Founded over one hundred years ago by Richard Ohnsorg the company receives a small amount of state subsidy but is classed as a private theatre, deriving its income from box-office and and sponsorship. It has a permanent company of sixteen actors and produces some eight new productions each year, mainly farce, new and old, and in recent years, in order to try and broaden its audience, the odd mainstream: *Cat On a Hot Tin Roof*, *Moon for the Misbegotten*, *Uncle Vanya* etc. transposed to Northern Germany. It goes without saying that in the cultural snob cauldron that is the German Staatstheater system, where anything is looked down on that is not performed in Hochdeutsch, it is dismissed contemptuously as Volkstheater, 'peoples theatre', as if 'the people' who go to such theatre are another race.

In 2010 Christian Seeler the Intendant – Chief Executive – of The Ohnsorg Theater, approached me to say that the theatre was moving from its then premises in the centre of Hamburg to a new site across from the central station and opposite my old stomping ground of the Deutsches Schauspielhaus, where I had been Intendant for three years in 1989. It was to be a new, custom built theatre specially to house the Ohnsorg company and would cost 15,000,000 Euros to build. Would I like to do the opening production?

*A Midsummer Night's Dream.*

I, who must have turned down at least a dozen requests around the world to direct the play, refusing on the grounds of my close encounter of the Brook kind, jumped at the chance to help protect an endangered species . . .

In the event the production turned out to be a bit of a curate's egg for I wasn't able to shake off entirely the memory of the Brook *Dream* and, among other things, failed to solve the fairies and went arse up in an area that should have been log-falling for me – the Mechanicals play at the conclusion of the piece. Great 'lovers' scenes mind.

I was too eager to solve the one area, that it seemed to me in retrospect, Peter had fallen down on.

What was it that he missed? In the nightmarish drug-fuelled psychedelian Chinese Circus Zeitgeist of a production that Brook conjured up there wasn't much emphasis on the tyrannical regime of Theseus – marry the choice of your father or it's the chop, or at best a pair of knee pads for the rest of your life. Maybe it's that our awareness and sensitivity to gender politics has changed enormously in the intervening period, but nevertheless it is strange in a play that is such a powerful analysis of the battle between the male and the female psyche that the gender politics were of little interest to him. Even the famous psychological doubling of Theseus / Oberon and Hippolyta / Titania was a last minute decision to make them look the same – the costumes and silver and copper wire wigs of Alan Howard and Sarah Kestelmann (Oberon and Titania) didn't look right and were abandoned at the preview stage in favour of the King and Queen of mortals and myth wearing just the one outfit.

'They're the same people really, aren't they?', Peter said to me, 'One's just the dark side of the other. . . .' Art by accident and a legend – and a casting imperative – were born. (Although the doubling of the roles had previous form. Freud had been around a long time.)

Whose dream is it anyway? That was where I got hung up. In all the years of carrying the play around in my head and witnessing countless other variations – stupidly from American extravagance to Germanic and Rumanian deconstruction – I had never really put my mind to the question. It hadn't seemed so important before in a play that spans the world of illusion and reality, shifting in and out of focus in a shimmer of fantasy. But suddenly it did.

Is it Bottom's – a weaver's dream of fame and fortune? The Bristol Old Vic / Handspring production appeared to think so.

**BOTTOM: I have had a most rare vision. I have had a dream past the wit of man to say what dream it was. Man is but an ass if he go about to expound this dream. Methought I was – there is no man can tell what. Methought I was – and methought I had – but man is but a patched fool, if he will offer to say what methought I had. The eye of man hath not heard, the ear of man hath not seen, man's hand is not**

**able to taste, his tongue to conceive, nor his heart to report, what my dream was! I will get Peter Quince to write a ballad of this dream: it shall be called 'Bottom's Dream', because it hath no bottom; . . .**

**(Act IV, Scene i)**

One can imagine the class revenge of an overweight artisan dreaming of ravishing a Queen, but there also appears to be something transformative in the experience, lifting Bottom's experience on to a higher plane. 'Bless thee Bottom, thou art translated!' says Peter Quince on viewing the asses head. Translated and transformed he is, as are many of the other characters after the long night in the forest. (Compare the wish-fulfilment dream of the tinker Christopher Sly in the *The Taming of the Shrew*, or Prospero's in *The Tempest*).

Is the fantasy Theseus's – another wish fulfilment dream: this time revenge up on the Amazon who he has conquered by force but has yet still to tame? Is Oberon's vicious voyeuristic abuse of Titania – the induced sexual congress with an ass – the dark erotic side of every male / female Fifty Shades fantasy? Or merely bestial perversity *in extremis*? Is it funny or repellent? Is the romantic image of Titania cradling an asses head crowned with a garland of flowers the innocent, true picture of the relationship? Or did Shakespeare knowingly couple Titania (possibly a name invented by Shakespeare – tit and anus? – but more probably derived from the gigantic race of the Titans) with the animal reputed to have the largest cock in the corral? (In an American production Titania was played by a 2 metres tall, 16 stone man . . .).

From early times the sexual prowess of a donkey has been legion. It is all too easy to avoid the implications of the troilic Oberon / Titania / Bottom affair and turn the episode into a harmless comedic exercise.

**'Tie up my lover's tongue, lead him to my bower'.**

**[paraphrase Act III, Scene ii]**

No more talking, let's fuck.

In 1986 on the occasion of a production of *Julius Caesar* at the Deutsches Schauspielhaus Hamburg, lighting designer Mark Henderson and I went on a trawl of the Reeperbahn. (Research you understand). The Reeperbahn then still had echoes of its pre-pole dancing sailors' past, a sleazy ragbag of bars, and girls tethered to hitching posts like so many horses. In amongst dodging the champagne sharks (or sharkesses) at thirty marks a shot, we happened upon a bar with a small red be-curtained stage. A braying behind the curtain announced the entertainment for the night.

Did I immediately think – 'Oh it's just like Titania in *A Midsummer Night's Dream*'? I didn't. Mark and I beat a hasty retreat, amazed at what was publicly and legally allowed. (It wasn't but happened none the less.) It was later that the similarity with the *Dream* and the brutal bestiality of the scene struck me. Being confronted with the stark reality of Shakespeare's supposedly comic coupling provided a fresh insight with regard to the play that I hadn't experienced in years. It is one thing to acknowledge intellectually the content of the scene, quite another to be confronted with the evidence of the unbelievably callous revenge that Theseus / Oberon in his mind brutally perpetrates on Hippolyta / Titania as a punishment for holding out on him.

Is then the dream Hippolyta's –

**My Oberon, what visions have I seen!**
**Methought I was enamoured of an ass.**

(Act IV, Scene i)

Is her desire to teach Theseus a lesson intertwined with erotic images of her ravishing equating to being skewered by a donkey? The danger with that one is that she takes pleasure in it. Is Theseus 'translated' in her mind into an avenging animal with a monstrous weapon? At the time it was great but on waking she says – 'O how mine eyes do loathe his visage now!'. His visage mark, nothing else . . . It seems the only way that Theseus can possess Hippolyta is by raping her. Her body he can ravish by force, but her mind remains closed to him. He must prise it open, will her to want him, to enjoy him, glory in his manhood – (and they say size doesn't matter). But watching her copulate with an ass? Shakespeare understood only too well the fount of subterranean impulses that flood the dark areas of our psyche. Our fears and our fetishes.

> . . . in the night, imaging some fear,
> How easy is a bush supposed a bear?

(Act V, Scene i)

Is it Puck's dream? Headlong Theatre made him an exasperated film director, Robin Goodfellow, who at night dreams of his fighting co-stars, his bickering support cast, and his technical crew performing a play at the wrap party.

Is it Hermia's? Queen Elizabeth 1st'? Many commentators have seen in Oberon / Titania's struggle over the 'little Indian boy' a parallel with the populace's obsession with the Queen's lack of conception and the constant speculation about her love life.

Is it the audience's? And does it matter? Is the play not the release of fantasy in each and every beholder's imagination – a what you will, an as you like it? As with so much of Shakespeare nothing is what it seems, and particularly so in a play of shadows, fantasy and dreams where the boundaries between illusion and reality are continually crossed.

**RALPH COTTERILL: (fairy) Tell us what the play is about**

**PERTER BROOK: I'll tell you after the first performance. It's a fairy-tale, it can mean anything you like.**

The case for it being Theseus's dream is a strong one. It is he who is the ultimate beneficiary of the harmony established at the end of the play. His chauvinism has triumphed, his queen has been brought to heel: the rebellion quelled. As Petruchio in *The Taming of the Shrew* says, after battering Katherina into submission –

> Marry, peace it bodes, and love and quiet life,
> An awful rule and right supremacy;
> And, to be short, what not that's sweet and happy

(Act V, Scene ii)

No amount of fairies blessing the house, and we the spectators applauding at the end, (in Brook's *Dream* Puck's 'Give me your hands, if we be friends' was literally interpreted by the cast coming down into the audience) can obliterate the fact that it needed a drug (and bestiality) to transform two of the recalcitrant parties; and the male part of one pair, Lysander, is still under the influence. What are we to make of that? What will happen if the effect wears off? Will he return to his original obsession with Hermia? Has Theseus learnt a chastening lesson through his wild encounter with the dark and passionate forces of the entangled wooded recesses of his mind? It would be nice to think so.

> HERMIA: . . . I beseech your grace that I may know
> The worst that may befall me in this case
> If I refuse to wed Demetrius.
> THESEUS: Either to die the death, or to abjure
> For ever the society of men.

(Act I, Scene i)

How does Hippolyta react to this form of enforced rape, yielding your virginity to one who you patently abhor or choose between death and a nunnery? Hippolyta has been there. She too was forced to marry and yield her 'virgin patent' on pain of death.

> THESEUS: . . . I wooed thee with my sword
> And won thy love doing thee injuries . . .

(Act I, Scene i)

It is significant that Hippolyta says not a word during the attempt to force Hermia to change her mind. Sometimes the silence of a character at particular moments of high drama in the plays speaks volumes. Having issued his verdict Theseus turns to Hippolyta and says –

> Come Hippolyta. (*Pause*) What cheer my love?

The pause is mine. The line seems to indicate at the very least a certain disapproval of what has just taken place. Does she sweep out leaving Theseus to then brood on his condition? Dream of revenge? Do they part and go their separate ways? Let battle commence.

\* \* \*

Mighty Oberon, king of the fairies, enters the story in Act Two, Scene One. He is ushered in by these words from Puck,

> The king doth keep his revels here tonight.
> Take heed the queen come not within his sight,
> For Oberon is passing fell and wrath
> Because that she as her attendant hath
> A lovely boy stolen from an Indian king.

Adultery is in the air. Oberon and Titania are experiencing marital difficulties, not because of their mutual infidelity, if it can be called that for a fairy, but because of a power struggle over this changeling child. Their first encounter is marked by Titania's comment,

> . . . Why art thou here . . .
> But that, forsooth, the bouncing Amazon,
> Your buskined mistress and your warrior love,
> To Theseus must be wedded?

and Oberon's

> How canst thou thus for shame, Titania,
> Glance at my credit with Hippolyta,
> Knowing I know thy love to Theseus?

'These are the forgeries of jealousy.' Theseus, it would appear, has done the rounds. Not only has he forced himself on Hippolyta but Perigouna, Ariadne and Antiope are just three more of the notches carved with force on his bed-post. Oberon / Theseus deals with Titania's infidelity in much the same way as he does with the mortals: he places a love spell upon her. Cupid 'loosed his loveshaft' and it fell upon

> . . . a little Western flower,
> Before, milk-white; now purple with love's wound:
> And maidens call it 'love in idleness'.

> (Act II, Scene i)

(Note the erotic suggestion of menstruation and swollen labia)

> And with the juice of this I'll streak her eyes
> And make her full of hateful fantasies.

> (Act II, Scene i)

And while she is engrossed with some monstrous lover, he will ask her for the changeling, and then 'all things shall be peace',

> When I had at my pleasure taunted her,
> And she in mild terms begged my patience,
> I then did ask of her her changeling child,
> Which straight she gave me, and her fairy sent
> To bear him to my bower in Fairyland.
> And now I have the boy, I will undo
> This hateful imperfection of her eyes.

(Act IV, Scene i)

In coupling Theseus and Hippolyta together Shakespeare has pitted a warrior king against the ultimate man-hating, battling Queen of the Amazons. Task? To bring about harmony in the war of the sexes. The withholding of the Indian boy in the fantasy world of the fairy kingdom has its roots in the rape of Hippolyta. Theseus wishes for Hippolyta to give willingly what he has taken by force. He desires that she submit meekly to his demands, give her sexual favours of her own free will. In the subconscious world of Oberon and Titania this translates into the withholding of an exotic child, something that once again can only be gained by subverting the natural order, this time not with a sword but a drug. The exotic and erotic nature of Titanias's description of how she came by the boy has something of Theseus's latent desire to conceive a child in such circumstances:

> Her mother was a votaress of my order,
> And in the spicèd Indian air by night
> Full oft has she gossiped by my side,
> And sat with me on Neptune's yellow sands
> Marking th'embarkèd traders on the flood,
> When we have laughed to see the sails conceive
> And grow big-bellied with the wanton wind;
> Which she with pretty and with swimming gait
> Following – her womb then rich with my young squire –
> Would imitate, and sail upon the land
> To fetch me trifles, and return again.
> As from a voyage rich with merchandise.

> And she, being mortal, of that boy did die,
> And for her sake do I rear up her boy;
> And for her sake I will not part with him.
>
> (Act II, Scene i)

The coupling of the Amazon Queen from somewhere along the shores of Libya and Duke Theseus (did Greece have Dukes?) would indeed produce a child of such dusky beauty.

Puck says the child was stolen by Titania from an Indian King. Titania says she cared for the child after the death of the mother. Which story are we to believe? There are always two sides to the problems in a relationship. Why does Oberon need the little boy? To be his 'henchman'? He could easily find himself someone else. In fact, if Titania were to give up the boy to her king, then the rift would be mended. But, in this the fairy King and Queen are far too human. Both are headstrong, powerful creatures, who refuse to bow to the wants of the other. They are childish in their need to be in control, and their conflict is only resolved through the application of a drug. Oberon / Theseus, chauvinist, haughty, autocratic requires submission. He is king of the fairies, and even though he doesn't care if his wife is faithful to him, he does demand that she submit when he asks her for something. Putting his own interests above those of all others, his designs work out exactly as he intends. How does Titania cope with the realisation, and the memory, that he's induced her to fornicate with a donkey?

> How came these things to pass?
> O, how mine eyes do loathe his visage now!
>
> (Act IV, Scene i)

But were we all to behave as Theseus / Oberon the world would be in a state of 'chassis'. Titania's apocalyptic speech on how Oberon / Theseus has disturbed the natural order (rape is wrong – period) has uncanny modern resonances of the man-made destruction of the environment through the rape and exploitation of our natural resources.

> TITANIA: . . . As in revenge, have sucked up from the sea
> Contagious fogs which, falling in the land,
> Hath every pelting river made so proud,

That they have overborne their continents.
The ox hath therefore stretched his yoke in vain,
The ploughman lost his sweat, and the green corn
Hath rotted ere his youth attained a beard.
The fold stands empty in the drownèd field,
And crows are fatted with the murrion flock.
The nine men's morris is filled up with mud,
And the quaint mazes in the wanton green,
For lack of tread, are undistinguishable.
The human mortals want their winter cheer.
No night is now with hymn or carol blessed.
Therefore the moon, the governess of floods,
Pale in her anger, washes all the air,
That rheumatic diseases do abound;
And thorough this distemperature we see
The seasons alter; hoary-headed frosts
Fall in the fresh lap of the crimson rose,
And on old Hyems' thin, and icy crown
An odorous chaplet of sweet summer buds
Is, as in mockery, set. The spring, the summer,
The childing autumn, angry winter change
Their wonted liveries, and the 'mazèd world
By their increase now knows not which is which.
And this same progeny of evils
Comes from our debate, from our dissension.
We are their parents and original.

(Act II, Scene i)

This is no midsummer night's dream – this is for real, this is now. As the ice cap melts, sea levels rise, arable land turns to desert, and flood, drought, famine, and disease stalk the world: as the spring, the summer, autumn, angry winter change their wontèd liveries – we are their parents and original.

* * *

The problem with any production of *The Dream* is the fairies . . . those naughty little elves that transport us to a world of romantic make believe – bringing out our latent Tinkerbell lurking somewhere in the sunlight dappled shadows. They're as elusive and insubstantial a bunch as one might expect when dealing with the occupants of a magic wood.

For a start, they give radically different impressions of themselves at different points. When we first meet Puck (in Act II, Scene i), he is addressed by a fairy as 'that shrewed and knavish sprite / Called Robin Goodfellow.' This very quintessential English name is reinforced by the tricks he is described as playing: crouching in your beer glass; scaring the girls; letting the horses loose. Likewise the fairies that held on Bottom have homely, rural names: Cobweb, Peaseblossom and Mustardseed.

However, the play takes place not in the English countryside, but in Athens and the wood nearby. The wood – invariably the forest of Arden – a Shakespearean metaphor for the tangled, subconscious confused world of the mind: of all our hopes, wishes, flights of fancy, despairs: a place that is both threatening and benign, both dark and sun dappled.

**If you go down in the woods today, be sure of a big surprise . . . (The Teddy Bears' Picnic)**

Titania and Oberon by contrast have distinctly classical-sounding names and the basis of their quarrel, the child who Titania claims as her surrogate, suggests that her power stretches well beyond the Athenian wood, even to having an order of votaresses, or worshippers, in India. Even our Robin, when called away from the bum-bumping milk-maids, can boast that he'll 'put a girdle round the earth / In forty minutes', a supersonic speed for a rural hobgoblin. (He walks off-stage one side and later reappears from the other, out of breath . . . ) But of course so can we. In my head I've just beaten Usain Bolt. There – I've done it again!

What are they, these fairies, who are they? We're never even entirely sure how big they are supposed to be. Titania and Oberon apparently must be the same size as Bottom and his mates, but their attendants are described as hiding in acorn cups when the royal couple scrap. At one moment Puck is small enough to be mistaken for a roasted crab in a drink, then large enough to change himself into a stool.

Some parallels can be found with folklore, classical mythology, ballads and plays, but the fairies in *A Midsummer Night's Dream* don't fall precisely into any particular category. Just as Oberon can become invisible by declaring himself so, the fairies' words can make them any size and transport them to any place – products of our imagination, transforming themselves at will as our subconscious (and conscious) thoughts: juxtaposing the mischievous with the vicious.

However, on stage? Puck and the fairies are life size actors. (The 19th century got round this by casting children, as did maybe Shakespeare) Only the imagination transforms them into different shapes and sizes. Punk, boiler suits, narcissists, naked – productions struggle to identify their function, grappling to fit them into some coherent conceptual straightjacket. Are they agents for good, bad? Are they those idle thoughts that mix the comic with the serious; that feeling that comes over us as we dream; as Steve Bell the cartoonist does, of turning Prime Minister David Cameron's head into a condom: sticking a long nose, large ears and buck teeth on Prince Charles? Or of humbling those that have done us wrong by imagining some harm. However, the indignities to which humans are really subjected by the malignity of Shakespeare's fairies are not so terrible,

> . . . Are not you he
> That frights the maidens of the villagery,
> Skim milk, and sometimes labor in the quern,
> And bootless make the breathless housewife churn,
> And sometime make the drink to bear no barm,
> Mislead night-wanderers, laughing at their harm?

> (Act II, Scene i)

It is something of an inconvenience that they intrude nightly into household life. But fair dos, what comes round comes round, and the fairies are pretty even handed. Good servants are rewarded by finding money in their shoes, and rings in their pails, by finding the house swept clean, the corn ground, the wheat threshed, and the wool carded: with exemplary justice, the sluttish are punished with pinches till black and blue; invisible hands strip the bed-clothes from the lazy.

Do right by them, and they'll do right by you by conferring a blessing on the house and its inhabitants. Thus Puck blesses Theseus' dwelling—

> . . . Not a mouse
> Shall disturb this hallowed house.
> I am sent with broom before
> To sweep the dust behind the door.

And Oberon commands,

> Through this house give glimmering light,
>     By the dead and drowsy fire;
> Every elf, and fairy sprite,
>     Hop as light as bird from briar.

and

> With this field dew consecrate,
> Every fairy take his gait,
> And each several chamber bless
> Through this palace with sweet peace;
> And the owner of it blessed
> Ever shall in safety rest.

(Act V, Scene i)

If Oberon is the director of the action, Puck is his chief actor, and one who doesn't mind taking a bit of creative license. While assisting Oberon in his plan for Titania to 'wake when some vile thing is near', it is Puck who changes Bottom's head into that of an ass rather than the 'cat, or bear, / Pard, or boar' that Oberon suggests for the purpose. In Act II, Puck innocently drops the love potion intended for Demetrius into Lysander's eyes, causing the latter to reject Hermia and fall in love with Helena. When Oberon berates him for his 'knaveries', Puck explains,

> Believe me, King of shadows, I mistook. . . .
> [But] so far am I glad it so did sort,
> As this their jangling I esteem a sport.

(Act III, Scene ii)

Puck is commonly known as Robin Goodfellow or Hobgoblin. Hob is the diminutive form of Robert or Robin, making Hobgoblin mean roughly Robin the Goblin. Originally the name Puck was a general term for any old fairy. 'Puck' or 'Pouke' is possibly an old word for devil and is found in many countries in many forms. In Iceland it is the 'Puki'. In Denmark and Northern German Platt it is simply 'Puk'. The Irish have the annual Puck Fair in Glenbeigh Kerry where a goat is (metaphorically) sacrificed and the word 'Pooka' is the invisible friend of James Stewart in the film *Harvey*.

The Vale of Neath, in South Wales, (from where I stem incidentally) is a land of wooded glens, mountain torrents, turbulent waterfalls and crystal clear pools. There is a theory that this sylvan paradise was the setting for *A Midsummer Night's Dream* and there is yet another site in the vicinity associated with Shakespeare generally, and *A Midsummer Night's Dream* specifically, in the Clydach Valley. Cwm Pwca, just downstream from a huge waterfall translates as Puck 'Valley'. Frederick Harries in his book, *Shakespeare and the Welsh* claims of this valley that:

> There is a Welsh tradition to the effect that Shakespeare received his knowledge of the Cambrian fairies from his friend Richard Price, son of Sir John Price of The Priory, Brecon. It is even claimed that Cwm Pwca, a part of the romantic glen in Breconshire, is the original scene of *A Midsummer Night's Dream*, a fancy as light and airy as Puck himself. Anyhow, there Cwm Pwca is, and in the sylvan days before Frere and Powell's ironworks were set up it is said to have been as full of goblins as a Methodist's head is full of piety. Unhappily today this area has long since been swamped by industrial development and I am reliably informed that spirits may no longer inhabit Cwm Pwca.

Wherever he comes from in all these countries the Puck, while generally obedient, is the prankster to out-April all fools.

What separates Puck out from Ariel in *The Tempest*? Both are agents of their master. The one, Ariel perpetrating vicious torment on Prospero's enemies, the other wilfully confusing and obfuscating Oberon's requests for his own amusement. What would happen if Ariel and Puck were to swap places? *The Tempest* would be a comedy of errors and *The Dream* a dark vicious play of sexual revenge. So no change there then . . . and the endings would be the same. On waking from the respective dreams the world would still be as it was – nothing would have altered.

Fairies are obviously inconstant creatures. They are not beings into deep emotion or thought, but into fun, revelry and mischief. Teenage hoodies? I still don't really know how to handle them.

\* \* \*

What of the Mechanicals – workers 'who never laboured in their minds till now'? Are we in at the birth of theatre – of the imagination?

'In the night, imagining some fear, / How easy is a bush supposed a bear'. Or a lant-horn the moon; a bush a forest; a man with two bricks a wall. Their amateur efforts to create a play within a play expose the artificiality of acting. These 'hard handed men', obviously nothing to do with Athens – Snout, Flute, Starveling, Bottom, Snug, Quince, names and professions straight out of Warwickshire – provide a down to earth balance to the illusory world of the fairy kingdom. It would appear that Shakespeare's sympathies lay ultimately with these earnest artisans and not with the court, appreciating the effort needed to create a piece of imaginative theatre, despite the patronising and supercilious remarks of the privileged onlookers. It is the heckling aristocrats who are left looking foolish in the face of such honest effort.

The tragedy of Pyrramus and Thisbe is the comical/tragical side of what happens when Capulet and Montague refuse to allow Romeo and Juliet freedom of choice of whom to love. Or Egeus and Hermia. But – 'The wall is down that separated their two fathers'. Compassion, understanding – true love will find a way, although, in the manner of Shakespeare's silent characters which leads either to unhappy endings or stories yet to be told: (Orlando, Antonio in *The Tempest* and *The Merchant of Venice*; Bassanio, Nerissa, Olivia, MacDuff – 'Such welcome and unwelcome things at once / 'Tis hard to reconcile.' *Macbeth* (Act IV, Scene iii) )

Egeus says nothing when Theseus over-rules his will and orders the marriage of Demetrius and Hermia. What will happen to that father / daughter relationship? It's lucky that Hermia didn't end up like Juliet – dead. But this is a dream. . . . We are out of the wood, blinking in the day-light, confronted with reality, the fumes of the night blown away on the wind as the morning mist.

Nothing is real but what is not.

# The Merchant
# of Venice

if money be the food of love . . .

What makes *The Merchant of Venice* at one and the same time so fascinating and so repugnant? Anti-Semitic it isn't – anti-racist it is. It has been lumped in with other plays as a romantic comedy, presumably because it results in three pairings and three marriages, a girl impersonates a judge and there is multiple mayhem over some ring swapping. Oh yes, and there's that hilarious scene of a Jew trying to cut a pound of flesh off nearest to a man's heart. Has them rolling in the aisles, that one. Of course, once that nasty man Shylock is out of the way we can get on with resolving the love stories. But who carves who up?

The romantic view. A young girl wanting to marry someone forbidden by her faith elopes disguised as a young man, taking with her money for survival. A young Venetian, desperate to win the hand of the wealthy lady he loves, borrows money to visit her and, in an inspired piece of guesswork, hazards all on the least likely of three caskets to contain her portrait. His best friend falls in love at first sight with milady's maid.

The cynical view. A Christian layabout of little faith persuades a young Jewish girl to leave her father, steal from him a fair size of his fortune in the process, and change her religion. A profligate gambler borrows money to buy himself a ticket to spot-the-lady in one of three caskets and gets lucky. An urban yob hitches himself to the maid of the aforementioned rich lady on five minutes' acquaintance on condition that the aforementioned gamble pays off. If not – *ciao*.

To subscribe to the romantic view one has to ignore the warning sign: Danger – Shakespeare At Work. The play may be set in Venice and based on an old Italian story but it presents a devastating picture of the emergent merchant capitalism of the Elizabethan era. Chivalry is dead (did it ever exist other than as a concept?) and London laddism rules. Racism, class, money – Shakespeare nails them all to the consumer pinboard.

Venice – a world centre of commerce. The Rialto – a medieval stock exchange where merchants come to trade. They're a right bunch of bastards on the Rialto. It's all that fast money, easy come easy go, desperate dealing, FTSE, NASDAQ, Dow-Jones, names that jump straight out of a Potter spell. It's not that Shylock doesn't behave badly, but if you drive a dog into a corner don't be surprised if it bites you.

It has been argued that given Shakespeare's Catholicism and the Elizabethan attitude to usury, audiences in 1600 would have seen nothing wrong in the treatment of Shylock as a Jew. This historical view of the play ignores the accuracy with which Shakespeare prefigured and fingered Thatcher's Children and the twenty-first century's obsession with consumerism and market forces. Broken oaths, broken promises, wild speculation, betting, wagering, betraying, deceiving – *The Merchant of Venice*, masquerading as a romantic comedy, leaves an unsavoury trail of capitalism and racism in its wake. Not much hope then for the various marriages floating precariously on this Venetian Lagoon of mercenary opportunism.

\* \* \*

Let us look at the givens.

Bassanio, a layabout lad-about-town, is broke. Not only broke, he has squandered the money he borrowed from Antonio, a rich merchant venturer, and now is on the cadge again:

> I owe you much, and like a wilful youth,
> That which I owe is lost; but if you please
> To shoot another arrow that self way

91

Which you did shoot the first, I do not doubt,
As I will watch the aim, or to find both
Or bring your latter hazard back again
And thankfully rest debtor for the first.

(Act I, Scene i)

But this time he is determined to sort himself out once and for all.
If Antonio will stake him again he will try and win the hand and fortunes
of a rich heiress, Portia. This is not the first time he has tried this ruse.

BASSANIO: In my schooldays, when I had lost one shaft,
I shot his fellow of the self-same flight
The self-same way, with more advisèd watch,
To find the other forth; and by adventuring both
I oft found both.

(Act I, Scene i)

It's all about show, a con. Arrive in town with a retinue of servants,
a new suit, a flashy tie, and pretend to be something you are not. The
Italian and French Rivieras used to be full of such seeming gentlemen,
gently easing rich spinsters and widows out of their fortunes by playing
the class card.

The clue to the real social status of Bassanio comes with his sidekick,
Gratiano, a bit of rough straight out of the champagne-swilling, jumped-
up, get-rich-quick city yob culture. Gratiano hitches a ride on Bassanio's
Belmont charm chariot, making off in the process with Portia's maid –
contingent of course on Bassanio securing the prized Portia.

BASSANIO:    . . . But hear thee, Gratiano:
Thou art too wild, too rude and bold of voice,
Parts that become thee happily enough
And in such eyes as ours appear not faults,
But where thou art not known, why there they show
Something too liberal. Pray thee take pain
To allay with some cold drops of modesty
Thy skipping spirit, lest through thy wild behaviour
I be misconstered in the place I go to,
And lose my hopes.

(Act II, Scene ii)

And how much does Bassanio need from Antonio for this further throw of the dice? This second arrow?

**PORTIA: What sum owes he the Jew?**

**BASSANIO: For me, three thousand ducats.**

**PORTIA:** What, no more?

**Pay him six thousand, and deface the bond.**

**Double six thousand and then treble that . . .**

(Act III, Scene ii)

Three thousand ducats. Three thousand ducats!? Is that all, says Portia when she finds out, is that all I am worth? You've put a man's life in jeopardy for a paltry three thousand ducats? Thrice three times and it would still be an insult.

Portia is seriously rich, Bassanio is seriously out of it. From now on the trousers will be firmly on the female. Bassanio will probably only be allowed pocket money.

Antonio, however, wealthy though he may be, does not have the money – it is a question of cash flow. Speculate to accumulate. International trade. His wealth is all ventures abroad. When his ships come home he will be worth a fortune, but for the moment it is all collateral. Antonio's WASP-like world is a self-protective club, a lodge of Masons, the MCC, the Garrick, Balliol and Trinity – one falls, we all fall.

**ANTONIO: I am a tainted wether of the flock,**

**Meetest for death. The weakest kind of fruit**

**Drops earliest to the ground, and so let me.**

(Act IV, Scene i)

Bond and bind together, help each other out. No punitive interest rates here but plenty of golden handshakes. Corporate business. Globalisation. Antonio believes he must be sacrificed for the health of the club.

In such a world outsiders are not just unwelcome, they are positively discriminated against. Never mind Jews – Germans, French, Moroccan, Spanish, Eastern, Scots (lot of North of the Border prejudice running around in Elizabeth's reign) and – to make sure nobody gets off – the English, all are despised and verbally if not literally spat on. Colour, race, creed – who cares? If your face doesn't fit, forget it. 'Let all of his complexion choose me so.' Lucky that Bassanio (is he one of ours?), braggart, penniless gold-digger that he is, is out of the right drawer.

\* \* \*

Much has been made of the homosexual current coursing between Antonio and Bassanio, although it appears to be decidedly one-way. Antonio playing Cyrano to Bassanio's Christian. Winning the lady's love in pounds in place of poetry. But this time Cyrano is in love with Christian, not Roxane. As Christian climbs the balcony to claim the kiss won by Cyrano's voice, so Bassanio besieges Belmont with Antonio's money.

Antonio the loser. Antonio the symbol of closed class wealth. Antonio, the older man in love with the younger (echoes of another Antonio and Sebastian in *Twelfth Night*). It must hurt. Is this the real reason for Antonio's sadness in the opening scene? He knows that Bassanio is on the woo again.

> Well, tell me now what lady is the same
> To whom you swore a secret pilgrimage . . .
>
> (Act I, Scene i)

Solanio and Salerio (salt – rub it in), those gossiping muppets on the Rialto, touch on it nearly. Solanio: 'Why then you are in love.' Antonio: 'Fie, fie' (The Merchant doth protest too much methinks!) A lot of jealously around, bitchiness, emotional blackmail.

> BASSANIO: [reads] . . . *all debts are cleared between you and I if I might but see you at my death. Not withstanding, use your pleasure. If your love do not persuade you to come, let not my letter.*
>
> (Act III, Scene iii)

How do you measure love? With a pound of flesh? Or a ring? Antonio cannot believe, having narrowly escaped losing his life, that Bassanio is unwilling to part with the ring given him by Portia as payment to Balthasar / Judge. Just as Portia asks the question of Bassanio over the sum of three thousand ducats (what's my love worth?), so Antonio asks it over the ring.

ANTONIO: **My Lord Bassanio, let him have the ring.**
**Let his deservings, and my love withal,**
**Be valued 'gainst your wife's commandèment.**

(Act IV, Scene I)

Are you measuring my love for you against Portia's in the form of a ring? And Bassanio gives it away. An oath broken. Light love, as easily given away as a pair of socks. Shylock refused to break his oath. He had made it in the eyes of the Lord and such is his faith that he expects the Christians to understand.

SHYLOCK: **An oath, an oath! I have an oath in heaven;**
**Shall I lay perjury upon my soul?**
**No, not for Venice!**

(Act IV, Scene i)

But the Christians swear, take oaths, make vows of marriage that are worthless. This Christian world is not one of faith, but of Bank Holidays where Whitsun is celebrated not according to the religious calendar but on the last Monday in May. Yet Antonio is a nice man, a gentle man, a noble man, it just so happens that he hates and despises Jews – 'our sacred nation' – spits on them, spurns them, calls them misbelievers, cut-throat dogs, voids his rheum upon their beard. Nothing wrong with that is there? Doesn't stop him being 'a nice man', 'a gentle man', 'a noble man', does it?

As for Shylock, that's a different matter. His daughter Jessica calls her home a hell. Yet the only time we see Shylock and Jessica together he treats her with trust and civility, giving over to her keeping the keys and custody of his house. He doesn't lock her in and forbid her to go out, merely asks her to make his house safe from Christians on a carnival rampage. In fact, compared with some other fathers of our Shakespearean acquaintance, Shylock's regime seems pretty lax. Jessica obviously has had plenty of opportunity to meet, play and sport with Lorenzo. Of course she may have climbed out of the window and spent nights on the tiles while Shylock thought she was safely tucked up in her little bed or swotting for GCSEs. The 'hell' of her home seems more like the hell of a teenager's home without TV and stereo – and no tobacco, alcohol or ecstasy if you please. (To some, this would smack of responsible parenting.)

Her envy of the life of the young Christians on the Rialto is palpable – she can't wait to join them. No stifling orthodox Judaism for her. Get out there and live a little as soon as she can. And while she's about it she'll take a load of money and jewels with her. 'Here, catch this,' (throws down box of ducats to Lorenzo), 'I'm going back to get some more.'

And Lorenzo? That will keep him happy. He can't believe his luck. He won't be able to back out after that. He needs it too much. Off they go on a trans-European spree (last seen disappearing in a gondola in the direction of Genoa). Spend like there's no tomorrow. Eighty ducats on a meal, swap a priceless ring given to Shylock by his wife for a monkey. The insouciance, the frivolity of it all. Bassanio and Gratiano give away their rings without a third thought. Shylock would not part with his for 'a wilderness of monkeys'. But here the ring is reduced to the level of a cheap bauble for a cheap thrill. Buying the moment. Living in the present. A nasty bit of work, Jessica. Some may say a chip off the old block. But we see no evidence in Shylock's relationship with her that he deserves such treatment. Certainly her betrayal of faith and family and her robbing Shylock of his wealth contribute mightily to Shylock's desire for revenge on the whole pack of Christians. Lorenzo's act of stealing Jessica away becomes a symbol for the whole decadent behaviour of Antonio and friends, and Antonio's forcing Shylock to become a Christian is a punishment worse than any loss of wealth.

Launcelot Gobbo calls Shylock a devil. Yet apart from telling us that Launcelot eats a lot and is lazy (possibly true), Shylock treats Launcelot more with resignation than anger. He even discusses Launcelot's defection from his service with Bassanio.

**BASSANIO: Shylock thy master spoke with me this day,**
**And hath preferred thee . . .**

(Act II, Scene ii)

All seems to be amicable between them; Launcelot even admits that he has a bad conscience, that it is the Devil himself urging him to leave Shylock. Reason? Bassanio has come into money (Antonio's) and is hiring men at a good rate, poaching them, and giving them flash uniforms (to impress). It's called bettering oneself, trading up. Just as Jessica destroys Shylock with her betrayal, so Launcelot Gobbo reduces his father to tears of despair with a cruel trick, unleashing in his sand-blind father a passion of grief that he had not bargained for, by pretending to be dead. Yet another of Shakespeare's clown/nobility parallels, this one involving offspring.

> LAUNCELOT: Ergo, Master Launcelot . . . is indeed deceased, or as you would say in plain terms, gone to heaven.
>
> GOBBO: Marry, God forbid! The boy was the very staff of my age, my very prop.
>
> (Act II, Scene ii)

Thus do Christians play so lightly with emotions. Life and death, marriage and money are jokes, oaths are to be broken and parents laughed at.

* * *

And so to Shylock.

All right, so he is careful with his money. Usury was frowned on in Elizabethan society. For us it is par for the course. We call them banks. They bleed us dry for profit. The twenty-first century pound of flesh is negative equity, exorbitant interest rates, repossession. Shylock would have been in good company with Barclays, RBS, NatWest and others and Antonio with Enron. Shylock hates Antonio because he is a Christian – more, because he lends out money gratis. Antonio hates Shylock because he is a Jew – more, because he lends out money for profit, thus breaking up the cartel, the gentleman's club.

However, Shylock is not a gambler. Antonio is. So what makes Shylock gamble on what has to be a very long shot? What are the chances of *none* of Antonio's ships coming back before three months have elapsed? After all he sent them out to the four corners of the globe, covering his options.

ANTONIO: . . . My ventures are not in one bottom trusted,
Nor to one place; nor is my whole estate
Upon the fortune of this present year.

(Act I, Scene i)

SHYLOCK: . . . He hath an argosy bound to Tripolis, another to the
Indies; . . . a third at Mexico, a fourth for England, and other ventures
he hath squandered abroad.

(Act I, Scene iii)

He hasn't put all his eggs in one argosy. He expects them *all* back
within two months. Shylock cannot have expected the bond ever to be
forfeit. It's like backing the outsider at the Grand National at a thousand
to one. Or playing Lotto. But of course, he can't charge Antonio
interest. That would be playing into the Christian's hands. He has to be
bigger than that. He devises a method which he calls 'a merry sport'. Is
it that? 'If I can catch him once upon the hip . . .' Yet it can hardly be
serious. Even when he gets the news that Antonio has possibly lost a
ship, his first thought is that he might not get his money back, not that
he'll get his pound of flesh.

SHYLOCK: There I have another bad match! A bankrupt, a prodigal,
who dares scarce show his head on the Rialto, a beggar that was used
to come so smug upon the mart!

(Act III, Scene i)

The situation only turns real after Jessica's defection, spurred on by
the unbelievable chance that all the ships have indeed been lost at sea. Or
have they? Where did Portia get the letter which she produces back in
Belmont that tells him that some of his boats have safely come to
harbour? How long had she had it? Has she known all along? Is it
possible that both Shylock and Antonio have been put through the mill
needlessly?

PORTIA: . . . you shall not know by what strange accident
I chancèd on this letter.

(Act V, Scene i)

The quality of Portia's mercy may well indeed have been strained if this is the case. Merciless would then be a better description of her handling of the situation.

The play is finely balanced between disgust at Shylock's insistence on exacting his pound of flesh and disgust at the racism that has brought him to it. Yet he has two speeches that in any context could be seen as a plea for racial tolerance and equality.

> SHYLOCK: . . . Hath not a Jew eyes? Hath not a Jew hands, organs, dimensions, senses, affections, passions? Fed with the same food, hurt with the same weapons, subject to the same diseases, healed by the same means, warmed and cooled by the same winter and summer as a Christian is? If you prick us, do we not bleed? If you tickle us, do we not laugh? And if you poison us, do we not die? And if you wrong us, shall we not revenge? . . .
>
> (Act III, Scene i)

The speech finishes with the key line that defines the whole rationale behind Shylock's revenge: 'The villainy you teach me I will execute, and it shall go hard but I will better the instruction.' Shylock's bloodthirsty act is not simply the result of the way the Venetians have treated him but an exact replica of Christian values. His cruelty will mirror theirs. In the eyes of the law he is 'doing no wrong'.

> SHYLOCK: . . . You have among you many a purchased slave,
> Which like your asses and your dogs and mules
> You use in abject and in slavish parts,
> Because you bought them. Shall I say to you,
> 'Let them be free! Marry them to your heirs!
> Why sweat they under burdens? . . .'
>     . . . . .
>             You will answer,
> 'The slaves are ours.' So do I answer you.
> The pound of flesh which I demand of him
> Is dearly bought, 'tis mine, and I will have it.
> If you deny me, fie upon your law!
>
> (Act IV, Scene i)

Here Shylock shows a clinical insight into the mercenary motives of Christian Venetian behaviour. He speculates with money, they speculate with lives and goods. He tries to join them and is defeated. There are too many of them and they are better at the game than he is. The lesson is, don't try and step over the class / race divide – they'll beat you every time. And as Shylock trails off into the sunset – stripped of his wealth, his faith, his hearth and home, that is the last we see of him. Yet there is still more flesh to be extracted.

\* \* \*

And so to Belmont. They come from all corners to try and guess which casket contains Portia's portrait. It is like trying to guess the weight of the ram at the village fair. Rather like Bianca in *The Taming of the Shrew* – will it be the octogenarian Gremio or the young Tranio bartering for her hand who'll win her? For Portia it's touch and go. Will it be the German drunk or the English idiot? Life and love are a lottery. Try and put them off – make them sign a piece of paper swearing that if they choose wrongly they will never marry. It works with some. Never mind that it is impossible to enforce – it's the thought that does it. Dad certainly knew what he was doing. If anybody is going to get the wealth that he has left behind, at least make them sweat for it. Presumably Portia was too young to wed when he was alive or he would have sorted it all out before he popped off.

So choose. Gold. Silver. Lead. Marriages are a convenience, a cementing of property and fortunes. Love plays no part. So who composed the rhymes to go in the caskets? Who thought up the effigies – skull and puppet – to go inside the gold and silver, cruelly mocking the choosers? Die – loser! Who chose lead as the one in which to place the portrait – the least alluring? What must Portia feel as Morocco and Arragon are contemplating the choice? It's crucial that Bassanio chooses right. Do they help him (Cough – n-o-o-o! After all there's more than a million at stake.) Daddy obviously didn't want some gold-digger frittering away his fortune and it could so easily have been some wealthy prince or potentate not put off by some sworn unenforceable oath. But he reckoned without Bassanio's cunning. *Faute de mieux*, Portia ends up with the biggest chancer of the lot, a crow with feathers painted green. The gambler, not even waiting to suss out the lie of the land, all the chips on one number, pulls it off. The hard-bitten bitch of an heiress gets the footloose and fancy free buccaneer. It's a marriage made in lead.

Three marriages, three recipes for disaster. Against the backdrop of a moon going in and out of the clouds, now light now dark, we get the feeling that all is not exactly roses between Jessica and Lorenzo.

LORENZO: The moon shines bright. In such a night as this,
When the sweet wind did gently kiss the trees
And they did make no noise, in such a night
Troilus methinks mounted the Troyan walls,
And sighed his soul toward the Grecian tents
Where Cressid lay that night.

JESSICA: In such a night
Did Thisbe fearfully o'ertrip the dew,
And saw the lion's shadow ere himself,
And ran dismayed away.

LORENZO: In such a night
Stood Dido with a willow in her hand
Upon the wild sea banks, and waft her love
To come again to Carthage.

JESSICA: In such a night
Medea gathered the enchanted herbs
That did renew old Aeson.

LORENZO: In such a night
Did Jessica steal from the wealthy Jew,
And with an unthrift love did run from Venice
As far as Belmont.

JESSICA: In such a night
Did young Lorenzo swear he loved her well,
Stealing her soul with many vows of faith,
And ne'er a true one.

LORENZO: In such a night
Did pretty Jessica, like a little shrew,
Slander her love, and he forgave it her.

JESSICA: I would out-night you, did nobody come;
But hark, I hear the footing of a man.

(Act V, Scene i)

No playful banter this, it is a no-holds-barred battle of the sexes, the classical allusions hardly masking the full-blown row into which it is about to degenerate when interrupted by the arrival of a messenger. Jessica will not be mollified even by music. Portia arrives back, her mood bitter and acerbic. The music also turns her off.

PORTIA: . . . Methinks it sounds much sweeter than by day
. . . . .
The crow doth sing as sweetly as the lark
When neither is attended, and I think
The nightingale, if she should sing by day.
When every goose is cackling, would be thought
No better a musician than the wren.
How many things by season seasoned are
To their right praise and true perfection!
Peace! . . .

(Act V, Scene i)

Out of nothing a row erupts between Nerissa and Gratiano. It's those rings. Gratiano is damned if he is going to carry the can all on his own. He fingers Bassanio. No honour among friends. The women twist the knife. Once again Portia shows no mercy. No comic scene this. A deadly earnest extraction of a metaphorical pound of flesh.

PORTIA: If you had known the virtue of the ring,
Or half her worthiness that gave the ring,
Or your own honour to contain the ring,
You would not then have parted with the ring.

(Act V, Scene i)

Antonio is silent. And is silent. Until finally he is forced to intervene and admit that the ring was given away on his behalf and in a rush of blood to the head pledges an oath once again on behalf of his friend:

ANTONIO: I once did lend my body for his wealth,
Which but for him that had your husband's ring
Had quite miscarried. I dare be bound again,
My soul upon the forfeit, that your lord
Will never more break faith advisedly.

(Act V, Scene i)

Will he never learn? He was almost fatally wrong once. He could be so again. There is nothing in Bassanio's past or personality that says he will stay true to Portia. It obviously hurts Antonio to deal with this lady who is now legitimately Bassanio's wife, his rival for Bassanio's affections. He needn't have worried – Portia has Bassanio wriggling on a hook and intends to keep him there for the rest of his life. Lorenzo's boat too comes home (what did he do to deserve it?).

NERISSA: . . . There do I give to you and Jessica
From the rich Jew, a special deed of gift,
After his death, of all he dies possessed of.

LORENZO: Fair ladies, you drop manna in the way
Of starvèd people.

(Act V, Scene i)

What happened to the monkey?

Gratiano rounds off a bad night's work with a few dirty jokes about keeping safe Nerissa's 'ring'. And Shylock? He has probably committed suicide. They're a nasty lot on the Rialto.

# Othello

'The forgeries of jealousy . . .'

Michael Billington complained in *The Guardian* of April 24th 2013 that Nick Hytner, in placing his production of *Othello* in a modern war context, elevated Iago to the centre of the action at the expense of Othello.

> 'But for all the brilliance, it confirms something I have long suspected: the more naturalistic the production, the more Iago becomes the play's focal figure . . . the crucial consequence of the production's modernity is that it puts Iago at the heart of the play . . . [the production] denies Othello something of his musical grandeur and makes Iago's diseased mind the main event. . . .'

Thus Michael Billington in his *Guardian* (24th April 2013) critique of Nicholas Hytner's production of *Othello* at the Royal National Theatre.

I do not understand Mr. Billington. After a lifetime of reviewing (forty years?) he has only just come to the conclusion that the pivotal figure in Othello is Iago, and worse, he is so susceptible to visual influence that he believes the play means one thing in period dress and another in modern dress. If the production were in Elizabethan dress and the language rhetorically expressed, he seems to be saying, Iago would be relegated to second lead and Othello regain his rightful place at the heart of the play. How can the play change? The actors are the same, they say the same words, in the same way, with the same inflexions. Either Iago is at the centre of the play or he isn't, regardless of whether the production is in Roman togas, Napoleonic riding gear, or Hawaian shorts. Michael Billington is displaying the naivety of an uninitiated theatre goer who on being confronted with contemporary images that are familiar – in Hytner's production straight out of *The Hurt Locker* – rather than the distancing effect of period costume, suddenly has a revelation: 'Oh. So that's what the play means!' Bollocks.

That the play is about jealousy is a given. But whose? Criticism has long focused on that of Othello, consigning Iago to the 'evil' basket. That his amorality is first cousin to Macbeth is clear, but the mainspring of the play, the factor that kicks everything off, is Iago's jealousy: crucially, the form this jealousy takes is pro-active and that of Othello re-active. Iago does, Othello is done to. Mr. Billington has obviously shied away from confronting the political reality of the play all of his forty odd critical years.

In *The Merchant of Venice* it is not Antonio who occupies the hot seat (except in court) it is Shylock. We remember Hal and Falstaff rather than Henry IV (whether cleft in two or not), both roles being considerably greater. Therefore it is no surprise that Iago emerges from any proper reading of the play as a central figure. After all, he has nearly 25% more lines than Othello – 1,098 to Othello's 887. If Iago is in the driving seat then it is only natural that he will grab the attention. No wonder he sometimes dominates the action.

There is only one jealous party at the start of the play and that is Iago, an unrelenting protagonist in his pursuit of revenge. The passion of Othello is only aroused at a later point by a series of lies and subterfuge as we see him impaled on the prongs of Iagos hatred.

As often with Shakespeare, one simple (inexplicable?) action kicks of events of monumental significance. The play begins with Iago already plotting against Othello, the reasons for which instantly emerge. He, an experienced soldier has been passed over for promotion by Othello, his commanding officer, in favour of one Cassio, in Iago's eyes a greenhorn cadet from a privileged background: the equivalent of a Non-Commissioned Officer, a regimental sergeant major, losing out to the son of an Earl graduating from Sandhurst.

'I know my price: I am worth no worse a place' says Iago. 'War is my trade'.

And, what is worse, Iago is Othello's Ancient, his personal right-hand man, his batman, and he's lost out to –

**One Michael Cassio, a Florentine**
**. . .**
**That never set a squadron in the field,**
**Not the division of a battle knows**
**More than a spinster . . .**
**. . . Mere prattle without practice**
**Is all his soldiership. But he, sir, had th' election.**

(Act I, Scene i)

What a snub! Jealous of Cassio, Iago determines to have his revenge on Othello. But why was he passed over? Is this some kind of inverted snobbery on the part of Othello, a belief that the Old Etonian Oxbridge brigade will win out every time against the working class state educated proletariat? Certainly we don't have any evidence that Othello mistrusts Iago (or else Iago's plan wouldn't succeed) and we do not get the impression that he's a bad soldier – quite the opposite. Can we believe Iago? Is this bitter prejudice? Is Cassio really that inexperienced or is he already battle worn?

Iago instantly plans a plague on both their houses and uses Roderigo, in his gullibility a sort of second cousin to Sir Andrew Aguecheek, a young man thwarted in his love by Othello's marriage to Desdemona, as cover to gain access to Brabantio, Desdemona's father. Without revealing his identity Iago informs Brabantio of his daughter's clandestine marriage to 'thick lips' Othello.

**IAGO: Zounds, sir, you're robbed . . .**
**Your heart is burst you have lost half your soul.**
**Even now, now, very now, an old black ram**

That seems clear enough but there's more –

**. . . you'll have your daughter covered with a Barbary horse, you'll have your nephews neigh to you, you'll have coursers for cousins and jennets for germans.**

Spanish horses, aka Arab stallions, as your bloodline. Even clearer, and in case Brabantio still hasn't got it –

**BRABANTIO: What profane wretch art thou?**

**IAGO: I am one, sir, that comes to tell you that your daughter and the Moor are making the beast with two backs.**

(Act I, Scene i)

And Roderigo rubs it in by revealing that his daughter has been spirited away by a gondolier into 'the gross clasps of a lascivious Moor'. Can't say fairer than that, guv.

If ever there was debate about Othello's colour, all this seem to point pretty conclusively to him being, if not coal black, then a goodly shade of black. The confusion has come about by use of the term 'Moor' with some persuaded that Othello is the dusky colour of an Arab from Morocco, and earlier, racially inclined critics, Coleridge for one, unable to believe that Shakespeare would have deliberately married an attractive white girl to an older black man. But Shakepeare often uses the word 'moor' as in 'blackamoor' to mean black and Othello even says of himself – 'I am black' and 'begrimed and black As mine own face'(Act III). Even allowing for the prejudice on the part of Iago, Roderigo and others the descriptions are graphic: 'thick lips', 'old black ram', 'sooty bosom'. Barbary horses, Spanish stallions – all the imagery is of blackness.

We don't know if Richard Burbage, who played the role in Shakespeare's company, ever sported black make-up, but one suspects that the willing suspension of disbelief on the part of Shakespeare's audiences made it unnecessary. If a white actor could play a black role in 1600 it has taken nearly four hundred years to accept that a black actor can play a white role, although it would be a brave actor indeed that would emulate Laurence Olivier and put on black make up to play Othello in the 21st century. In an attempt to get round the problem Patrick Stewart was the only white face in an all black cast in a Jude Kelly 'photo negative' production at the Shakespeare Theatre in Washington in 1997. I'm not sure what that adds to our understanding of the play except to reiterate that there was racism around in the 16th / 17th centuries. Surprise. (Let's have more black Henry Vs, white Othellos. Queen Lears.)

If Act I, Scene i kicks off Iago's revenge, we wait until his soliloquy at the end of Act I to discover the real reason why Iago 'hates him

(Othello) as I do hell pains'. The slight at being denied promotion, it turns out, was only the tip of the iceberg, the final straw. Othello, it would seem, is not only tupping Desdemona but the old ram has been sticking it to Emilia, Iago's wife, into the bargain.

> IAGO: . . . I hate the Moor,
> And it is thought abroad that 'twixt my sheets
> He's done my office. I know not if't be true . . .
> But I, for mere suspicion in that kind,
> Will do as if for surety . . .

(Act I, Scene iii)

No smoke without fire. Plenty of willing gossip-mongers to whisper the salacious rumour in his ear. If further confirmation were needed of the worm gnawing at his gut, in Act II, Scene i he says –

> IAGO: . . . I do suspect the lusty Moor
> Hath leapt into my seat; the thought whereof
> Doth, like poisonous mineral, gnaw my innards;
> And nothing can, or shall content my soul
> Till I am evened with him, wife for wife.

Whether ill-founded or not, it is a genuine suspicion, as Emilia's exchange with Desdemona in Act IV, Scene iii shows.

> DESDEMONA: . . . O, these men, these men!
> Dost thou in conscience think – tell me, Emilia –
> That there be women who do abuse their husbands
> In such gross kind?
>
> EMILIA: There be some such, no question.
>
> DESDEMONA: Wouldst thou do such a deed for all the world?
>
> EMILIA: Why, would not you?
>
> DESDEMONA: No, by this heavenly light!
>
> EMILIA: Nor I neither by this heavenly light: I might well do it i'th' dark.
>
> DESDEMONA: Wouldst thou do such a deed for all the world?
>
> EMILIA: The world's a huge thing: it is a great prize for such a small vice.

> DESDEMONA: In troth, I think thou wouldst not.
>
> EMILIA: In troth, I think I should and undo it when I had done it. Marry, I would not do such a thing for a joint ring, nor for measures of lawn, nor for gowns, petticoats, nor caps, nor any petty exhibition. But for the whole world! . . . ? Ud's pity, who would not make her husband a cuckold to make him a monarch? I should venture purgatory for it.

Interesting. Is there a sense here that Emilia, the maidservant of Desdemona, has slept with the 'Noble Othello', pre nuptials, on a mission to secure Iago promotion? Certainly, Othello would represent a prize worth catching were she to succeed in getting him between the sheets. No whore she but an ambitious pragmatist, of the kind who throughout history have used their bodies to ensure survival.

She continues to strike a further blow for female emancipation and equality:

> EMILIA: . . . But I do think it is their husbands faults
> If wives do fail . . .
> . . . Let husbands know
> Their wives have sense like them: they see and smell,
> And have their palates both for sweet and sour
> As husbands have. What is it that they do
> When they change us for others? Is it sport?
> I think it is. And doth affection breed it?
> I think it doth. Is't frailty that thus errs?
> It is so too. And have not we affections,
> Desires for sport, and frailty, as men have?
> Then let them use us well: else let them know
> The ills we do, their ills instruct us so.
>
> (Act III, Scene iii)

And Phillip Larkin said that sex began in 1963. Three hundred and seventy years ago, at the point where the Puritans closed the theatres, Hester Prynne is being pilloried in the town of Boston for having an adulterous affair, being forced to wear, embroidered on her breast for life, an 'A', a Scarlet Letter, in the novel of the same name by Nathaniel Hawthorne. Chaucer's maxim 'Do and be done by as you did' here finds more than an echo in Emelia's demand for sexual equality. There is also an echo of Shylock's refusal to accept the treatment meted out to him by the Christians, 'The villainy you teach me I shall execute, and it shall go hard but I will better the instruction'. (Act IV.i)

Emilia is in a long line of emancipated Shakespearean women who defy convention and cock a snook at male dominated morality: Juliet and Miranda, girls who do not wait to be asked for their hand but declare their love openly and propose first, not waiting four years for February 29th; Olivia and Rosalind, both appropriating their husbands; sorry, no arguing, we'll sort it out later. Hermia, refusing to bow to the will of her father and fleeing with her lover. Katherina, who has to be battered into submission before succumbing to the domination of Petruccio.

There is enough in Emilia's philosophy for us to believe that she too could have made the beast with two backs with Othello, though of course holding such views does not necessarily make the wish father to the thought. But coupled with the gondoliers' gossip around the canals of Venice there's enough to give Iago pause.

So, Iago gradually feeds poison into Othello's ear, fanning the flames of Othello's (and his own) jealousy until it culminates in the deaths of four people. Two mirror murders; two husbands, Othello and Iago, killing their wives. However the one kills himself through remorse, the other attempts a cowardly escape. As the magnitude of Iago's deception is revealed to him, Othello says,

> . . .Then you must speak
> Of one that loved not wisely but too well;
> Of one, not easily jealous but, being wrought,
> Perplexed in the extreme; of one whose hand
> . . . threw a pearl away,
> Richer than all his tribe . . .

(Act V, Scene ii)

One not easily jealous. Not envious of others. It is more his credulity, his innate – maybe naïve – faith in the honesty of man that shatters his world with such passionate and all-consuming force. Once the dyke is breached the green water floods the plain. And yet he has every cause to be jealous of others more fortunate. He has suffered slavery, torture, humiliation: it is this that has captured Desdemona's heart in the first place:

> OTHELLO: . . . my story being done,
> She gave me for my pains a world of sighs;
> She swore, in faith, 'twas strange, 'twas passing strange'
> 'Twas pitiful, 'twas wondrous pitiful;
> She wished she had not heard it . . .
> She loved me for the dangers I had passed,
> And I loved her, that she did pity them.
>
> (Act I, Scene iii)

One not easily jealous. But another one is, and we are left in no doubt as to the origins of the green eyed monster. There is however a substantive difference in the quality of their jealousy. While Othello's language is passionate, poetic, sensitive, and emotional when roused, that of Iago is blunt, earthy, his passion in public for effect only. He is to the world 'honest Iago', a rough diamond, hail-fellow-well-met, rough talking, bawdy in the company of men. But alone we are privy to the thoughts and plans of a malevolent Richard III directed towards one end only.

One not easily jealous. Othello is a man of essential nobility debased and brought low by his passion. Shakespeare treats jealousy in a number of ways. Iago is closer to Edmund in *King Lear* than Othello is to Leontes in *The Winter's Tale*, or Ford in *The Merry Wives of Windsor*. In many ways Leontes begins where Othello leaves off. We are right in the middle of irrational suspicion as the play opens, of a smouldering, soul consuming jealousy. Ford wears his jealousy on his sleeve – irascible, apoplectic, a victim of his wife's incorrigible sense of humour in the face of his ridiculous, unwarranted behaviour. They are people who, as Emilia says 'are not ever jealous for the cause, / But jealous for they are jealous'. Edmund however – 'Now God stand up for bastards' – has, like Iago, 'something of the night about him', and plans his revenge on his brother Edgar as a campaign. He too, like Iago, has been passed over.

How does Iago think it will all end? Does he already have the deaths of Othello and Desdemona on his mind? Their demise only becomes imperative at a late stage as Iago feels the net closing in on him. Having learnt the tactics of attack and retreat on the battle field, he adapts his purpose to circumstance. There is a sense that much of what he plans is on the hoof, that, carried away by the exhilaration of his success, Iago is driven to further and further extremes in an attempt to divert attention and blame away from himself. I do not believe that he sets out with the deaths of Othello and Desdemona in mind; rather he aims at the collapse of the marriage, but events overtake him as both his and Othello's jealousy spin out of control.

Does Othello have reason to mistrust Desdemona? After all they were only a few hours married before they embarked for Cyprus and Othello is straight away into action – the military kind – and they can't have had much time to consummate the marriage. So when on earth could Desdemona have betrayed him with Cassio unless in the twenty-four hours after the marriage, a case of the bride having one last freedom fuck with the best man? A pretty impossible scenario had Othello stopped to think about it but then what does Othello know of Desdemona's sexual past or her predilections? An older man, a younger woman, the fascination of racial taboo?

> OTHELLO: Villain, be sure thou prove my wife a whore;
> Be sure of it: give me the ocular proof,
> Or by the worth of mine eternal soul,
> Thou hadst been better have been born a dog,
> Than answer my waked wrath.'
>
> (Act III, Scene iii)

This really puts the shits up Iago. Probably for the only time in the play he is genuinely frightened. He realises that he has to do something to save his reputation and his skin. To insinuate that Othello has been cuckolded by Cassio he invents the story of Cassio talking in his sleep – they share a room together – and, as proof, later comes up with the story of Desdemona's handkerchief, which fortuitously Emilia has found and innocently given to Iago.

> IAGO: . . . Tell me but this:
> Have you not sometimes seen a handkerchief,
> Spotted with strawberries, in your wife's hand?

**OTHELLO:** I gave her such a one: 'twas my first gift.

**IAGO:** . . . such a handkerchief –
I'm sure it was your wife's – did I today
See Cassio wipe his beard with.

(Act III, Scene iii)

Why do we listen to such people? They only mean us harm. The well meaning neighbour reporting on the comings and goings of the husband's / wife's lover(s). Do we not suspect their motives for thus informing us? But we are susceptible, gullible, suspicious. The merest suggestion of our partner's infidelity kicks us in the gut.

**OTHELLO:** O, blood, blood, blood!'

Good old 'honest' Iago!

From now on Iago is in a revenge play up to his neck, there's no turning back. (Question: how do you deal with the handkerchief in a modern dress production? Or Friar John locked up in a house of plague and unable to deliver the Friar Laurence's letter in Romeo and Juliet? Or Richard's horse for which he would give his Kingdom in the heat of battle? Mmm.)

In Act V, Scene i Iago winds Roderigo up, preying now on Roderigo's jealous belief that Cassio has slept with Desdemona. He prevails on Roderigo to lay in wait in the dark and kill Cassio. He confides,

**IAGO:** . . . whether he kill Cassio,
Or Cassio him, or each do kill the other,
Every way makes my game. Live Roderigo,
He calls me to a restitution large,
Of gold and jewels, that I bobb'd from him
As gifts to Desdemona.
It must not be. If Cassio do remain
He hath a daily beauty in his life
That makes me ugly: and besides, the Moor
May unfold me to him – there stand I in peril.
No, he must die . . .

Work it out as you go along. Iago retires to watch. In the confrontation Cassio stabs Roderigo but only succeeds in wounding him. Roderigo is still alive – and so is Cassio. Oh dear! There follows a stage direction, omitted by some editors. In the dark, unseen – [*Iago from behind wounds Cassio in the leg and exit*] Another botched attempt. Oh dear again! (In a comic version both Cassio and Roderigo would be limping and hopping around the stage, cursing). Iago enters for a third time, pretending to arrive on the scene by chance.

> **IAGO:** (*To Cassio*) O, my lieutenant! What villains have done this?

> **CASSIO:** I think that one of them is hereabout
> And cannot make away.

> . . .

> **RODERIGO:** O, help me here!

> . . .

> **IAGO:** O murd'rous slave, O villain!
> [*He stabs Roderigo*]

Done. Roderigo no longer lives to tell the tale, and although Cassio is still alive Iago can spin him any story he likes. Here is evidence enough that the tail is wagging the dog. The situation spirals out of control and in a desperate attempt to save his own neck Iago kills his wife and succeeds in destroying both Othello and Desdemona.

Iago has no quarrel with Desdemona. He enmeshes her in the plot as a necessary means to get back at Othello, but that he had initially thought of her death . . . I doubt it. Similarly he misreads the depth of Othello's passion that is unleashed at the suggestion of Desdemona's infidelity. A good soldier and reader of battle plans he may be, but his ability to read human nature is rudimentary. It does not occur to him the action Othello might take when driven 'even to madness'.

Of the four great tragedies, *Hamlet*, *King Lear*, *Macbeth* and *Othello*, *Othello* is the only domestic play concerned with the lives and deaths of ordinary people. The highest rank (and smallest role) is that of a Duke and the audience occupies the world of soldiers and their wives. No Kings or Queens, Princes and Princesses. The plot is simple, there are no side issues, and the action relentless over a condensed period of time. A steel arrow pierces the heart of the story.

Given such a scenario any production worth its salt, modern or otherwise, throws the twin jealousies of Othello and Iago into stark relief. And if it is Iago who stands out in the memory, not only is it because the devil has all the best tunes, he also has the most lines.

# Twelfth Night

## . . . Malvolio in paper chains

The skeletal tree lists drunkenly, brown needles strew the carpet; paper chains dangle brokenly from the sellotape; the remnants of an unexploded cracker litter the fireplace; a cat cuffs a silver bauble as it bobbles down the hallway; the star is packed away for another year up in the attic. The bones have been boiled down for soup, and the last lump of Christmas pud is in the kids' lunch-box.

It's Twelfth Night. For some, the party's over. Others swig the dregs from empty bottles, refusing to leave. How far can you push your luck before the music stops? Watch out, boys, the neo-cons are coming and the hangover's about to kick in.

Time to get back to the serious business of January: the bills, the bills . . .

Except it's probably not January, it's probably early summer. Olivia describes Malvolio's deranged behaviour as – 'a very Midsummer madness' – although naturally this is a phrase that could be used at any time of the year, akin to 'mad as a March hare'. It is warm enough for the three lads to hide in a Boxtree in the garden – well it could be in the snow I suppose – but Maria says of Malvolio that he is 'yonder i' the sun, practicing behaviour to his own shadow this half hour'. The lads carouse through the night – no sense of being wrapped up against the winter cold. More conclusive perhaps is Fabian's description of Sir Andrew Aguecheek's challenge of Sebastian to a dual as being 'more matter for a May morning', and when Maria warns Feste that he will be thrown out of the house for going AWOL he replies 'let summer bear it out'. Whatever: it's summer.

Is the title *Twelfth Night* simply then a metaphor, an ominous portent of the looming Puritanism that is just around the corner? Let the bad times roll. Enter left Malvolio.

Way back in 1974 I stripped the play down in an experiment aimed at investigating the content of the Malvolio scenes. I cut the play down to about seventy minutes, focusing on the cruel treatment meted out to Malvolio by Sir Toby, Feste, Fabian and Maria. I was in my 'everything must be played in bright, open white light' phase of directing – a legacy of Peter Brook's *A Midsummer Night's Dream* – and in order to simulate the darkness of the cell in which Malvolio is bound and incarcerated I placed a paper bag over his head.

Then, a couple of years later, we were looking at pictures in the press of IRA prisoners in the Maze prison in the North of Ireland with paper bags over their heads. My theatrical solution of the disorientation caused by the bag had preceded the political reality. Obviously, in my subconscious the image had come from somewhere: I certainly didn't believe that the device of the paper bag was original.

**SIR TOBY: Come, we'll have him in a dark room and bound.**

(Act III, Scene iv)

Wind forward thirty years to the Ludlow Festival and the brown paper had bag morphed into a black hood which Malvolio's tormentors placed over his head, having first bound his hands behind his back, leaving a long length of rope which was wielded mercilessly by Maria, as Feste, his voice disguised as Sir Topas, torments Malvolio by attempting to convince him that he's lost his marbles. It immediately lifted *Twelfth Night* out of the realm of the parochial, a rather nice little festive (Feste) celebration of self-indulgent love and rampaging drunkenness, into the realm of the – then – contemporary images of torture issuing forth from Abu Graib. Malvolio was then thrust into a pit in the stage floor and the trap, in the form of a grill, closed over him.

Immediately I was accused of being gratuitous and gimmicky.

'How dare I put Malvolio in *Twelfth Night* in a black hood, tie him up, and turn a scene that is essentially comic into something grotesque!' was the rough tenor of a number of letters and several critics.(*Pace* Sam Marlow of *The Times*).

What? Locking somebody in a pitch black cell, tying them up, and trying to convince them that they are mad is comic? I'm sorry, I think I have a good sense of humour, but I don't see the comedy in that. It may have been comic in 1600 but it isn't now, and can't be played as such. And anyway I don't believe Shakespeare wrote comedy in that way.

I was attempting to interpret truthfully the demands of the text in a manner that would confront the audience with the reality of the situation, and finding a theatrical way of showing it. I added the rope that is held by Maria in order to emphasise that it is she who is the instigator of the events that lead to Malvolio's imprisonment. And naturally of course the picture was identified with that of Lindy English, the American soldier who had recently been photographed with Iraqi prisoners in the prison of Abu Graibh in Baghdad. And equally naturally I can't pretend that I didn't have that in mind.

But theatre is about those kind of statements; it makes you think, 'What did they really do to Malvolio? Did he really deserve that treatment? What is funny about the way that they treat him?' Then, in asking the audience to confront their reactions, a prime motive of theatre is fulfilled: a quest for how we can make this world a better place to live in by analysing our actions and the consequences of those actions. Particularly with a Shakespeare play, where often there is so much inherited confusion, there is an imperative to offer an audience an image that they see every day: ask what they *really* think. Even Sir Toby Belch thinks they've gone too far: 'I would we were well rid of this knavery'.

One cannot avoid confronting the fact that the punishment to which the vanity of Malvolio is exposed is both brutal and excessive and that there is nothing in his behaviour to justify his unscrupulous persecution. Comic interludes, romantic self-indulgence, cross-dressing gender-bending with homosexual under and overtones the play may have. But there is a dark, cruel streak running through it. No wonder he'll be revenged.

Part of the problem is that audiences tend to look at a play in one way if it is in Elizabethan or Renaissance costume, and look at it another way if it is in modern dress. And yet the actors say the same words, delivered in the same manner. So the perception is in the eye of the audience, and not in the ear for what is actually being said. The appearance is of modernity, whereas the actuality is that the accoutrement of expectation is being stripped away, and something else supplied that forces an audience to think in a contemporary fashion.

I am making a blanket generalisation here because obviously there are those audience, and critics, who would look at the plays, no matter how they were costumed, and identify their political content. But in my production of *Twelfth Night* the confrontation was forced on the audience, some of whom were maybe not accustomed to seeing the play in any political light.

So, what is Malvolio's crime? His name perhaps? 'Mal' – bad: 'volio' – I wish. I wish you ill.

Maria says, 'He is sometimes a kind of Puritan'.

Well is he, or isn't he? A pompous, humourless git maybe but we don't see much evidence of a *Mayflower* link. No pious prayers or the invoking of God's wrath to threaten the revellers. He is much more concerned with ensuring that Olivia's household is run as a tight ship and that the hooligan element does not get out of hand. He is not deliberately Malicious, although his language is intemperate when lambasting the behaviour of the carousers. Is it this that gets up their collective drink-infused nostrils?

> **MALVOLIO:** My Masters, are you mad? Or what are you? Have you no wit, manners, nor honesty, but to gabble like tinkers at this time of night? Do you make an alehouse of my lady's house, that you squeak out your coziers' catches without any mitigation or remorse of voice? . . .

> (Act II, Scene iii)

To which Sir Toby replies contemptuously, 'Art any more than a steward?' How dare this commoner presume to criticise we of noble blood in such a manner! Class you see. As early as the nineteenth century some commentators saw Malvolio not as an object of fun but as a victim of social discrimination.

Olivia says of him that he is 'sad and civil' and that he 'suits as a servant with her fortune'. In other words his grave and solemn demeanour is in tune with her melancholy and mourning. Dressed soberly he is not initially a figure of fun and we do not sense the consuming passion of the religious zealot. He presents a picture of a conscientious Steward going about his household duties with sergeant-major-like efficiency. The revenge exacted is out of all proportion to the crime. Humourless he may be but as Lamb says, Malvolio is not essentially ludicrous: he becomes comic but by accident, as a result of the madness that overtakes him through the false hopes engendered by the misinterpretation of Maria's letter.

> MARIA: I shall drop in his way some obscure epistles of love, wherein by the colour of his beard, the shape of his leg, the manner of his gait, the expressure of his eye, forehead and complexion, he shall find himself most feelingly personated. I can write very much like my lady, your neice; on a forgotten matter we can hardly make distinction of our hands.
>
> (Act II, Scene iii)

What is this forgotten matter – forging a cheque with Olivia's signature? Deceit is Maria's middle name. The trick played on Malvolio turns him into a posturing, ludicrous clown. So is this Shakespeare's attack on the Puritanism of the Reformed Church of England, holding the movement up to ridicule? Possibly, Will.i.am was ever topical. And subversive, for in the final analysis Malvolio invites our sympathy. His final speech lays out the cruelty of the 'jape' in terms that cannot fail to shame.

> MALVOLIO: Lady . . . pray you, peruse that letter.
> You must not now deny it is your hand.
> Write from it if you can, in hand or phrase,
> Or say 'tis not your seal, not your invention;
> You can say none of this. Well, grant it then,
> And tell me in the modesty of honour,
> Why you have given me such clear lights of favour?
> Bade me come smiling and cross-gartered to you,
> To put on yellow stockings, and to frown
> Upon Sir Toby and the lighter people?
> And, acting this in an obedient hope,
> Why have you suffered me to be imprisoned,

Kept in a dark house, visited by the priest,
And made the most notorious geck and gull
That e'er invention played on. Tell me why?'

. . .

OLIVIA: Alas, poor fool! How they have baffled thee!

(Act V, Scene i)

Olivia's affection for him is plain, even if he is an impossible suitor. Earlier she has said at the first hint of his supposed madness that she 'would not have him miscarry for half her dowry' and as he exits she says 'he has been most notoriously abused'. He is her faithful and trusted servant and remains so.

Nevertheless Malvolio's final cry of 'I'll be revenged on the whole pack of you!' has an ominous ring to it. There is a hint that the audience is under threat, as well as the instigators of his humiliation. It is here that the first real sign of fundamentalism rears its head, ironically brought about and self inflicted by the antics of the four japers. Malvolio, driven into a corner, will fight back and crush those who have heaped humiliation on him. The cry indicates a turning point in his behaviour, the sanguinity and composure as Steward now the steely and dangerous demeanour of the avenger. It is on a par with Shylock's chilling 'The villainy you teach me I will execute, and it shall go hard but I will better the instruction' (*The Merchant of Venice*, Act III, Scene i) as Malvolio transforms himself into a forerunner of those early seventeenth century neo-conservatives who, historically in 1640, closed the theatres down for twenty years in the name of religion.

In the modern world, the invasion of Iraq, the looming threat of war with Iran or North Korea, the use of Drones – unmanned bombers targeting civilians in Afghanistan and Pakistan – all under the pretext of preserving Western democracy, are basically the product and thinking of a similar bunch of 21st century puritans. Such men are dangerous, amoral fundamentalists yet professing to possess 'the word of God'. Their actions belying their faith, they are determined to conquer and rule by force, by aggression, by sanctions, by deprivation. Guantanamo Bay is still open for torture, despite the pledge of Obama to close it down.

The final words of Malvolio, whether ice cold, snarling or howling, encompass all those contemporary images of revenge – *The Zero Dark Thirty* moments of water-boarding, the ruthless hunting down of Bin Laden. No wonder that at the time the image of Malvolio, hooded, bound, on the end of a rope, disturbed audiences. I suspect that with a certain distance between the events and now the image would not be as contentious, but coming hard as it did on the heels of the Abu Ghraib revelations the parallel was too new and raw, demanding of audiences (and critics) a stance with regard to both torture and Shakespeare. No going to the theatre for a nice escapist interlude.

Malvolio's story (to be continued) joins the other group of sequels that intrigue at the end of the play. Rather than reconciliation, the conclusion of *Twelfth Night*, opens more cans with more worms wriggling out of them than are contained in your average expanse of suburban lawn. Of that, more later.

* * *

If do and be done by as you did haunts the story of Malvolio his chief tormentor is not Maria but Feste. If Sir Toby is the hedonistic opposite of Malvolio's rectitude – 'Dost thou think because thou art virtuous there shall be no more cakes and ale?' – Feste is the intellectual irritant that gets under Malvolio's guard.

Feste is like an old dog who has an itch that he has to scratch, cynical, sardonic, bitter, dancing to the tune of whoever pays the piper, often under protest. There is a sense that he is past his sell-by date, a hanger-on who is growing old disgracefully, a crabby old bugger who would just like to be left alone to read his newspaper in the sun. Formerly in the service of Olivia's father, the old fool is now simply tolerated, one who Malvolio has to put up with perforce, in a household that is poor in comparison with that of Orsino's.

All too often Feste is played as some terrible demonstration of how one thinks fools used to behave four hundred years ago (who knows?). But Shakespeare's fool / clowns invariably display a streak of bitterness, betraying the hidden humiliation of the lot that has befallen them.

... Come away, come away, death,
And in sad cypress let me be laid.

(Act II, Scene iv)

Feste's dealing with the other figures is characterised by an insouciance and a toughness of behaviour which the opening scene with Maria establishes, demonstrating his intransigence and his belief that he can talk his way out of any situation.

MARIA: Nay, either tell me where thou hast been, or I will not open my lips so wide as a bristle may enter, in way of thy excuse. My lady will hang thee for thy absence.

FESTE: Let her hang me. He that is well hanged in this world need fear no colours.

...

MARIA: Yet you will be hanged for being so long absent; or to be turned away – is that not as good as a hanging to you?

FESTE: Many a good hanging prevents a bad marriage; and for turning away, let summer bear it out.

(Act I, Scene v)

Does Olivia throw him out. She does not.

OLIVIA: What think you of this fool, Malvolio? Doth he not mend?

...

MALVOLIO: I marvel your ladyship doth take delight in such a barren rascal. I saw him put down the other day with an ordinary fool that has no more brain than a stone. Look you now, he's out of his guard already; unless you laugh and minister occasion to him he's gagged. ...

(Act I, Scene v)

Ouch. That hit home. Feste is obviously furious at this denigration of his linguistic dexterity. And so there you have it. To someone of Malvolio's rectitude it is incomprehensible that such an old scrounging lay-about is tolerated in Olivia's household. The enmity between them is intense and Feste festers: bides his time to get his own back.

In Act V.i Maria and Toby's plot and Feste's part in it is revealed.

FESTE: . . . I was one, sir, in this interlude, one Sir Topas, sir – but that's all one. 'By the Lord, fool, I am not mad!' But do you remember: 'Madam, why laugh you at such a barren rascal, and you smile not, he's gagged'? And thus the whirligig of time brings in his revenges'.

But that's all one. A fitting catch phrase for a play who's subtitle is *What You Will*. Feste's 'but that's all one' sums up his existential cynicism, a shrug of the shoulders, take it or leave it, echoed in the melancholy mood of his final song,

'A great while ago the world began,
With a hey-ho, the wind and the rain;
But that's all one, our play is done . . . '

(Act V, Scene i)

But not before the mayhem of confusion has wreaked havoc with a number of lives.

How much did the fact that Shakespeare could only work with a male company influence the way he looked at gender? Was it always expediency that allowed him to put boys in women's costumes only for them to then don men's gear and act as realistic men again? Or did it give him the licence to explore cross-dressing gay and lesbian sexuality in a more overt sense? Amongst a number of gender-bending plots, none is more complex and homo-erotic than *Twelfth Night* and leads to some startling conclusions.

We are fond of believing that the Elizabethan / Jacobean society held a completely different attitude towards male relationships, openly acknowledging homosexuality, but contemporary Britain has only recently come to terms with this very human aspect of sexual behaviour and the Church (and many tories) are still struggling. But whereas only fifty years ago it was impossible to display such behaviour without recourse to a private club performance, in the last period of time it has been possible to explore such relationships on our stages almost without fear of prejudice. We tend to forget that the Lord Chamberlain was only abolished in 1968.

Viola's cross-dressing may not present audiences today with a moral frisson, but for 17th century Puritans, it was possibly *infra-dig* to say the least. Critics of the day argued that cross-dressing was sinful, wicked, and monstrous and that it promoted sexual deviance, turning women into hermaphrodites. The possibility of women becoming men and to a lesser extent men becoming women confronted the Elizabethan / Jacobean audience with the idea of transvestism as a reality.

How is it that England was alone in Europe in pursuing the custom of young male actors playing women's parts? Is it that the probably pre-dominantly male audience was turned on by the sight of young boys in dresses, or young boys in male attire being wooed by older men in dresses? Stephen Orgel claims that 'homosexuality in this Puritan culture appears to have been less threatening than heterosexuality' because it avoided 'a real fear of women's sexuality.' Sooner or later though there was bound to be a clash between what was seen as the licentiousness of the stage and the Puritan ethic that was beginning to sweep the country in the late 17th century. The stage was being denounced from the pulpits as 'effeminate' and the wearing of female dress by boy players as 'an occasion of wantonness and lust.' Shades of Mary Whitehouse four hundred years later. *Plus ça change*. Malvolio's revenge was to see the theatres closed down.

The gender ambiguity of Viola / Cesario lets a whole flood of desire out through the lock gates: homo-erotic attraction between Orsino and Cesario, heterosexual attraction between Orsino and Viola, and lesbian attraction between Viola and Olivia. On the surface, the passion that Olivia finds herself unable 'to hide' by means of 'wit or reason' is directed at a young man, but our senses tell us that her hidden passion is for a girl (Act III.i.153–54). When, after their first meeting, Olivia sends Cesario her ring for him to slip his finger into (an act of erotic symbolism) Cesario / Viola suddenly realises, 'I am the man: if it be so, as 'tis, / Poor lady, she were better love a dream' (Act II.ii.24–25). So good has her chav charm been, she has seen off not only Orsino but every other contender sniffing round Olivia's skirts. In cockily taking the liberty of lifting Olivia's veil Viola is hoist with her own petard, releasing a flood of homo-erotic feelings in both Olivia and herself. 'But if you were the devil,' Cesario / Viola exclaims upon seeing her face, 'you are fair' (Act I.v.255). All else follows.

'How quick bright things come to confusion.' (*A Midsummer Night's Dream*)

The sudden denouement at the end of the play, which turns all these relationships inside out, leaves a dozen unresolved stories hanging in the air.

'Nothing is but what is not'.

How much then is Olivia attracted to the feminine / masculine side of Cesario / Viola? And what does she do about the revelation that she has been in love with a girl but now is suddenly married to an unknown 'real' boy? And Olivia is a boy playing a girl anyway. Sebastian suddenly finds himself married to an unknown heiress (who is a boy) who he met five minutes before. We know what he thinks. He can't believe his luck.

> OLIVIA: Blame not this haste of mine. If you mean well,
> Now go with me, and with this holy man
> Into the chantry by; there before him
> . . . Plight me the full assurance of your faith,
> . . . What do you say?
>
> SEBASTIAN: I'll follow this good man and go with you;
> And having sworn truth, ever will be true.

> (Act IV, Scene iii)

What on earth will Olivia's future be with this unknown opportunist, this chancer, this Bassanio? The mere act of Sebastian's deceiving her into marriage is at odds with the integrity and honesty of Viola's character, the very thing that Olivia has mistakenly fallen in love with in the first place. Twins, Sebastian and Viola may be in outward appearance: in morals? Poles apart. The little shit.

> SEBASTIAN: (*To Olivia*)
> So comes it, lady, you have mistook.
> But nature to her bias drew in that.
> You would have been contracted to a maid.
> Nor are you therein, by my life, deceived:
> You are betrothed both to a maid and man.

> (Act V, Scene i)

Shell shocked, Olivia says absolutely nothing about her mistake right to the conclusion of the play. In this she joins a host of other characters in Shakespeare who remain dumb in the face of astonishing revelations that turn their lives upside down, other cross-dressers and victims who have similar problems to contend with – Rosalind / Orlando, Portia / Bassanio *et al*.

At what point does the revelation that Cesario/Viola is a girl in boys clothes (and is in fact a real boy) turn Orsino on? All that self-indulgent sighing and mooching, was for what? In a five minute *volte face* he abandons all thought of Olivia, intrigued by the confession that a boy / girl is in love with him

> **ORSINO: . . . I shall have share in this most happy wrack.**
> **(*To Viola*) Boy, thou hast said to me a thousand times**
> **Thou never shouldst love woman like to me.**
> **. . . Give me thy hand . . .**

Though already aware that Cesario is a girl Orsino still calls her / him 'boy'. Smirk, smirk? Ironic? Or Freudian slip?

> **ORSINO: . . . Cesario, come;**
> **For so you shall be while you are a man. . . .**
>
> **(Act V, Scene i)**

Titillating or what? Orsino seems to relish the fact that he's going off to consummate the marriage with Viola still in male attire, and who he will still call by his/her male name. Until she / he's got a dress on, that is. (And even then, who knows?)

One relationship stands outside the Orsino / Olivia / Viola / Orsino convoluted love and marriage carousel – that of Antonio and Sebastian. The sea captain Antonio rescues Sebastian from drowning. Though Antonio faces danger of almost certain death in Illyria for crimes he has committed against Orsino during an earlier visit, when Sebastian goes off to seek his fortune – having borrowed money of Antonio for that purpose (cf. Bassanio and the other Antonio in *The Merchant of Venice*) – Antonio states

ANTONIO: The gentleness of all the gods go with thee!
I have many enemies in Orsino's court,
Else would I very shortly see thee there –
But come what may, I do adore thee so
That danger shall seem sport, and I will go!

(Act II, Scene i)

Is this mere male bonding or do we sense the yearning for a deeper relationship? Love at first sight? After all Antonio's only just met Sebastian barely an hour beforehand (Act I.v), has only just discovered his name is Sebastian and yet 'I do adore thee so'. Does Antonio wish, like Sir Andrew Aguecheek, to be 'adored once' in return? He's willing to go through hell and high water, dare any danger, to just have sight of him. Sounds like love to me. Or lust.

His sense of rejection when denied by Viola, in the mistaken identity of Sebastian, is painful.

ANTONIO: . . . This youth that you see here
I snatched one half out of the jaws of death;
Relieved him with such sanctity of love;
And to his image, which methought did promise
Most venerable worth, did I devotion.

(Act III, Scene iv)

Saw a hint of a promise in the way Sebastian looked at him? Fell in love with his looks?

ANTONIO: . . . That most ungrateful boy there by your side
From the rude sea's enraged and foamy mouth
Did I redeem; a wrack past hope he was.
His life I gave him, and did thereto add
My love without retention, or restraint,
All his in dedication. For his sake
Did I expose myself – pure for his love –
Into the danger of this adverse town;
Drew to defend him when he was beset; . . .

(Act V, Scene i)

On the surface this is a selfless love of an older man for a younger boy, but rather like the love of Antonio for Bassanio in *The Merchant of Venice*, it is doomed to perish unconsummated on the rock of rejection in favour of a woman (sorry – man dressed as a woman). When the real Sebastian turns up, though glad at first to meet up again with Antonio after wandering lost in Illyria, on being united with his twin sister, he immediately forgot him. As Antonio is dragged off by the officers to await trial for his crimes, Sebastian says not a word on his behalf – doesn't even return the purse of money he has borrowed. The little shit.

In the next episode:-

Malvolio's revenge. (A well kept secret).

Olivia and Sebastian. Domestic strife and a pending divorce.

Orsino and Viola. S&M and a threesome with Olivia.

Antonio is charged with abuse of a minor.

At home with Maria and Sir Toby. A Reality show.

Feste loses his licence.

Get the box set.

# The Winter's Tale
bohemian rhapsody – pulling the wool

### 'In the bleak midwinter . . .'

Modern analysis of this beautiful play has concentrated on Hermione's resurrection in an attempt to rationalise what appears to be a Christian 'miracle'. For many commentators *The Winter's Tale* (not *A Winter's Tale*, notice) is also a fairy tale. Reporting the reunion of Leontes and Perdita a courtier comments, 'This news, which is called true, is so like an old tale that the verity of it is in strong suspicion'. (Act V, Scene ii). In Act V, Scene iii when Hermione *'comes to life'* Paulina cynically observes:

> **That she is living,**
> **Were it but told you, should be hooted at**
> **Like an old tale.**

The Old Shepherd on finding a box of gold immediately believes it to be 'fairy gold'. Time and again we are reminded of the fantastical nature of events. And yet, as is so often the case with Shakespeare, these supernatural events are entirely explicable, the characters' gullibility mirroring the audience's desire to suspend disbelief and enter into the theatre world of make-belive. After all, we don't want the theatre to be like real life do we? We all want to believe in something don't we? Please don't spoil the story, daddy.

For Hermione's resurrection is a con. In collusion with Paulina she has kept herself hidden away for sixteen years waiting for Perdita's return.

> HERMIONE: . . . For thou shalt hear that I,
> Knowing by Paulina that the oracle
> Gave hope thou wast in being, have preserved
> Myself to see the issue.
>
> (Act V, Scene iii)

The 'miraculous' denouement poses more questions than it answers.

> MAMILLIUS: A sad tale's best for winter. . . .
> . . . . .
> There was a man – . . .
> Dwelt by a churchyard – I will tell it softly:
> Yond crickets shall not hear it.
>
> (Act II, Scene i)

And not only is this tale told softly, it is so soft that unless you listen carefully you can hardly hear it. . . .

The condition:

> OFFICER: Hermione, Queen to the worthy Leontes, King of Sicilia, thou art here accused and arraigned of high treason, in committing adultery with Polixenes, King of Bohemia, and conspiring with Camillo to take away the life of our sovereign lord the King, thy royal husband; the pretence whereof being by circumstances partly laid open, thou, Hermione, contrary to the faith and allegiance of a true subject, didst counsel and aid them, for their better safety, to fly away by night.

A Shakespeare tale never begins at the beginning. Just as winter is half-way between summer and spring, so we enter the tale of Leontes's jealousy slap bang in the middle. *The Winter's Tale* almost begins where *Othello* leaves off. 'Unmotivated', 'senseless', 'groundless', 'no cause', run the condemnatory phrases of his jealousy. Unmotivated? We soon learn that Hermione is heavily pregnant, and that Polixenes's stay in Sicilia has been nine months:

> POLIXINES: Nine changes of the watery star hath been
> The shepherd's note since we have left our throne
> Without a burden.
>
> (Act I, Scene ii)

131

Nine months – a chance length of time? What has the King of Bohemia been doing away from his country for nine months? And what about his son, some seven or eight years old? He hasn't seen his Dad in all that time. And how does Polixenes view him?

> POLIXENES: He's all my exercise, my mirth, my matter;
> Now my sworn friend, and then mine enemy;
> My parasite, my soldier, statesman, all.
> He makes a July's day short as December,
> And with his varying childness cures in me
> Thoughts that would thick my blood.
>
> (Act I, Scene ii)

If Polixenes loves his son all that much why has he been hanging around Sicilia so long? Has he a wife? If not, his son has had neither mother nor father around him at a critical age. If yes, then he has been away from both wife and son for an unconscionable amount of time. How has he occupied himself? Leontes would have been busy with the affairs of state, for he obviously runs a tight ship. Polixenes would have been thrown back on the company of the queen.

We learn that as lads Polixenes and Leontes hunted the lasses together. There's even the hint of a Hermione / Polixenes / his wife-to-be threesome and the news that Polixenes has put it about a bit.

> POLIXENES:            . . . Oh my most sacred lady,
> Temptations have since then been born to's: for
> In those unfledged days was my wife a girl;
> Your precious self had not then crossed the eyes
> Of my young playfellow.
>
> HERMIONE:                      Grace to boot!
> Of this make no conclusion, lest you say
> Your queen and I are devils. Yet go on:
> Th'offences we have made you do we'll answer,
> If you first sinned with us, and that with us
> You did continue fault, and that you slipped not
> With any but with us.
>
> (Act I, Scene ii)

Seems grounds enough for jealousy to me. And once the imagination is running riot, every gesture is misinterpreted. But no smoke without fire. Only if Hermione's behaviour can be misinterpreted, can Leontes's jealousy be justified.

> LEONTES:                    Is whispering nothing?
> Is leaning cheek to cheek? Is meeting noses?
> Kissing with inside lip? Stopping the career
> Of laughter with a sigh? – a note infallible
> Of breaking honesty. Horsing foot on foot?
> Skulking in corners? Wishing clocks more swift?
> Hours minutes? Noon midnight? And all eyes
> Blind with the pin and web but theirs, theirs only,
> That would unseen be wicked – is this nothing?
> Why, then the world and all that's in't is nothing;
> The sky covering is nothing; Bohemia nothing;
> My wife is nothing; nor nothing have these nothings,
> If this be nothing.
>
> (Act I, Scene ii)

Do we believe this or is Leontes now so far gone that it is pure invention? Hermione flirts, so much is clear. Playing with fire. Perhaps the fact that she is eight months pregnant gives her a sense of security that makes her dare to push the envelope of sexual banter and behaviour further than she would otherwise contemplate. She looks her best and knows it. Having stayed so long, why doesn't Polixenes wait to celebrate the birth of his best friend's child? It could be his – maybe he doesn't want to stay around to spot the likeness . . .

\* \* \*

We learn three things from the opening scene with Camillo and Archidamus. One, that Sicilia and Bohemia are totally different societies – the same contrasts that exist between Scandinavian and Mediterranean cultures. (Never mind that in Shakespeare's world Bohemia has a shoreline and Sicilia is more associated with puritanism and austerity than sun and sand.) In Sicilia the trains run on time. In Bohemia it's mañana. Two, that Polixenes and Leontes are best friends from childhood; that a bond exists between them that nothing will ever tear asunder. (Therefore we know immediately that the story will show just how that rift occurs.) Three, that the boy Mamillius is the great hope of the nation (so something is going to happen to him). The ground rules are clearly laid out and Leontes's paranoia precipitates all that follows.

This is an autocratic society. What the king says goes. Off with his (her) head. The fire raging in his heart leads him to excess. His belief that Polixenes has fathered his child causes him to demand its incineration, commuted to the 'lesser' punishment of being left in a wild and remote place:

> LEONTES:          ... This brat is none of mine:
> It is the issue of Polixenes.
> Hence with it, and together with the dam
> Commit them to the fire!
>
> (Act II, Scene iii)

Magnanimously he orders independent proof, smug in the knowledge that he is right:

> LEONTES: Yet, for a greater confirmation –
> For in an act of this importance 'twere
> Most piteous to be wild – I have dispatched in post
> To sacred Delphos, to Apollo's temple,
> Cleomenes and Dion, whom you know
> Of stuffed sufficiency. Now from the oracle
> They will bring all; whose spiritual counsel, had,
> Shall stop or spur me. Have I done well?
>
> (Act II, Scene i)

The second resolution on Iraq. We'll go to the UN if that will satisfy you, but it won't make any difference – we're going to war anyway.

In a play that mixes the pagan with the Christian, the oracle is a given. Where all else is supposition, Apollo must be believed. It exonerates all concerned. This is the only truth, for elsewhere in this play nothing is what it seems. Deception, self or otherwise, is endemic. Only the oracle does not deceive.

Let us look at the deception list.

Leontes: himself

Camillo: Leontes, Polixenes, Florizel and Perdita

Hermione: the world

Polixenes: Leontes, his subjects, his son

Paulina: the world, particularly Leontes

Florizel: his father, the village community, Leontes (she comes from Libya, lies Florizel to Leontes, I bring my father's greetings, etc.)

Perdita: her father, her brother, the village, Leontes

Old Shepherd: the entire parish

His son: ditto

Autolycus: everybody. Note however the honesty with which Autolycus – 'My revenue is the silly cheat . . . For the life to come, I sleep out the thought of it' – claims to do it.

> **AUTOLYCUS: The Prince himself is about a piece of iniquity – stealing away from his father, with his clog at his heels. If I thought it were a piece of honesty to acquaint the King withal, I would not do't. I hold it the more knavery to conceal it; and therein am I constant to my profession.**
>
> **(Act IV, Scene iv)**

He deceives to survive, makes no bones about it. Everyone else is practising deception, they would say, in the name of their own and others' good. Parallel scenes of honest roguery and self-righteous nobility are common in Shakespeare. The Duke in *Measure for Measure* has just procured Mariana to sleep undetected with Angelo in place of the Novice Isabella, when he runs into the pimp Pompey and begins to froth at mouth: 'Fie sir, a filthy bawd!' He then throws him in jail for living off immoral earnings. It is all right for the Duke to procure sex covertly but not for Pompey to ply his 'legitimate' trade. Double standards. One rule for the rich, another for the poor. So while the nobs deceive in defence of self-righteous behaviour, Autolycus risks hanging for picking pockets. One person only, Antigonus, isn't into deception, but he gets torn to pieces by a bear for his pains.

Camillo, from humble beginnings – 'Leontes, whom I from meaner form / Have benched and reared to worship' – rises to be Leontes's right-hand man and most trusted adviser, deceives him into thinking he will poison Polixenes – swears an oath indeed – and then heads off with Polixenes to Bohemia. Canny, a machiavellian survivor, he weighs up all the odds, susses out all the options:

> **CAMILLO:**                       . . . But for me,
> **What case stand I in? I must be the poisoner**
> **Of good Polixenes, and my ground to do't**
> **Is the obedience to a master – one**
> **Who, in rebellion with himself, will have**
> **All that are his so too. To do this deed,**
> **Promotion follows. If I could find example**
> **Of thousands that had struck anointed kings**
> **And flourished after, I'd not do't; but since**
> **Nor brass, nor stone, nor parchment bears not one,**
> **Let villainy itself forswear't. I must**
> **Forsake the court: to do't or no is certain**
> **To me a break-neck.**
>
> (Act I, Scene ii)

Sixteen years later, in Bohemia, he has worked himself into the same position with Polixenes:

> **POLIXENES: As thou lov'st me, Camillo, wipe not out the rest of thy services by leaving me now. The need I have of thee thine own goodness hath made. Better not to have had thee than thus to want thee. Thou, having made me businesses which none without thee can sufficiently manage, must either stay to execute them thyself or take away with thee the very services thou hast done . . .**
>
> (Act IV, Scene ii)

But the positions are now reversed, Leontes back home repenting and in mourning, Polixenes in Bohemia autocratic and laying a heavy scene on Camillo and his son, the Old Shepherd and Perdita. There is a distinct parallel between the tyrannical behaviour and language of Leontes when ordering Antigonus to do away with the baby:

> Thou, traitor, hast set on thy wife to this.
> My child? Away with't! . . .
>                         . . . take it hence
> And see it instantly consumed with fire:
>                 . . . Take it up straight!
> Within this hour bring me word tis done,
>                 . . . or I'll seize thy life,
> With what thou else call'st thine. If thou refuse,
> And wil't encounter with my wrath, say so:
> The bastard brains with these my proper hands
> Shall I dash out. . . .
>
> (Act II, Scene iii)

and the dire threats of death and torture that Polexenes utters to the Old Shepherd and his daughter:

>                 . . . Thou, old traitor,
> I am sorry that by hanging thee I can
> But shorten thy life one week. – And thou, fresh piece
> Of excellent witchcraft, . . .
>                 . . . . .
> I'll have thy beauty scratched with briars and made
> More homely than thy state. . . .
>                 . . . . .
> These rural latches to his entrance open,
> Or hoop his body more with thy embraces,
> I will devise a death as cruel for thee
> As thou art tender to't.
>
> (Act IV, Scene iv)

This is the second time that Perdita suffers such horrific threats – once as a baby and once as a teenager. There is more than an echo here of *The Tempest* and Prospero's dire threats to Ferdinand if he takes Miranda's virginity before they are married, a reminder that William was not above a bit of recycling if it suited his purpose. For Perdita it means that for a second time in her life, not of her own choosing, she will be at the mercy of the high seas as she tries to escape with Florizel.

So, if Camillo wants to get back to Sicilia it's time for him to deceive

Polixenes. He uses the escape of the two kids to furnish his own needs and instantly betrays them, persuades them to make for Sicilia.

> CAMILLO: What I do next shall be to tell the King
> Of this escape and whither they are bound;
> Wherein my hope is I shall so prevail
> To force him after: in whose company
> I shall re-view Sicilia, for whose sight
> I have a woman's longing.

(Act IV, Scene iv)

Which means of course that when Polexenes catches up with them in Sicilia, it will be the chop for the Old Shepherd and his son, a nunnery at best for Perdita (minus scratched out eyes) and a chain round his ankle (literally and metaphorically) for Florizel for the rest of his life. But none of this matters to Camillo – he's back in his beloved Sicilia. To hell with the rest. He deserves his marriage to Paulina (what a surprise) at the end of the play, perhaps Leontes's retrospective punishment for leaving him all those years ago, and for Paulina's sixteen-year deception?

\* \* \*

Bohemia. A Romany community? New Age travellers? A hippy compound? Arcadian nymphs and shepherds? The Bagwam, a maharishi? Pot-smoking, opium-filling, laid back, let it all hang out, communal living? Many interpretations are based on Achidamus's description:

> ARCHDAMUS: . . . We will give you sleepy drinks, that your senses, unintelligent of our insufficience, may, though they cannot praise us, as little accuse us.

(Act I, Scene i)

The truth is much nearer home, for what Shakespeare is describing is rural Warwickshire. In Polixenes's very first lines there is a mention of shepherds. We go from the austerity and sterility of the Sicilian court to the celebration at the end of shearing time in Bohemia. Shearing is hard. I know. I've done it. Two or three hundred times a day (not me, I hasten to add) wrestling with a hundredweight of sheep and wool, turning, twisting, shearing. It's communal and traditional. As long as there are sheep they have to be shorn, and for many farms shearing has been on the same day or days each year for centuries. In the days of hand shears the community moved from one farm to the next, the children rolling the wool and sweeping, the women rolling and cooking. The entire village would have spent several days at the Old Shepherd's farm, now the largest in the district thanks to the 'fairy gold' found with Perdita, and at the end of it all would celebrate. The hard work is over – eat, drink and be merry.

This is not about shepherdesses in frilly dresses or tipis and yurts. This is about 'hard-handed men' (and women) and a community binding round itself, ensuring its survival through the common work ethic, the antithesis of the court life of Sicilia. No Arcadian, Victorian, pastoral scene this, no tables groaning with pies and beef.

The transition from Sicilia to Bohemia is a symbolic one. And, just as winter must recede and spring and summer follow, so the sheep must shed their wool and the lightness and freedom that they experience after the heaviness and weight of the wool parallel the retreat of winter. Yet even here the dead weight of autocracy can descend. Liberal, sunny, free-living Bohemia feels the tyrannical hand of the king reach out to grip the Old Shepherd by the throat. There has been a hint of this conservatism on the part of Polixenes earlier in his treatment of Camillo: 'Of that fatal country, Sicilia, I prithee speak no more.' I'm not letting you go back.

Now he lays the Capulet / Juliet scene on his son Florizel. This is unusual in Shakespeare in that customarily the girls are forbidden to marry their choice. But rather like Hamlet, Florizel is not allowed to 'carve for himself'. What a bit of luck that Perdita turns out to be a princess, eh? Leontes and Polixenes have now reversed positions. Would Leontes have interceded on Florizel's behalf? Probably. Would Polixenes have listened? Probably not.

* * *

Nature or nurture? Is there any basis for genes dominating environment? Genetically Perdita will certainly have inherited her family's physical characteristics, but all her upbringing has been at the hands of the Old Shepherd and his son. How old was the son when Perdita was found?

Seven, eight – the same age as Mamillius and Polixenes's boy? Or about seventeen or eighteen? If the latter then he is at least thirty-four when Perdita reigns as queen of the feast. The mother is dead.

> SHEPHERD: Fie, daughter! When my old wife lived, upon
> This day she was both pantler, butler, cook;
> Both dame and servant; welcomed all, served all;
> Would sing her song and dance her turn; now here,
> At upper end o'th'table, now i'th'middle;
> On his shoulder, and his; her face o'fire
> With labour, and the thing she took to quench it:
> She would to each one sip. You are retired,
> As if you were a feasted one and not
> The hostess of the meeting.

(Act IV, Scene iv)

Presumably Perdita has been brought up in a male household, cared for by a wet-nurse hired with the gold found in the chest. The Shepherd, with his new-found wealth, careful though he would have had to be, would have put it about a bit. Farm-hands, helpers – certainly the Shepherd would have been at pains to ensure that Perdita has had the very best of care in order not to offend the 'fairies'. Read, write, sew, sing? All the accomplishments of a young lady. These are not innate – they are acquired. But something else is acquired too. A sense of value, of place, of community. Perdita would have helped in the house, around the farm; would know all about animals, the seasons, the countryside, wild flowers:

> PERDITA:                . . . Here's flowers for you:
> Hot lavender, mints, savory, marjoram;
> The marigold, that goes to bed with' sun
> And with him rises weeping; these are flowers
> Of middle summer, and I think they are given
> To men of middle age.

(Act IV, Scene iv)

She is unaccustomed to dressing up in anything other than everyday working clothes, disproving the theory that all girls love frilly dresses, and despises the outward show of something she is not: 'Most goddess-like pranked up' . . . 'in these my borrowed flaunts'. She hates affectation:

> PERDITA: Methinks I play as I have seen them do
> In Whitsun pastorals: sure this robe of mine
> Does change my disposition.
>
> (Act IV, Scene iv)

These values are those of an unpretentious rural community at one with itself. She will carry them with her to the Sicilian court, along with her accent. (Rural. How broad?)

It is these values that Florizel falls in love with.

The Old Shepherd must have indulged in a fair bit of subterfuge to keep his secret. Did he ever bother to find out whose baby Perdita was? What yarn did he spin his neighbours? Did he say that he had found the baby, or did he pass it off as the illegitimate and unwanted offspring of some distant rich relative that he had taken in out of pity? Perdita never for one moment thinks that she is anything other than the legitimate daughter of the Shepherd. What happened to her mother? Did she die in childbirth or when Perdita was too young to remember? Another story to sort out for the folks next door. Sixteen years ago the Old Shepherd and his son obviously couldn't read or they would have known from Antigonus's letters who she was. Or is it that they kept the secret to themselves? How else would they have known that her name was Perdita? But the story hinges on their belief that Perdita is a changeling, so they cannot have read the letters.

\* \* \*

How does Perdita feel about suddenly finding out that her real mother and father are a king and queen? Will she change? A fair old shock to the system, really, to find out that, far from inheriting a few chunks of your mother's old furniture, you're in line to land up owning two countries. Could this be the retrospective reward for the Old Shepherd's humanity? Maybe old Will believed in fairies after all.

Hoops to jump through everywhere. How many did Hermione and Paulina have to jump through to disguise the continuing existence of

Hermione? Leontes defies the oracle, and instantly receives the news that his son has died. Hermione collapses – 'Look down and see what death is doing!' – and is carried out. Paulina comes back in and announces that Hermione is indeed dead. Leontes asks to be taken to her and view the dead body.

Questions abound:

(a) Is Paulina already pretending?

(b) Has she cooked up the survival plan with Hermione in the short interval between Hermione being carried off and Paulina's return?

(c) Does Paulina genuinely believe that Hermione is dead – some death-like faint, just like Juliet, that causes her to be buried alive and then hammer on the coffin at a later point to be let out? If so, who lets her out? There must have been a funeral so –

(d) Was a body substituted?

(e) Was the coffin empty?

(f) Was Hermione in it and let out by Paulina?

(g) and (h) Who knew and colluded in what part of the charade?

Hermione is secreted away for sixteen years, growing older in the process.

**LEONTES: [of the statue] . . . But yet, Paulina,**
**Hermione was not so much wrinkled, nothing**
**So agèd as this seems.**

(Act V, Scene iii)

Fed in secret, exercising in secret, waiting for the moment when Perdita would return. There is to be no miraculous resurrection; the statue trick is a cold, careful, calculated plan. Deception as an art form. A huge con trick posing as a miracle. The clues are there from the moment that Antigonus goes off with the baby to Bohemia.

In his dream Hermione comes to him on board the boat. He jumps to all the wrong conclusions:

**ANTIGONUS: . . . Dreams are toys:**
**Yet for this once, yea superstitiously,**

142

I will be squared by this. I do believe
Hermione hath suffered death, and that
Apollo would, this being indeed the issue
Of King Polixenes, it should here be laid,
Either for life or death, upon the earth
Of its right father.

(Act III, Scene iii)

The baby is not Polixenes's – we know that from the oracle (and the oracle never lies). Therefore the conclusion that Hermione is dead is also false.

Sixteen years later with the pressure growing on the king to produce an heir (failure to provide for the succession breeds civil war and chaos), Paulina makes Leontes swear never to marry:

PAULINA:    Will you swear
Never to marry but by my free leave?
   . . . . .
      Unless another,
As like Hermione as is her picture,
Affront his eye.

(Act V, Scene i)

As Paulina is unaware at this moment of the existence of Perdita, the inference is obvious. Anyway Perdita is Leontes's daughter, although it is clear when he finds out that she is not married that he fancies her something rotten.

PAULINA:    Sir, my liege,
Your eye hath too much youth in't!

(Act V, Scene i)

Paulina knows that the time is fast approaching when the game will be up. She will not be able to hold off the heir-seeking court jackals much longer. After the revelations of Perdita's identity, comes the news of the statue carved in Hermione's likeness. Of course no one is allowed to touch it. The 'statue' comes alive. Shock, horror, not a dry eye in the house. The penny drops:

**LEONTES:**                 . . . for I saw her,
**As I thought, dead; and have in vain**
**Said many a prayer upon her grave.**

                                      **(Act V, Scene iii)**

Do you mean I have been on my knees for sixteen years for nothing? The deception boomerangs back.

What lessons have been learned? Polixenes has been let off the hook; he doesn't have to make a choice. Leontes is miffed that no one told him about Hermione and is throwing his weight around again. Hermione says not a word to Leontes in the last scene, preoccupied as she is with Perdita. But that silence is eloquent. Is she going to forgive Leontes for causing her to be incarcerated for sixteen years, for leaving her baby in the wilds (what a bit of luck it was found, eh?), for bringing about the death of her son? Is the winter over for the man who dwelt by a churchyard? Questions.

# Macbeth

the Scottish play – dealing with the English

*Macbeth* is known in theatrical circles as 'the Scottish play'. It is strange that this unconscious acknowledgement of the Celtic origins of the play about the struggle for the soul of Scotland is rarely reflected in production – give or take a kilt and a caber or two.

For this is a play about Scotland caught at a time of political transition. The battleground may be rooted historically in the Scotland of 1100, but the political action is firmly in James VI and I's English court. So how has the play come to be seen down the ages as the conflict of good and evil, with good (of course) triumphing in true pantomime tradition? Nowhere is this reflected more strongly than in the old stage superstition that even to mention the play by its title would be to bring down untold misfortune on the production, the theatre, the audience – the whole world – at the single utterance of that dreaded name. This ignores the fact that there are probably more accidents associated with the duel in *Hamlet,* or Juliets down the ages falling off the balcony, than any in *Macbeth*. So – The Scottish Play.

In his Introduction to the Arden edition of *Macbeth* Kenneth Muir cites with ideological certainty a number of conservative analyses of the play. It is 'a statement of evil'; 'a picture of a special battle in a universal war and the battleground is in the soul of Macbeth and his wife'; 'Shakespeare's most profound and mature vision of evil'; 'the whole play may be writ down as a wrestling of destruction with creation'; 'the contrast between light and darkness is part of the general antithesis between good and evil, devils and angels, evil and grace, hell and heaven'.

What examining board could resist such an inviting Christian analysis? With such deeply entrenched conservative views as a benchmark for study, what pupil would dare challenge such authoritative assumptions? For the problem that arises with the use of the word evil is one of metaphysical subjectivity. What is 'evil'? How do you define it? *Who* defines it? It is an abstract, dependant on a Christian theology that posits an opposite force in Satan and Mephistopheles.

Macbeth is not a man driven to extremes by forces of darkness beyond his control. He is the ultimate existentialist, someone for whom the awakening of the realisation that he alone is responsible for his actions leads to Shakespeare's most definitive existential statement of the nihilism of power, the astonishing

> **MACBETH:** Tomorrow, and tomorrow, and tomorrow,
> Creeps in this petty pace from day to day
> To the last syllable of recorded time;
> And all our yesterdays have lighted fools
> The way to dusty death. Out, out, brief candle!
> Life's but a walking shadow, a poor player
> That struts and frets his hour upon the stage,
> And then is heard no more. It is a tale
> Told by an idiot, full of sound and fury,
> Signifying nothing.
>
> (Act V, Scene v)

This is the creed of ruthless individualism, someone for whose 'own good / All causes shall give way' (Act III, Scene iv), a modern creed that strikes a resonant chord with generations of Thatcher's children.

So what kind of Scotland is left behind after his demise? What deal did Malcolm do with the English king to get the loan of ten thousand troops?

> **MALCOLM**          . . . before thy here approach,
> Old Seyward with ten thousand warlike men,
> Already at a point, was setting forth.
>
> (Act IV, Scene iii)

146

Ten thousand is worth a million now. And there is no country in the world that would take part in such an invasion without doing some kind of *quid pro quo* deal that involves the carving up of the country that it is invading. Witness the desperate attempt of Bush and the assembled might of the US Right to bribe and coerce other nations into helping it invade Iraq with promises of billions of aid. Malcolm has sold Scotland down the line in order to secure his throne – there is no way back from a deal that carves Scotland up with the English.

> **MALCOLM:** . . . My thanes and kinsmen,
> **Henceforth be earls, the first that ever Scotland**
> **In such an honour named.**
>
> (Act V, Scene vi)

Note the invisible bullet, the thanes, the chiefs of the clans, the leaders of Scottish society are to be transformed into earls, Anglicised, colonised, the passing of an era. 'Fair is foul and foul is fair'. This is the moment that prefigures the rule of Scotland from Westminster, the court of James VI and I. It is Malcolm's final speech that sets him apart from his predecessors and most clearly marks the transition of Scotland from a feudal power to a subservient colony.

For Malcolm is the apotheosis of *Realpolitik:* Malcolm the materialist; Malcolm the politician; Malcolm, like Prince John in *Henry IV* Part Two, heralding a new era of ruthless, pragmatic government. What is his reaction on being present when Macduff receives the news of the slaughter of his family?

> Be this the whetstone of your sword; let grief
> Convert to anger; blunt not the heart, enrage it.
>
> (Act IV, Scene iii)

Use it, Macduff, use it!

Malcolm seizes with alacrity the opportunity offered him on a plate. Here's the perfect guy to do the work of sorting out Macbeth for him. Macduff's consuming desire for revenge makes him the ideal weapon of mass destruction. Malcolm can send him in to do battle against Macbeth without having to put himself anywhere near the front line. Then walk in and claim the victory. What a shit.

As the play begins so the play ends – with conquerors high on bloodletting. Macduff has beaten Macbeth in an old, one-to-one, hand-to-hand, heroic duel. Macduff, concerned only with personal revenge, does the dirty work. Malcolm, without having to fight, picks up the crown, Macduff merely a means to an imperial end, a conduit through which Malcolm could vanquish his foe. But technically Malcolm himself is a usurper. Although 'named', he renounced the title and fled to England. Macbeth was then 'named' by the thanes and therefore ruled legitimately, albeit having ascended by illegitimate means.

And what sort of Scotland will it be? Macduff the 'patriot' was willing to accept a ruler who would ravish the womanhood of Scotland, embezzle the fortunes of the country, coerce the thanes. The volte-face on the part of Malcolm is astonishing.

> MALCOLM:  I . . .
>
>                         . . . here abjure
> The taints and blames I laid upon myself
> For strangers to my nature.
>
>           . . . . .
>                 . . . My first flase speaking
> Was this upon myself.

>                                    (Act IV, Scene iii)

It's all right, Macduff, you've passed the test. I was only joking. There's ten thousand English soldiers round the corner. No wonder Macduff says, 'Such welcome and unwelcome things at once, / 'Tis hard to reconcile.' Do we believe that Malcolm is telling the truth? That he has never before lied? It is immaterial. If he can lie like this to Macduff, what sort of lies will he tell in the future to get his way?

Yet what sort of Scotland would Macduff have? He would have been willing to put up with the most extreme excesses of Malcolm's behaviour merely to have Macbeth out of the way. Women would have been raped, defiled – 'we have willing dames enough', says Macduff. But I would take your lands, rob your coffers, insists Malcolm.

> MACDUFF:                 . . . All these are portable,
> With other graces weighed.

**MALCOLM:**                   **But I have none.**
**The king-becoming graces,**
**As justice, verity, temperance, stableness,**
**Bounty, perseverance, mercy, lowliness,**
**Devotion, patience, courage, fortitude . . .**

(Act IV, Scene iii)

It takes a hell of a lot to put Macduff off. I wouldn't want to live in a country that was willing to accept the conditions that Malcolm imposes. No equality there. The contrast with Macbeth's view could not be more marked:

> . . . Then fly, false thanes
> **And mingle with the English epicures.**

(Act V, Scene iii)

Macbeth indicates a pride in his own Scottishness and a total rejection of the fat, overfed English marching over the borders to usurp and dominate his homeland. The puritan versus the licentious. Duncan and Macbeth probably had more in common than meets the eye. Both believed in the innate sovereignty of Scotland, and Duncan would have been shocked to discover that his son had squandered his heritage. After all it is Macbeth at the start of the play who has saved Duncan's kingdom from being overrun by foreigners.

At the beginning of the play Duncan faces threats all round. Sensing a weakness in Duncan's rule, two thanes have stepped forward to claim the throne. Much has been made of Duncan's 'goodness', his 'saintliness', his 'chivalry'. The Duncan of history was a lot more ruthless, and reading between Shakespeare's lines there is more to Duncan than meets the eye. What is it about Duncan's reign that is so wonderful if two of his thanes are in rebellion and are in alliance with the invading Norwegian army under the command of the Norwegian king, Sweno, while the Western Isles, the Kerns and the Galloways are all up in arms against him? One is tempted to ask what is so rotten in the state of Scotland that he's got so many disparate factions threatening his rule. Or is it that it is merely a case of the old lion being tired? In Duncan's desperate defence of the realm there are echoes of other Shakespearean regimes – Old Hamlet's,

Prospero's – whose dominions have fallen on hard times through neglect and are thus prey to invading and usurping forces. These foreign and domestic aggressors in *Macbeth* show that, no matter how saintly Duncan may be, he is just like other rulers who cling to power. That the defence of 'the gentle weal' is carried out by the barbaric arts of war and that these barbaric arts find their apotheosis in the man who is the most savage butcher of them all. Thank you cousin. 'Only I have left to say, / More is thy due than more than all can pay' (Act I, Scene iv).

In the whole Shakespearean canon, there is an obsession with what it is that motivates people to take power. The killing of the king is a primal urge in society, whether at a national or boardroom level. Shakespeare was fascinated by the gulf that exists between the thought of action and the act itself, and if, with Richard III, he reaches new heights of butchery, then Macbeth begins where Richard leaves off. Notwithstanding Macbeth's conscience, his need to murder Duncan is imperative. And, if Hamlet attempts to objectify, to analyse, then Macbeth is 'In blood stepp'd in so far', that there is only one inevitable path to the end. He is the most extreme of Shakespeare's creations. There is no death speech, no soliloquy, no recantation, only a belief that, as a man, he had to act as he did. He goes heroically, existentially, to his death, flying in the face of what he knows is about to happen, symbolically replacing the Cawdor of the beginning of the play, as he had replaced him in title, of whom it was said, 'Nothing in his life / Became him like the leaving it'.

Could not such energy and poetic drive have been used otherwise? In Macbeth's demonic descent into the hell of civil butchery, and in his desperate search to give coherence to the blackness that wells up in his soul, we find echoes of Schiller's Franz Moor in *Die Raüber* who says 'God forgive me, I am no ordinary murderer.'

Like father like son. Duncan gets Macbeth to do his dirty work, Malcolm uses Macduff. Macbeth, though, is paying a 'soldier's debt'. And what a warrior.

> SARGEANT:      . . . But all's too weak:
> For brave Macbeth – well he deserves that name –
> Disdaining Fortune, with his brandish'd steel,

> Which smok'd with bloody execution,
> Like valour's minion carv'd out his passage
> Till he fac'd the slave –
> Which ne'er shook hands, nor bade farewell to him
> Till he unseam'd him from the nave to th' chops,
> And fix'd his head upon our battlements.

> (Act I, Scene ii)

A positive orgy of savagery. And later in the same scene the sergeant says:

> So they doubly redoubled strokes upon the foe.
> Except they meant to bathe in reeking wounds
> Or memorize another Golgotha,
> I cannot tell.
> – But I am faint; my gashes cry for help.

Such is the importance of the news that no one has been the least concerned that the poor chap is almost bleeding to death. Duncan says, only now concerned for his welfare:

> So well thy words become thee as thy wounds,
> They smack of honour both. Go get him surgeons.

'Bellona's bridegroom', Macbeth has saved Duncan's bacon. His tottering regime has been rescued by the barbaric heroism of one man – well, plus Banquo. Well may Duncan call him '. . . valient cousin! Worthy Gentleman!' For the 'gentle weal' is dependent on a worthy gentleman who was ready

> . . . to bathe in reeking wounds
> Or memorize another Golgotha.

He honours all his noblemen; he honours in particular his most powerful subject at the moment of his greatest triumph. And yet, in that moment of Macbeth's triumph, Duncan does an extraordinary thing. At the point where Macbeth might reasonably expect to be named the successor to the throne of Scotland (there being no automatic succession, the kingship passing by vote or designation), Duncan produces an astute political rabbit out of his hat:

> . . . Sons, kinsmen, thanes,
> And you whose places are the nearest, know
> We will establish our estate upon
> Our eldest, Malcolm . . .

> (Act I, Scene iv)

What a hammer blow this is to Macbeth we learn from his soliloquy after the event.

> . . . That is a step
> On which I must fall down, or else o'erleap,
> For in my way it lies.

> (Act I, Scene iv)

He might reasonably have expected the succession to fall to him, and so might his companions and thanes. For, prior to this, we have no evidence of anything other than that Macbeth was very popular, a trifle unimaginative perhaps, but much liked, and that his one great attribute was that of being a magnificent warrior, the saviour of the kingdom. Duncan, having survived the traitorous attack on behalf of two of his thanes, decides that maybe the time is coming when he will lose his kingship and hastens to cement it by naming his son. Even in triumph Duncan feels himself to be vulnerable and psychologically moves to protect himself. This 'naming' is important because it implies a legitimacy of inheritance that is not in fact there, the successor being arbitrarily chosen by the king in power. This of course often meant handing down to the next of kin, but if the king died without 'naming', then the thanes elected the successor. (Compare Hamlet's position *vis-á-vis* the throne of Denmark.) It is this 'naming' of Malcolm that undoes Duncan. There is a devastating irony when Duncan, on receipt of the news of Cawdor's treachery, looks into the face of Malcolm his son and says:

> There's no art
> To find the mind's construction in the face:
> He was a gentleman on whom I built
> An absolute trust.

> (Act I, Scene iv)

He is looking into the face of the man who turns out to be the most consummate liar of them all.

\* \* \*

What of the prophecies of 'the weird sisters'? Notwithstanding Lady Macbeth's belief that the events of the play are the result of 'Fate and metaphysical aid', what we actually see is a series of man-made choices, decisions taken without a fate or a fury in sight. The witches appear at just the right psychological moment, at the point where Macbeth and Banquo are riding across the heath, high on killing, exhilarated after the bloodbath of the battle. The seeds of his downfall and his ambition are already contained within Macbeth himself: the savagery, the power released by the strength in his arm. The blood lust, the ambition, the belief in invincibility. That seed is nurtured by the weird sisters, but it would not have grown to fruition if the thought had not already been present in Macbeth. His is an existential choice: he chooses to make the witches' prophecy come true. He could have chosen to ignore their advice (after all, he doesn't *have* to kill Duncan), but they feed his ego, they feed his ambition. It is not so much a question of prophecy, more one of autosuggestion. The witches only articulate things that are known, or could be deduced. We the audience know before the witches tell Macbeth that he has been made Thane of Cawdor. It is common knowledge. And if Macbeth had been patient, despite Malcolm, the step over which he must stumble, it is odds-on that given his popularity and prowess, one day he would have possessed the 'golden round' legitimately. A bit old maybe. The witches only articulate the 'black and deep desires' that are already fermenting in his mind. Making the prophecies come to pass depends entirely on Macbeth's desire to make them concrete. The wish is father to the thought, though it may take a little while for him to put two and two together. (With a little help from his wife.)

> . . . **equivocation of the fiend**
> **That lies like truth.**

> (Act V, Scene v)

The supernatural element gradually weakens as the strength of Macbeth grows. The imaginary dagger, Banquo's ghost and the apparitions all gradually disappear, and witchery is replaced by the plausible and the practical. Ultimately, the two great prophecies, Birnam Wood coming to Dunsinane, and Macbeth succumbing to 'a man of no woman born' are confidence tricks. The first is no more than a tactical military exercise in camouflage that was well known in the history of European battles. If the story had not come such a long way in its power, it would be laughable. In the second, Macbeth meets his nemesis, not at the hands of a superman, someone 'not of woman born', but an ordinary mortal in the shape of Macduff born by Caesarean, 'who was from his mother's womb untimely ripped'. In such a closed and small community of ruling thanes the circumstances of Macduff's birth would have been universally known. Had Macbeth not at this moment been subject to his own psychological doubts and fears, and had he logically and pragmatically analysed the 'prophecies', he might have come to the right conclusions. The imagination for Shakespeare is a dark, primordial labyrinth where the battleground of our fantasies wrestles with the daylight of action. ('In the night, imagining some fear, / How easy is a bush supposed a bear!', *A Midsummer Night's Dream,* Act V, Scene i.) There are no miracles. Woods do not move. Men are born of women. Dragons are a myth. But, by then, his mind is too far gone, he has succumbed and become a victim, like Brutus, like Richard III, of his own fantasies and persuasions.

The witches, those 'black and midnight hags', complicate our reading of the story, imposing as they do a false trail of reliance on external forces to explain Macbeth's actions. Yet they themselves have their origin in entirely explicable circumstances, creatures on the fringes of society, outcasts. In Elizabethan terms, witches were often single women, spinsters, living on the outskirts of villages, midwives, nursemaids. Their magic is not black or satanic. It is practical, the use of herbs for healing. Some of the viler-sounding ingredients of the cauldron turn out to be nothing more than harmless country names for wild flowers and roots. But the witches represent a typical Shakespearean sociologic reversal of the natural order. Those with nothing ostensibly control the life of he who has everything. A contrast between those who have and those who have not. The single female was often thought to have supernatural powers which gave rise to the fear in men that she could be credited with certain kinds of knowledge to do with life and death. A society that does not give women power fears their mystery. In this kind of climate witchcraft grew as men came to fear this unknown power. James VI and I, who wrote a book on witchcraft, managed to have more witches killed during his reign than at any other time throughout British history.

As Terry Eagleton says:

> The witches are exiles from a society based on routine oppression and incessant warfare. They are poets, prophetesses and devotees of female cult. Radical separatists who scorn male power, they strike at the stable social, sexual and linguistic forms which the society of the play needs to survive. As their teasing riddles and deadly nonsense rhymes make plain, they scorn male power and lay bare the hollow sound and fury at its heart. Their words and bodies mock rigorous boundaries and make sport of fixed positions, unhinging received meanings as they dance, dissolve and rematerialise. Their rhyming jingles, their tantalising prophecies and the spectral dynasty of future kings they summon to torment his eyes, hold up an ironic mirror to the specifically male fantasies of supremacy and violence fostered in 'Bellona's bridegroom', by the cut-throat warrior's world which defines him. The witches cordon off and qualify Macbeth's thoughts and actions as symptomatic of the kind of life he had learned to lead, thwarting any urge we may feel to accept them without questioning their character or their causes.

> (*William Shakespeare*, 1986)

Lady Macbeth invokes the black art of witchcraft:

> Come, you spirits
> That tend on mortal thoughts, unsex me here.

> (Act I, Scene v)

Maleness is macho, women are weak. Lady Macbeth fears that her husband is not in fact the stuff of which ruthless individualists are made because he is 'too full o'the milk of human-kindness / To catch the nearest way.'

Here is a challenge to his masculinity, a gauntlet thrown down by his lady in the true spirit of a jousting knight, the Dark Age equivalent of the white feather. Macbeth, from being a hitherto unexceptional, uncreative person save for his physical prowess, unleashes a wild creative and poetic imagination by the one peacetime act of a single murder. Lady Macbeth has looked no further than the simple act of killing Duncan. Beyond that she has not seen what the consequences of killing a king might be.

Macbeth – 'To know my deed t'were best not know myself' – has looked into the future and seen that this one act of regicide will unleash a whole chain of killing. And what does Lady Macbeth think she is going to do? Sit on the throne in comfort for the rest of her days? As Macbeth came by the throne, so he might lose it. While Banquo lives – the only other figure privy to the prophecies, ambitious for himself, his son, waiting frustrated in the wings, being fobbed off continuously by the promise of a talk about things some day – there is danger.

Macbeth has already transgressed the bounds of moral acceptability once in time of peace. Killing in war is legitimate, of course. He has, through the strength of his fighting ability, killed and butchered, 'and seamed from the nave to the chops' a thousand opponents. What a good chap, they all cry. But this one act of killing in peacetime is unacceptable. Where is the moral line to be drawn? Kill a thousand in the name of some dubious cause and be praised? Or one, and be judged. 'God forgive me, I am no ordinary murderer.' The line, like the story of Macbeth, is as direct as an arrow – from Nietzsche, down through Schopenhauer, to Hitler *et al*. It is a question that we still must answer in the twenty-first century. Do we paradoxically admire the poetic imagination of Macbeth while celebrating his departure? Does he appeal to those latent forces that lie dormant within us all waiting to be unleashed? Duncan, Malcolm, Macbeth, Macduff – who would you choose? Hands up.

Though set in 1100 Shakespeare's play is rooted firmly in the politics of 1606. As Prince John in *Henry IV Part Two* signifies the passing of the heroic age of Hotspur, so the death of Macbeth prefigures the rise of Malcolm. No longer the 'boy' of Macbeth's contemptuous dismissal, he lays to rest the ghost of his father with a Bush-like 'peace and all that we long for'. The consequences are still being felt four hundred years later.

# As You Like It

If you go down to the woods today

Why don't I like *As You Like It*?

I just don't. Shakespeare sets too many rabbits running that he can't catch. It's as if he set out full of confidence on a stroll through the Forest of Arden, changed his mind about the direction he was going in, went back a few times to try different paths and in the end, lost, settled down in the sun in a quiet glade for a spot of gentle tanning and day dreaming until the sun went behind a cloud and he was forced to find his way home. He'd had better days.

Then, while he was dozing, a number of interesting characters strolled by: a couple of girls with punk hair and jeans, easily taken for boys, escaping the clutches of a dysfunctional family looking for a father figure: a farm hand attempting to get a cow-girl legs akimbo in the hay. But she gets the hots for the tall punk girl who she thinks is a guy. A disenfranchised Posh boy with the abs of a wrestler (it's part of the plot), comes by, accompanied by a doddery old bloke, who should have been in a home. Posh boy runs into Punk girl, who he too thinks is a fellah and to whom he becomes peculiarly attracted . . . (The outfit is really convincing, not to mention the lack of boobs). Strangely Punk girl, (haven't I seen you somewhere before?) insists Posh boy should pretend that her / him is not a him but a her and practice a bit of tonguing. Whoa! Things are getting a bit steamy here in the woods. And she could talk for Arden that girl. She certainly has a way with words. So Posh boy writes him / her a load of bad poems: would you believe it! 'Kill him for his bad verse!' cry the rabble in *Julius Caesar* of the poet Cinna.

A miserable git keeps turning up and regaling all and sundry with his (interesting) thoughts on life and art, and a stand-up his own artist has blagged his way into the knickers of a country girl, blinding her with science.

Good Lord! There's an impoverished Duke, roasting squirrels over a fire and slurping nettle soup. Ah, this is the life! Who needs cash in a wood anyway? And he's brought Bates with him and the rest of the Downton bunch. It's more crowded round here than a Stones concert.

And worst of all, everybody keeps singing. You go into the woods for a bit of peace and quiet and suddenly it's like the x-factor – Warwickshire has got talent. Then, before Will can shift his ground to another part of the forest, suddenly they're all there, glee in the glade, Sir Role an' da boyz singing and dancing and getting married – surprise, surprise, the punk boys were posh girls after all! Or boys – I'm not sure. Things always get confused around this point, Bill.

The Posh boy looked *really* glum, didn't say a word at the news that he'd been writing soppy sonnets to a bird all along. I think he hoped the girl would stay a boy and he could have a Gay Gordons, but no such luck. And who the fuck was that pantomime figure in drag tying the knot in bad rhyming couplets? (Hi men!) You never wrote that, did you Bill?

Absolutely not. Don't you know who I am, sir? I'm William Shakespeare, a celebrity (some think), having a day off. Get me out of here. If I can find the way.

And they all lived happily ever after – LOL.

I exaggerate.

But not much.

# King Lear

the world turned upside down

I have never directed *King Lear*. I am not sure why, there have been several opportunities. The nearest I have come is a workshop in the woods in Taos in New Mexico with students from the Southern Methodist University, Dallas. (Lear staggering waist high in water along a stream bearing the body of Cordelia. Howl.)

There is something in the play that worries me. Each time I see it or read it I am conscious of the weight of opinion (only in the last fifty years, I have to add) that regards the play as Shakespeare's greatest achievement, his crowning masterpiece accomplished at the height of his powers in his great creative purple patch. I look at the fairy-tale structure – more than a passing resemblance to Cinderella minus the happy ending, try to get behind the less than soaring poetry, apply all the usual rules of political engagement that pertain to Shakespeare's power plays, recognise the kinship with Beckett, as a madman, a fool and a blind man wander the heath in a storm in a codified world comprised of *non sequitur* and subtext, and still I am uneasy. Why? For the engaged director, *Lear* seems to be the ultimate play about equality, examining as it does the way in which autocratic power ruthlessly divides and brings about the downfall of humanity.

There are in fact three versions of the play. There is the Quarto version published in 1608, known as Q1, or the 'Pide Bull Quarto'. And then there is the first Folio version published in 1623. The Folio contains a hundred lines not in the Quarto and the Quarto contains some three hundred lines not in the Folio. Both contain passages and lines that we would be very sorry to lose. Most editions combine the two texts thus constituting the third version of the play. Would the real *King Lear* please stand up?

For over three hundred years, until the second half of the twentieth century, the play was not regarded in any way as a masterpiece. It was imperfect and unplayable in the view of many. What is it in our own twenty-first-century culture that has reversed a view held over the years by poets, dramatists, critics, actors, theatregoers, Tolstoy and Dr Johnson alike? They can't all be blind and stupid. And was it Shakespeare himself who cut from both the Quarto and Folio versions some of the most famous lines?

If there is one play, then, that exemplifies more than any other the changing nature of historical perspective then it is *King Lear*. What do we mean by *King Lear* today? What did the seventeenth century mean? And which version are we talking about? I suspect that the thinking of the last fifty years that has catapulted *Lear* to the top of the critical tree has much to do with the globalised spread of war and the increasing awareness of what that means. The holocaust of 1939–45 and the involvement of the world in a struggle against the forces of Nazism, and now, the nightly beaming of battle and devastation into our living rooms under the auspices of the BBC, Sky and CNN, have brought a new universal awareness of the nihilistic mayhem in *King Lear.* Not that other eras were unaware of this, but today its images seem more present, more urgent. The more we recognise inhumanity and injustice, the more we witness the disintegration of the family unit, the more urgent and accessible the themes of *Lear* become, not because they were not understood in the past, but because they are now more to the fore and the imperfections of the play have become less important.

Shakespeare's play goes back to a time of pre-literature, to legend, of the tribal, Celtic world of hierarchy and division. It can be no coincidence that the date of the Quarto is given as 1608, the same year that James VI and I passed the Act of Union, bringing together all the warring factions of Great Britain and uniting them for the first time under one banner. Henceforth England, Scotland and Wales would have to bury their religious, cultural and linguistic hatchets and lump it under Westminster. (It is significant that James's three children were the Duke of Albany, the Duke of Cornwall and Princess Elizabeth.) Four hundred years later the discontent that this caused reverberates in the Celtic lands today.

The story is simple enough, taken from an account of Geoffrey of Monmouth around the twelfth century. The old (pagan) king decides to divide up his kingdom, in this case Britain, between his three daughters, on the basis of how much love they are willing to accord him. He calls it his 'darker purpose'. Two come across, in his eyes, with the goods, one backs off. The kingdom is divided into two. The dissenter (now penniless) is taken up by the King of France and comes back with an army to try and claim the lot. The two ugly sisters bite the hand that feeds them and have their autocratic, tyrannical father thrown out of house and home to wander the heath in a storm, gradually going mad. He is joined by a fool, a blind man and another outcast posing as a beggar. Just about all of them end up dead. It was a bad move or what? And the moral is: If you are going to give your stuff away make sure you leave something for yourself. There is no good deed that goes unpunished, and there is none so ungrateful as those who have been unduly favoured. Make sure, out of self-interest, that you share equally. But that wasn't in Lear's nature, hence the tragedy.

Why does he give up the kingdom at this point? The theme is worked out with equal vituperation in *Timon of Athens*. Timon gives away his possessions to all and sundry and then, when he is broke, throws himself on the mercy of his erstwhile friends. Of course, the rats desert the ship. Love in Shakespeare is valued by land, possessions, gold, silver – anything but pure unalloyed emotion (well, rarely). So Lear comes to recognise Cordelia's love when it is too late.

But what was Cordelia doing returning with the French army to invade?

> KENT: . . . But true it is, from France there comes a power
> Into this scattered kingdom, who already,
> Wise in our negligence, have secret feet

In some of our best ports and are at point
To show their open banner.

(Act III, Scene i)

What did Cordelia intend? Defeat the armies of Albany and
Cornwall (Regan and Goneril) and return the kingdom to her father
(who had given it away in the first place), or keep it for France? What
would she have done with Regan and Goneril? Where would Lear have
fitted in? For all she knows, at the point where we hear of the army, Lear
is having a good time with his hundred knights rampaging up and down
the land – authority without responsibility.

The play deals in inheritance through legitimacy. Once again the
question is raised as to who are real and who are assumed parents. The
offspring resulting from union with a wife are 'legitimate', those from
union with a woman from outside marriage 'illegitimate', even though
Edmund's conception was the occasion of 'great sport'. (Was his wife as
good in bed? The implication is not.) However the mother–child
relationship in the play is non-existent. The only source of love and
authority is the father. Leaving aside Shakespeare's convenient pragmatic
solution to the lack of females in his acting company, the conclusion
must be that the best mother is an absent or dead mother. Goneril and
Regan have no children. How old are they? Cordelia, the youngest, is
the favourite – an afterthought? Are there fifteen to twenty years
between her and her sisters? It gives a spur to the jealousy if there are.

Love is confused with lust. Edmund, a whore's son, born out of
wedlock and 'sport', is belittled and passed over. Edgar is favoured.
Britain is a paradise lost as Satan in the guise of Edmund becomes the
most attractive character on offer, seducing male and female alike.

* * *

The play begins by reducing a land and its people to a map:

LEAR: Meantime, we shall express our darker purpose.
Give me the map there. Know that we have divided
In three our kingdom; and 'tis our fast intent
To shake all cares and business from our age,

> Conferring them on younger strengths, while we
> Unburdened crawl toward death.
>
> > (Act I, Scene i)

The culture and terrain of this world are a few lines drawn on a piece of paper, an inhuman act to the level of the absurd as people and boundaries are shifted around at will and whim. Maps simplify, relegate culture to a few place-names. Here kingship is reduced to the level of a landlord, converting an old family home into three apartments. The theme is repeated in *Henry IV Part One*, where Hotspur, Glendower and Mortimer attempt to divide up the kingdom between them. The unreal world of the map is reduced to the level of farce, as Hotspur simply seeks to alter the course of the 'smug and silver Trent / . . . It shall not wind with such a deep indent' because it 'cuts me from the best of all my land / A huge half-moon, a monstrous cantle out.' He'll have the river straightened. Easy. Just get the rubber and the pencil out. Change the world at a stroke. (In Geoffrey of Monmouth's account, Albany and Cornwall, the names of the dukes married to Regan and Goneril, are the old names for Scotland, and Wales and the West of England. Cordelia, in the play, presumably represents the rest of Britain.)

Lear's offer of land for love reduces emotion to a formula. Tell me in so many words how much you love me. Tap it in and the amount will measure on the screen.

> GONERIL: Sir, I love you more than word can wield the matter,
> Dearer than eyesight, space, and liberty,
> Beyond what can be valued rich or rare,
> No less than life, with grace, health, beauty, honour,
> As much child e'er loved or father found;
> A love that makes breath poor and speech unable;
> Beyond all manner of 'so much' I love you.
>
> > (Act I, Scene i)

This is a mercenary world of calculation where words have a numeric value. Add them all up at the end and see who has the highest score. Where emotion plays no part in the calculation, someone is always bound to come out a loser.

**LEAR:** . . . When she was dear to us we did hold her so;
But now her price is fallen.

(Act I, Scene i)

Love for land is a symptom of the material problems of the decaying
system of kingship, into which Cordelia is unwilling to buy. It measures
price at the expense of value; Britain is a cake to be cut into three with
Lear retaining the right still to eat it.

**LEAR:**                          **Ourself by monthly course,**
**With reservation of an hundred knights,**
**By you to be sustained, shall our abode**
**Make with you by due turn.**

(Act I, Scene i)

Having it all ways or what? The metaphor of land for love and price
for value continues over the vexed question of Lear's hundred knights.
The daughter who allows him the largest number is the one who loves
him best. Sorry dad. Fifty is the limit.

**LEAR:** I prithee, daughter, do not make me mad.
I will not trouble thee, my child. Farewell.
We'll no more meet, no more see one another.
But yet thou art my flesh, my blood, my daughter –
Or rather a disease that's in my flesh,
Which I must needs call mine. Thou art a boil,
A plague-sore, or embossèd carbuncle,
In my corrupted blood. But I'll not chide thee.
Let shame come when it will, I do not call it.
I do not bid the thunder-bearer shoot,
Nor tell tales of thee to high-judging Jove.
Mend when thou canst, be better at thy leisure;
I can be patient, I can stay with Regan,
I and my hundred knights.

(Act II, Scene iv)

In a reverse auction his emotions are auctioned off and knocked
down to the one that allows him the least number. One hundred – one
hundred – any decrease on a hundred? Fifty, do I hear fifty? Twenty-five

164

on the right. Twenty-five – NONE! Sold to the lady in the iron petticoat. Terms and conditions apply. Big Brother has voted you out. You must leave the house instantly.

> CORNWALL: Let us withdraw; 'twill be a storm.
>
> REGAN: This house is little; the old man and's people
> Cannot be well bestowed.
>
> > (Act II, Scene iv)

People here are so many cattle. There is no King like an ex-King.

But ethics cannot be reduced to mere numbers. This is a male world that cedes power to the women, where stability depends on legitimacy, and both Lear and Gloucester become involved in the struggle to secure succession. Illegitimate Edmund seethes with emotion and far from suffering the yoke around his neck fights back in a bitter machiavellian counter-move to secure his inheritance.

> EDMUND: Thou, Nature, art my goddess; to thy law
> My services are bound. . . .
> . . . . .
> Legitimate Edgar, I must have your land.
> Our father's love is to the bastard Edmund
> As to the legitimate. Fine word 'legitimate'!
> Well my 'legitimate', if this letter speed
> And my intention thrive, Edmund the base
> Shall top the legitimate. I grow. I prosper.
> Now gods stand up for bastards!
>
> > (Act I, Scene ii)

\* \* \*

This is an old Shakespearean trick – Richard III, Shylock, Iago, Macbeth – a long line of characters from the dark side of the moon who act from motives of exclusion. Orthodox, conservative society has excluded these outsiders and they fight back the only way they know how, by punishing the perpetrators. The message is that a community and a system must embrace differences, have moral and cultural equality and harmony, or it will shore up problems for itself. The boil will burst if it is not treated.

Edmund stands for nature on the rampage. If he is not accommodated then he will be trouble. Gloucester, yet another 'good old man', belittles him in his presence, is patronising and disparaging:

> GLOUCESTER: His breeding, sir, hath been at my charge. I have so often blushed to acknowledge him that now I am brazed to it.
>
> KENT: I cannot conceive you.
>
> GLOUCESTER: Sir, this young fellow's mother could; whereupon she grew round-wombed, and had indeed, sir, a son for her cradle ere she had a husband for her bed. Do you smell a fault?
>
> KENT: I cannot wish the fault undone, the issue of it being so proper.
>
> GLOUCESTER: But I have a son, sir, by order of law, some year elder than this, who yet is no dearer in my account. Though this knave came something saucily to the world, before he was sent for, yet was his mother fair; there was good sport at his making, and the whoreson must be acknowledged.
>
> (Act I, Scene i)

If this is how Gloucester treats him on this occasion, can we wonder at the cumulative effect of this constant derision? 'Speak what we feel, not what we ought to say', says Edgar at the close. 'We that are young / Shall never see so much nor live so long.' He returns us to the beginning where Goneril and Regan utter what they think they should say, while Cordelia says 'nothing', speaks what she feels. If I should marry, she says, whom should I love, my father or my husband? My sisters are fools:

> CORDELIA: . . . You have begot me, bred me, loved me.
> I return those duties back as are right fit,
> Obey you, love you, and most honour you.
> Why have my sisters husbands, if they say
> They love you all? Haply, when I shall wed,
> That lord whose hand must take my plight shall carry
> Half my love with him, half my care and duty.
> Sure I shall never marry like my sisters,
> To love my father all.
>
> (Act I, Scene i)

In this Cordelia shows great prescience, for neither Goneril nor Regan loves her husband enough to stay faithful to him, the glamour of Edmund proving too much for them as they implode with jealousy. In true fairy-story style, the moral should be that good will out, if it weren't for the fact that, Edgar excluded, all those with a shred of goodness in them end up dead or maimed. This is wholly compatible with Shakespeare's bleak view of the world and *Realpolitik*. Cordelia is no Fortinbras, Alcibides or Richmond. No, France has gone home leaving Cordelia alone. There is too much danger in turning your back on government and going abroad at a crucial time even if it is to fight your wife's battles and Britain is the prize, as Richard II found out to his cost.

\* \* \*

Cordelia will not play the word game. 'Nothing', she says.

> **LEAR: Nothing?**
> **CORDELIA: Nothing.**
> **LEAR: Nothing will come of nothing. Speak again.**
> **CORDELIA: Unhappy that I am, I cannot heave**
> **My heart into my mouth. I love your majesty**
> **According to my bond, no more nor less.**
>
> > (Act I, Scene i)

Language versus silence. Education has narrowed the gap between emotion and intellect. We now have a shorthand for everything and communication is often reduced to words of a few syllables. What colour is it? Red. We have an instant image of a sort of homogeneous catch-all generalised red – no texture, no character to it. How does it feel, taste, smell, look? What are its dimensions? Red. Reduced. Nothing. Lear learns to express his emotions through the use of language and only at the cost of his reason.

> **LEAR:** . . . **You think I'll weep.**
> **No, I'll not weep.**
> **I have full cause of weeping;**
> *(storm and tempest)*
> **but this heart**

Shall break into a hundred thousand flaws
Or ere I'll weep. O Fool, I shall go mad!

(Act II, Scene iv)

When at last he is stripped of everything, wandering the heath homeless in the storm, 'a bare forked animal', then and only then does he appreciate the value of sharing.

LEAR: Poor naked wretches, whereso'er you are,
That bide the pelting of this pitiless storm,
How shall your houseless heads and unfed sides,
Your looped and windowed raggedness, defend you
From seasons such as these? O, I have ta'en
Too little care of this! Take physic, pomp;
Expose thyself to feel what wretches feel,
That thou mayst shake the superflux to them
And show the heavens more just.

(Act III, Scene iv)

The heath and the mind shelter the homeless on an equal footing and as he staggers brokenly from prison bearing the dead body of Cordelia in his arms, then and only then does he realise the inadequacy of language to express the well of emotion and love that he feels:

LEAR: Howl, howl, howl! O, you are men of stones!
Had I your tongues and eyes I'd use them so
That heaven's vault should crack. She's gone for ever.
I know when one is dead and when one lives;
She's dead as earth. Lend me a looking-glass;
If that her breath will mist or stain the stone,
Why then she lives.

(Act V, Scene iii)

Nothing. In death Cordelia's silence says everything.

\* \* \*

Having said 'nothing', Cordelia disappears from the play until almost the end and her place and voice are effectively occupied by the Fool.

FOOL: Sirrah, I'll teach thee a speech.

LEAR: Do.

FOOL: Mark it, nuncle:
Have more than thou showest,
Speak less that thou knowest,
Lend less than thou owest,
Ride more than thou goest,
Learn more than thou trowest,
Set less than thou throwest;
Leave thy drink and thy whore
And keep in-a-door,
And thou shalt have more
Than two tens to a score.

KENT: This is nothing, Fool.

FOOL: Then 'tis like the breath of an unfee'd lawyer: you gave me nothing for't. Can you make no use of nothing, nuncle?

LEAR: Why no, boy. Nothing can be made out of nothing.

FOOL: (to Kent) Prithee tell him; so much the rent of his land comes to. He will not believe a fool.

LEAR: A bitter fool!

FOOL: Dost thou know the difference, my boy, between a bitter fool and a sweet one?

LEAR: No, lad; teach me.

FOOL: That lord that counselled thee
To give away thy land,
Come place him here by me;
Do thou for him stand.
The sweet and bitter fool
Will presently appear:
The one in motley here,
The other found out – there.

LEAR: Dost thou call me a fool, boy?

FOOL: All thy other titles thou hast given away; that thou wast born with.

(Act I, Scene iv)

His is the lone voice raised in Lear's company that articulates Lear's foolishness. The Fool, non-rational, is wise.

FOOL: . . . Nuncle, give me an egg, and I'll give thee two crowns.

LEAR: What two crowns shall they be?

FOOL: Why, after I have cut the egg i'th'middle and eat up the meat, the two crowns of the egg. When thou clovest thy crown i'th'middle, and gavest away both parts, thou borest thine ass on thy back o'er the dirt. Thou hadst little wit in thy bald crown when thou gavest thy golden one away.

(Act I, Scene iv)

'He will not believe a fool.' Like Feste in *Twelfth Night* and Touchstone in *As You Like It*, the Fool acts as a counterbalance to the action, keeping us up to speed on the issues at stake. This is nowhere more apparent than at the end of Act III, Scene ii, when the Fool addresses the audience directly:

FOOL: . . . I'll speak a prophecy ere I go:
When priests are more in word than matter,
When brewers mar their malt with water,
When nobles are their tailors' tutors,
No heretics burned, but wenches' suitors –
Then shall the realm of Albion
Come to great confusion.
When every case in law is right,
No squire in debt, nor no poor knight,
When slanders do not live in tongues,
Nor cutpurses come not to throngs,
When usurers tell their gold i'the field,
And bawds and whores do churches build –
Then comes the time, who lives to see't,
That going shall be used with feet.
This prophecy Merlin shall make; for I live before his time.

(Act III, Scene ii)

The world turned upside down. There is a bitter cataclysmic quality to this speech of two halves, which on the one hand posits a world of peace and harmony, and on the other one that consists of nihilistic devastation. As the world of the stage is divided between the play and the audience, so the Fool captures the sense of both illusion and reality, examining once again the power of the imagination and the actuality. This contradiction seems to me to be the nub and crux at the heart of *King Lear*, turning the very idea of a class-divided society on its head, a golden thread that runs through all the plays.

> GLOUCESTER: I see it feelingly.
>
> LEAR: What, art mad? A man may see how this world goes with no eyes. Look with thine ears. See how yon justice rails upon yon simple thief. Hark in thine ear – change places and, handy-dandy, which is the justice, which is the thief? Thou hast seen a farmer's dog bark at a beggar?
>
> GLOUCESTER: Ay, sir.
>
> LEAR: And the creature run from the cur? There thou mightst behold the great image of authority: a dog's obeyed in office.
> Thou rascal beadle, hold thy bloody hand.
> Why dost thou lash that whore? Strip thy own back.
> Thou hotly lusts to use her in that kind
> For which thou whipp'st her. The usurer hangs the cozener.
> Thorough tattered clothes great vices do appear;
> Robes and furred gowns hide all. Plate sins with gold,
> And the strong lance of justice hurtless breaks;
> Arm it in rags, a pygmy's straw does pierce it.
>
> (Act IV, Scene v)

Although the story seems to conform to the conservative restoration of order through the triumph of 'legitimate Edgar' over 'the bastard Edmund' who despises 'the plague of custom', the text ultimately rejects a view of a world that is such, in favour of one that is built on equality and partnership rather than exploitation and dislocation.

It is too simplistic to follow Orwell's unimaginative interpretation based on the theory of the fatal flaw, which determines a view of the play that merely makes the cataclysmic consequences Lear's fault for the stupendous folly of surrendering his sovereignty in the first place. This wagging finger, 'I told you so' approach that categorises much of orthodox thinking on Shakespeare's protagonists makes you wonder why he wrote the plays in the first place, if it is only to show that those who challenge established order get what they deserve. Such a reading of *Lear* misses the whole point of a play that puts an all-powerful patriarchal ruler through the mangle of traumatic experience, turning on its head the whole question of kingship and the unequal distribution of wealth and power associated with it. Lear comes to an understanding of what it means to have an egalitarian society: that a world governed by the dominant ideologies of war, economic and sexual exploitation is patently wrong. It looks forward to an era when human beings may act with understanding and compassion and not be caught up in the inevitability of the dog-eat-dog syndrome, one that allies itself with the mad, the blind, the poor, the homeless, the powerless, the disenfranchised, and with all those who 'with best meaning have incurred the worst'. If ever there were a play for today's leaders, it is *King Lear*. They would do well to read and see it, in order to understand the consequences of the needless suffering and pain they inflict by pursuing imperial and global economic goals. Maybe I shouldn't worry.

I am indebted to Terence Hawkes for some of the thinking in this essay. (Terence Hawkes, *King Lear: Writers and their Work*, Northcote House 1995).

# The Taming
# of the Shrew

a male wish-fulfilment dream of revenge

Probably no other play in the entire canon has aroused such divergent opinion and passion in the last twenty years as *The Taming of the Shrew*. For many it is a barbaric document dedicated to male domination and brutality, a perfect example of Shakespeare the conservative. However, those who believe it should be kept locked in its Elizabethan cupboard to be viewed only from an historical perspective, a treatise on the humiliation of women – keep 'em in their place, if they complain bash them – are themselves contributing to a species of conservatism that is the obverse side of the same coin. To shut up literature of any kind is the sharp end of censorship, and the burning or banning of books and the shutting out of debate are perilously close to a world to which they would be horrified to subscribe. A reading of the other plays, never mind the *Shrew* itself, makes it abundantly clear to the most hardened misogynist that Shakespeare carried not just a torch for women's rights but lit a bloody big bonfire.

*The Taming of the Shrew* cannot in the twenty-first century be looked on as a domestic, marital comedy, with an erring wife rightly and meekly subjecting herself to the will of her husband, wrapped up in comedy and fun as in the Burton and Taylor film. It has to be viewed as the ruthless subduing of a woman by a man in a violent excess of male savagery, couched in the form of a class wish-fulfilment dream of revenge.

In this, it is much the same as *The Tempest*, but the starting point is the other end of the social scale. In *The Tempest*, Prospero, the Duke, is thrown out of Milan for not ruling the state properly. In the *Shrew*, Christopher Sly, a drunken tinker, is thrown out of a pub for breaking glasses. The key to the play lies in the very first scene, the Induction, often cut (as in Greg Doran's 2003 Bridget Jones production for the RSC and the all female version at the Globe Theatre), but which is in fact crucial to our understanding of the class structure of the play.

A drunken tinker is thrown out of a pub by a woman (the lady of the house). In a society that is basically controlled by males, this is the first indignity suffered by a man who has nothing – a tinker, a pauper, who has no money, drunk every night, humiliated at the hands of a woman. He protests that he is of royal lineage, descended from a long line of Norman tinkers. The hostess says 'So you won't pay for the glasses?' 'No I won't.' 'Right, I'm going to call the police.' 'OK, go and call the police and see what happens.' And then he falls asleep. Now, contained in those few lines is the essential character-conflict of the play. Christopher Sly has an inferiority complex about his position – social, financial and to do with the reversal of what he sees as the rightful role of a man in a world where men are dominant. As he sleeps, out of the dark emerge some huntsmen:

LORD: Hunstman, I charge thee, tender well my hounds.
Breathe Merriman, the poor cur is embossed,
And couple Clowder with the deep-mouthed brach.
Saw'st thou not, boy, how Silver made it good
At the hedge corner, in the coldest fault?
I would not lose the dog for twenty pound.

FIRST HUNTSMAN: Why, Belman is as good as he, my lord.
He cried upon it at the merest loss,
And twice today picked out the dullest scent.
Trust me, I take him for the better dog.

LORD: Thou art a fool. If Echo were as fleet,
I would esteem him worth a dozen such.
But sup them well, and look unto them all.
Tomorrow I intend to hunt again.

(Induction 1)

The huntsmen are talking about their dogs, betting on them: 'I would not lose the dog for twenty pound', almost the exact same sentiment expressed in the final scene, where the men bet on the women. The link between this moment of dogs and wives is of paramount importance.

> HORTENSIO:   . . . What's the wager?
>
> LUCENTIO: Twenty crowns.
>
> PETRUCHIO: Twenty crowns?
> I'll venture so much of my hawk or hound,
> But twenty times so much upon my wife.
>
> LUCENTIO: A hundred then.
>
> HORTENSIO: Content.
>
> PETRUCHIO: A match! 'Tis done.
>
> (Act V, Scene ii)

Huntsmen hunt stags or hares, husbands hunt wives. And not only that, when the huntsman says, 'Tomorrow I intend to hunt again', there is a forewarning, a presaging of what is about to happen. The dog of today that will tear down its quarry, will, in the shape of Petruchio tomorrow, tear down Kate.

> LORD: What's here? One dead, or drunk? See, doth he breathe?
>
> SECOND HUNTSMAN: He breathes, my lord.
> Were he not warmed with ale,
> This were a bed but cold to sleep so soundly.
>
> LORD: O monstrous beast, how like a swine he lies!
> Grim death, how foul and loathsome is thine image!
> Sirs, I will practise on this drunken man.
> What think you, if he were conveyed to bed,
> Wrapped in sweet clothes, rings put upon his fingers,
> A most delicious banquet by his bed,
> And brave attendants near him when he wakes,
> Would not the beggar then forget himself?
>
> FIRST HUNTSMAN: Believe me, lord. I think he cannot choose.
>
> SECOND HUNTSMAN: It would seem strange unto him when he waked.

LORD: Even as a flattering dream of worthless fancy.
Then take him up, and manage well the jest.
Carry him gently to my fairest chamber,
And hang it round with all my wanton pictures.
Balm his foul head with warm distillèd waters,
And burn sweet wood to make the lodging sweet.
Procure me music ready when he wakes,
To make a dulcet and a heavenly sound.
And if he chance to speak, be ready straight.
And with a low submissive reverence
Say 'What is it your honour will command?'
Let one attend him with a silver basin
Full of rose-water and bestrewed with flowers,
Another bear the ewer, the third a diaper,
And say 'Will't please your lordship cool your hands?'
Some one be ready with a costly suit,
And ask him what apparel he will wear.
Another tell him of his hounds and horse,
And that his lady mourns at his disease.
Persuade him that he hath been lunatic,
And when he says he is Sly, say that he dreams,
For he is nothing but a mighty lord.

(Induction 1)

The huntsmen come out of the dark and say, 'We will transport this man to an unknown world, a foreign paradise of gentility, of nobility, of privilege. We will invest in him all the accoutrements of a nobleman, of a lord.' At this point, the wish-fulfilment dream of Sly is already taking shape. As he sleeps and dreams he begins to project himself, in his fantasy, into a position of power, authority and affluence. Gradually, at the hands of the huntsmen, he loses his lower-class complex and is transformed. The dawning, the awakening, the realisation that he is all those things that were once beyond his reach, brings about a change in manner, language and confidence.

SLY: Am I a lord and have I such a lady?
Or do I dream? Or have I dreamed till now?
I do not sleep. I see, I hear, I speak.
I smell sweet savours and I feel soft things.

Upon my life, I am a lord indeed,
And not a tinker nor Christophero Sly.
Well, bring our lady hither to our sight,
And once again, a pot o'th'smallest ale.

SECOND SERVINGMAN: Will't please your mightiness to wash your
hands?
O, how we joy to see your wit restored!
O, that once more you know but what you are!
These fifteen years you have been in a dream,
Or when you waked, so waked as if you slept.

SLY: These fifteen years! By my fay, a goodly nap.
But did I never speak of all that time?

FIRST SERVINGMAN: O, yes, my lord, but very idle words,
For though you lay here in this goodly chamber,
Yet would you say ye were beaten out of door,
And rail upon the hostess of the house,
And say you would present her at the leet [court],
Because she brought stone jugs and no seal'd quarts.
Sometimes you would call out for Cicely Hacket.

SLY: Ay, the woman's maid of the house.

THIRD SERVINGMAN: Why, sir, you know no house, nor no such
maid,
Nor no such men as you have reackoned up,
As Stephen Sly, and old John Naps of Greece,
And Peter Turph, and Henry Pimpernell,
And twenty more such names and men as these,
Which never were nor no man ever saw.

SLY: Now Lord be thankèd for my good amends.

ALL: Amen.

(Induction 2)

Dream. Sleep. Sleep. Dream. The world of *The Tempest* is never far
away. Oh that we could live forever in our heads, but we have bad
dreams. We are bounded in a nutshell.

A number of key lines. Fifteen years, the length of time that Sly
himself could have been married. The obsession that he has with the
woman of the house who has thrown him out of the pub: 'You would

say you were beaten out of the door, and rail upon the hostess of the house, and say you would present her at the court.' A repetition of what he says immediately prior to falling asleep. In his dream, that same paranoid obsession consumes him, that desire for male revenge. 'Sometimes you'd call out for Cicely Hacket.' 'Aye, the woman's maid of the house, that's the one I'd like to get.' 'Why, you know no such house, nor no such maid.' They channel his paranoia.

A play is presented for Sly's benefit. And contained in that play, is the very mirror image of the situation that he, himself, has been replaying over and over again in his mind: the story of a man demonstrating how to tame a woman. This is what you do.

\* \* \*

Now, let us examine a scene that isn't in *The Taming of the Shrew*; it comes from *The Taming of a Shrew*, a play which most commentators now accept is an early version by Shakespeare, which contains a number of scenes that were left out of the Folio edition when it was first produced in 1623. In the very last scene of the play, Petruchio has left with Kate, the players have disappeared, Sly is still asleep on the ground. The play is over. It is six o'clock in the morning with the dawn coming up. Sly, dew-decked on the dank ground, discovered by the Tapster, is waked from his drunken stupor.

> TAPSTER: Now the dark of night is ever past and dawning day appears in the crystal sky, now must I haste abroad. Soft, what's this? What, Sly? Oh wondrous. He's lain here all night? I'll wake him. I think he's starved by this, but that his belly was so stuff'd with ale. What ho, Sly! Wake, shame!
>
> SLY: Sirra, give us some more wine. What? All the play is gone? Am I not a lord?
>
> TAPSTER: A lord? With a moraine. Come on, thou drunken still.
>
> SLY: Who's this? Tapster! Oh lord, sir, I've had the bravest dream tonight that ever thou heardest in all thy life.
>
> TAPSTER: Aye, marry, but you'd best get you home, for your wife will thrash you for dreaming here tonight.

**SLY: Will she?** (*Laughs*) **I know now how to tame a shrew. I dreamt upon it all this night till now, and thou must wake me out of the best dream that ever I had in my life! But I'll to my wife presently and tame her to, and if she anger me . . .**

**TAPSTER: Hey, tarry, Sly. I'm going with thee and know the rest of thy story.**

Sly wakes up and says to the Tapster: 'I've had the best dream I've ever had in my life. I've dreamt how to tame a shrew', and the Tapster says, 'You'd better get home to your old woman, 'cos you won't half cop it.' He says, 'Oh-ho no, I know how to tame a shrew now, I'm going to show her what for.' And the Tapster says; 'Ho, ho I'm going to come with you, this I've got to see, baby.' Because he knows that as soon as Sly goes home and walks into that kitchen, he's going to bang on the table and say, 'Where's, my breakfast woman?' And his wife is going to say, 'What do you mean by coming home at this time of night and shouting for your breakfast – get out!'

Suddenly Sly is back where he started, the dream has come full circle. It has all been in his head; the Prospero of the pub. The waking moment, the diffusion of the fantasy, is different from the reality. Thought and action, the discrepancy between them, is one of the major themes of the plays. The wish-fulfilment dream of Christopher Sly is a direct link to Petruchio and the taming of Kate. Only with this difference; in his dream he can, in his life, he can't

\* \* \*

Sly / Petruchio. As the play / dream unfolds let us examine his reasons for embarking on the taming venture. We have already been introduced to Kate and the premise of the shrew – her wildness and her unorthodox behaviour. That she behaves as she does is indisputable. What is interesting is the psychological reason for why she behaves as she does. It is no use, for example, to try and turn Shylock into a nice man in an attempt to avoid anti-Semitism. It is much more important to understand the political and social reasons that have turned him into the vengeful figure that he is. Pretty soon you uncover a devastating indictment of the appalling class-behavioural politics of that bunch of bastards on the Rialto.

We have also met, crucially, the person that Shakespeare calls 'The Prize'. This is how Bianca, the younger daughter of Baptista is termed on the title page: 'The Prize'. And Baptista cannot let 'The Prize', Bianca, be married until he has found a husband for Katherina. (Compare the Nurse's description of Juliet: 'He that can lay hold on her, will have the chinks.') Obviously, if Bianca is Baptista's bargaining power, then he cannot possibly run the risk of Katherina being on the shelf for the rest of her days. He must obtain the best for both his daughters, get as much money and land as possible. Keep the Baptista estates and wealth pile growing. This is the point at which Petruchio enters.

PETRUCHIO: . . . Antonio, my father, is deceased.
And I have thrust myself into this maze,
Happily to wive and thrive as best I may.
Crowns in my purse I have, and goods at home,
And so am come abroad to see the world.

HORTENSIO: Petruchio, shall I then come roundly to thee
And wish thee to a shrewd ill-flavoured wife?
Thou'dst thank me but little for my counsel,
And yet I'll promise thee she shall be rich,
And very rich. But th'art too much my friend,
And I'll not wish thee to her.

PETRUCHIO: Signor Hortensio, 'twixt such friends as we
Few words suffice; and therefore, if thou know
One rich enough to be Petruchio's wife –
As wealth is burden of my wooing dance –
Be she as foul as was Florentius' love,
As old as Sibyl, and as curst and shrewd
As Socrates' Xanthippe, or a worse,
She moves me not, or not removes at least
Affection's edge in me, were she as rough
As are the swelling Adriatic seas.
I come to wive it wealthily in Padua;
If wealthily, then happily in Padua.

GRUMIO: Nay, look you, sir, he tells you flatly what his mind is. Why, give him gold enough and marry him to a puppet or an aglet-baby, or an old trot with ne'er a tooth in her head, though she have as many diseases as two and fifty horses. Why, nothing comes amiss, so money comes withal.

(Act I, Scene ii)

He's come to wive and thrive as best he may. If she's rich, then it doesn't matter what she looks like, whether foul, old, cursed, shrewd or worse. In other words, looks and behaviour are immaterial as long as she's got money. 'Nothing comes amiss, so money comes withal'. And Petruchio answers, 'Thou knowest not gold's effect.' Even before meeting Katherina he is hyped up, ready to take her on. Ready to possess her, her dowry, her wealth and her estates. A proper Elizabethan condition, I hear you cry. What's wrong with that? Shakespeare was only observing the social condition of his time. Petruchio marries her. So what? Rich families got richer and richer by bargaining and bartering their daughters to make sure they gained more power and influence.

But Shakespeare's treatment is radically different. As soon as Katherina is out of the way, Baptista bargains with young Tranio (disguised as Lucentio, his master) and with the octogenarian Gremio, as to who can give the most for his daughter's hand. 'Now I'll play a merchant's part.' Bianca will go to the highest bidder. Accepted practices in Elizabethan society are mirrored in this play, but are taken to a violent extreme in order to demonstrate the absurdity of the proposition. The ostensibly comic auction is a terrifying indictment of a system that will see a young girl married either to an eligible youth or a doddery old man, merely on the flip of a coin. *Romeo and Juliet* is based on the same premise: Juliet must be married to the wealthy nephew of the Prince and there is no question of her having any say in the matter whatsoever. This historical condition ignores the question of individual freedom of choice, and it is this freedom that Shakespeare explores from his egalitarian and humanist standpoint.

Petruchio marries Katherina. At the first sign of dissent, he lays down his submission laws:

PETRUCHIO: . . . Nay, look not big, nor stamp nor stare, nor fret, I will be master of what is mine own.

> She is my goods, my chattels, she is my house,
> My household stuff, my field, my barn,
> My horse, my ox, my ass, my any thing,
> And here she stands. Touch her whoever dare.
>
> (Act III, Scene ii)

That then is the definitive statement of possession – of owning lock, stock and barrel some *thing*, not some*body*, but some *thing*, using Katherina merely as a commodity as, later, Bianca is used by Baptista. Pretty nasty stuff. Ruthless, serious, and any comedy that arises comes from the commitment on the part of the actor to these beliefs of Petruchio, and not through a tongue-in-cheek attitude to the writing. In this way, not only are the women debased, but men too.

Petruchio has succeeded in his first objective – to get the ring on the finger and obtain the money, 'the Specialities', that were drawn up with Baptista before his first meeting with Kate, the business deal. He now embarks on the next part of his plan, which is to separate her from the society with which she is familiar and disorientate her through a form of processing, as in the Brian Forbes film *The Stepford Wives*, where the women are sent to a 'taming house'. Disorientation, classical anti-terrorist techniques of third-degree torture and brainwashing. And here is the question on which the answer depends, as to whether the *Shrew* is a modern play or not. Was Petruchio successful? If, as many arguments go, Kate got the man she deserved, the man she wanted, the only one who could match her guts, fiery spirit and self-willed determination, then the conclusion is dangerously close to the argument that women only get raped because they wish to be. That Kate is a willing participant in a masochistic experience.

Can the marriage be happy? Is it finally love? Or is it ultimately the brutalising and crushing of an independent spirit by a physical and mental force? The revenge of a male society on any woman who steps out of line? The class and sexual frustrations of Christopher Sly, tinker? Consider the impassioned speech by Emilia in *Othello* on the consequences of the inequality and injustice built into marriage:

> EMILIA: . . . But I do think it is their husbands' faults
> If wives do fall. Say that they slack their duties,

And pour our treasures into foreign laps;
Or else break out in peevish jealousies,
Throwing restraint upon us; or say they strike us,
Or scant our former having in despite –
Why, we have galls, and though we have some grace,
Yet have we some revenge. Let husbands know
Their wives have sense like them: they see and smell,
And have their palates both for sweet and sour
As husbands have. What is it that they do,
When they change us for others? Is it sport?
I think it is. And doth affection breed it?
I think it doth. Is't frailty that thus errs?
It is so too. And have not we affections,
Desires for sport, and frailty, as men have?
Then let them use us well: else let them know
The ills we do, their ills instruct us so.

(*Othello* Act IV, Scene iii)

Who in the face of such a plea can deny Shakespeare his place in the annals of radical reform? It is very easy to be seduced into believing that because some of us are part of an educated, Western liberal elite, consisting of some 0.05 per cent of the world's population, that this male behavioural pattern is a thing of the past. In Japan, until recently, some seventy-five per cent of all marriages were arranged in some form. Matchmakers were still common in the West of Ireland up to twenty-five years ago, old farmers marrying young girls in order not to die without heirs. Ethnic cleansing takes place in Bosnia fifty years after the world proclaimed that the lesson of Hitler had been learned. There is a Sly / Petruchio lurking in us all – brainwashing, processing, hunting, hounding. The old Elizabethan adage that England was 'hell for horses, purgatory for servants, but a paradise for women' was and is simply not true. And what is this Maze torture technique that Petruchio employs in the taming house?

PETRUCHIO: Thus have I politicly begun my reign,
And 'tis my hope to end successfully.
My falcon now is sharp and passing empty,
And till she stoop she must not be full-gorged,

For then she never looks upon her lure.
Another way I have to man my haggard,
To make her come and know her keeper's call,
That is, to watch her, as we watch these kites
That bate and beat and will not be obedient.
She eat no meat today, nor none shall eat.
Last night she slept not, nor tonight she shall not.
As with the meat, some undeservèd fault
I'll find about the making of the bed,
And here I'll fling the pillow, there the bolster,
This way the coverlet, another way the sheets.
Ay, and amid this hurly I intend
That all is done in reverend care of her.
And, in conclusion, she shall watch all night,
And if she chance to nod I'll rail and brawl,
And with the clamour keep her still awake.
This is a way to kill a wife with kindness,
And thus I'll curb her mad and headstrong humour.
He that knows better how to tame a shrew,
Now let him speak – 'tis charity to show.

(Act IV, Scene i)

The speech itself demonstrates the classic taming technique of bringing a falcon to hand – a falcon, a bird of prey, sharp talons, beak, claws, bringing it to rest on your wrist. No food, no sleep, deprivation. Waking the prisoner at four in the morning, shining the light in the eyes. Just as she is nodding off, drag the bolster away. No food, no sleep, disorientation. The technique has come down through the ages as part of the Political Prisoner Handy Torture Manual, direct from *The Taming of the Shrew*. This speech leaves no doubt as to the seriousness of Petruchio's intentions. It is a revenge play, a revenge dream, not in the classic, Jacobean sense of revenge, but of a man perpetrating revenge on a woman for being in a position of authority over him. Kate finally cracks:

KATHERINA: I know it is the moon.

PETRUCHIO: Nay, then you lie. It is the blessèd sun.

KATHERINA: Then, God be blessed, it is the blessèd sun.
But sun it is not, when you say it is not,

And the moon changes even as your mind.
What you will have named, even that it is,
And so it shall be so for Katherine.

(Act IV, Scene v)

If black is white, then that is what Kate will swear to. The taming trial is on the last leg.

And so to the wedding feast. As with all the plays, the final scene is riddled with visible and invisible bullets. No happy ending this, but fraught with sexual and social implication.

The guests: Lucentio, now married to 'the Prize', Bianca; Hortensio, Petruchio's best friend, married to a rich widow; Baptista; Gremio, the erstwhile octogenarian suitor; Tranio, now once more Lucentio's servant; Grumio.

It is the postprandial scene of brandy and cigars, the male province rather than the female. The moment when the ladies disappear leaving the gentlemen to the port – the male club. It begins with Petruchio saying, 'Nothing but sit and sit and eat and eat.' Boredom and *ennui* are already setting in for Petruchio. The chase, the excitement of the kill are over. He's restless; this inactivity is foreign to him.

BAPTISTA: Padua affords this kindness, son Petruchio.

PETRUCHIO: Padua affords nothing but what is kind.

HORTENSIO: For both our sakes, I would that word were true.

(Act V, Scene ii)

What's up with Hortensio? He's only just got married to a rich widow. Is he having a rough time already? It certainly doesn't sound like Padua is being very kind to him.

PETRUCHIO: Now, for my life, Hortensio fears his widow.

WIDOW: Then never trust me if I be afeard.

PETRUCHIO: You are very sensible, and yet you miss my sense:
I mean Hortensio is afeard of you.

WIDOW: He that is giddy thinks the world turns round.

PETRUCHIO: Roundly replied.

KATHERINA: Mistress, how mean you that?

WIDOW: Thus I conceive by him.

PETRUCHIO: Conceives by me! How likes Hortensio that?

HORTESNIO: My widow says this she conceives her tale.

PETRUCHIO: Very well mended. Kiss him for that, good widow.

KATHERINA: 'He that is giddy thinks the world turns round'
I pray you tell me what you meant by that.

WIDOW: Your husband, being troubled with a shrew,
Measures my husband's sorrow by his woe.
And now you know my meaning.

KATHERINA: A very mean meaning.

WIDOW: Right, I mean you.

KATHERINA: And I am mean, indeed, respecting you.

PETRUCHIO: To her, Kate!

HORTENSIO: To her, widow!

What an atmosphere. From the first moment of what should start as a celebration, the knives are out. The needles are digging in, the fur is flying. And something in Petruchio's personality at this moment, leads us to suspect that he is looking for some action, and at precisely this moment, as the two women start to quarrel with each other, so the betting starts, as in the Induction – only for dogs, substitute wives. The husbands are now the hunters. Due to the smallness of casts, usually not more than fifteen or so in Shakespeare's day, this would have been made even clearer by the doubling of roles.

PETRUCHIO: A hundred marks, my Kate does put her down.

HORTENSIO: That's my office.

PETRUCHIO: Spoke like an officer – ha' to thee, lad.

(*He drinks to Hortensio*)

BAPTISTA: How likes Gremio these quick-witted folks?

GREMIO: Believe me, sir, they butt together well.

BIANCA: Head and butt! An hasty-witted body
Would say your head and butt were head and horn.

VINCENTIO: Ay, mistress bride, hath that awakened you?

BIANCA: Ay, but not frighted me, therefore I'll sleep again.

PETRUCHIO: Nay, that you shall not. Since you have begun,
Have at you for a bitter jest or two.

BIANCA: Am I your bird? I mean to shift my bush,
And then pursue me as you draw your bow.
You are welcome all.

Sweet little Bianca, once the prize, the pride and joy of Baptista, whom everybody lusted after, dressed in her frills, she who plied her music, now has the ring on her finger and is unafraid to speak out, say her piece. Put the men down. Sweet little Bianca suddenly reveals a vicious streak: 'An hasty-witted body / Would say your head and butt were head and horn.' You stupid berk. I mean 'to shift my bush'. Pre-marriage, yes. Post-marriage, no. She sweeps out, shifts her bush, a deliberate, ominous sexual pun. Don't get clever with me, baby, or you won't get any pie tonight. The other women follow in a show of solidarity. The point is made that the women, now that they are married, have obtained social and sexual power. If those are the only rules by which this macho game can be played, so be it.

PETRUCHIO:                 Here, Signor Tranio,
This bird you aimed at, though you hit her not –
Therefore a health to all that shot and missed.

Note the repetition of the hunting images; Tranio continues the metaphor:

TRANIO: Oh sir, Lucentio slipped me like his greyhound,
Which runs himself, and catches for his master.

PETRUCHIO: A good swift simile, but something currish.

TRANIO: 'Tis well, sir, that you hunted for yourself.
'Tis thought your deer does hold you at a bay.

BAPTISTA: O, O, Petruchio! Tranio hits you now.

LUCENTIO: I thank thee for that gird, good Tranio.

HORTENSIO: Confess, confess, hath he not hit you here?

PETRUCHIO: 'A has a little galled me, I confess;
And as the jest did glance away from me,
'Tis ten to one it maimed you two outright.

Hunting, betting, gambling images are all intertwined.

PETRUCHIO: . . . And therefore for assurance
Let's each one send unto his wife,
And he whose wife is most obedient,
To come at first when he doth send for her,
Shall win the wager which we will propose.

HORTENSIO: Content. What's the wager?

LUCENTIO: Twenty crowns.

PETRUCHIO: Twenty crowns?
I'll venture so much of my hawk or hound,
But twenty times so much upon my wife.

LUCENTIO: A hundred then.

HORTENSIO: Content.

PETRUCHIO: A match! 'Tis done.

HORTENSIO: Who shall begin?

LUCENTIO: That will I. Biondello,
Go bid your mistress come to me.

BIONDELLO: I go.

BAPTISTA: Son, I'll be your half Bianca comes.

LUCENTIO: I'll have no halves. I'll bear it all myself.

Even Baptista wants to get in on the act. So, Bianca and the wives of Hortensio and Lucentio are sent for and refuse to come. This is already a reversal of the roles they occupied in the early part of the play when they would never have dreamt of refusing to obey. Kate acquiesces.

LUCENTIO: Here is a wonder, if you talk of a wonder.

HORTENSIO: And so it is. I wonder what it bodes.

. . .

BAPTISTA: Now fair befall thee, good Petruchio!
The wager thou hast won, and I will add
Unto their losses twenty thousand crowns –

> Another dowry to another daughter,
> For she is changed, as she had never been.
>
> PETRUCHIO: Nay, I will win my wager better yet,
> And show more sign of her obedience,
> Her new-built virtue and obedience.

The betting continues. Petruchio has gained into the bargain twenty thousand crowns. Money rules. But still he wants more.

> See where she comes, and brings your froward wives
> As prisoners to her womanly persuasion.
> Katherine, that cap of yours becomes you not.
> Off with that bauble, throw it under foot.
>
> (*She obeys*)
>
> WIDOW: Lord, let me never have a cause to sigh
> Till I be brought to such a silly pass!

This widow is not going to knuckle down for anybody's money.

> BIANCA: Fie, what a foolish duty call you this?
>
> LUCENTIO: I would your duty were as foolish too!
> The wisdom of your duty, fair Bianca,
> Hath cost me a hundred crowns since supper-time.
>
> BIANCA: The more fool you for laying on my duty.

How stupid can you get? A gross insult to my intelligence to bet a hundred crowns on blind obedience.

> PETRUCHIO: Katherine, I charge thee, tell these headstrong women
> What duty they do owe their lords and husbands.
>
> WIDOW: Come, come, you're mocking. We will have no telling.
>
> PETRUCHIO: Come on, I say, and first begin with her.
>
> WIDOW: She shall not.

The widow and Bianca do not want to be part of this humiliating process. They have gained some measure of independence by another route. They demonstrate that they now possess a quality, strength and position that they are not prepared to relinquish. Katherina is the one

189

who must now turn turtle and be submissive. Role reversal yet again. Bianca and the Widow are no shrews. They merely show how to bend the marital system to their will, using their newly acquired positions of wealth and power to assert their freedom of will. Blind obedience means to be treated like an animal, degrading and inhuman.

And so to the final speech. In recent years these forty lines or so have probably caused more dispute than any other scene in the complete canon of world drama.

KATHERINA: Fie, fie, unknit that threatening unkind brow,
And dart not scornful glances from those eyes
To wound thy lord, thy king, thy governor.
It blots thy beauty as frosts do bite the meads,
Confounds thy fame as whirlwinds shake fair buds,
And in no sense is meet or amiable.
A woman moved is like a fountain troubled,
Muddy, ill-seeming, thick, bereft of beauty,
And while it is so, none so dry or thirsty
Will deign to sip or touch one drop of it.
Thy husband is thy lord, thy life, thy keeper,
Thy head, thy sovereign; one that cares for thee,
And for thy maintenance; commits his body
To painful labour both by sea and land,
To watch the night in storms, the day in cold,
Whilst thou liest warm at home, secure and safe;
And craves no other tribute at thy hands
But love, fair looks, and true obedience –
Too little payment for so great a debt.
Such duty as the subject owes the prince,
Even such a woman oweth to her husband.
And when she is froward, peevish, sullen, sour,
And not obedient to his honest will,
What is she but a foul contending rebel
And graceless traitor to her loving lord?
I am ashamed that women are so simple
To offer war where they should kneel for peace,
Or seek for rule, supremacy, and sway,
When they are bound to serve, love, and obey.

Why are our bodies soft, and weak, and smooth,
Unapt to toil and trouble in the world,
But that our soft conditions and our hearts
Should well agree with our external parts?
Come, come, you froward and unable worms,
My mind hath been as big as one of yours,
My heart as great, my reason haply more,
To bandy word for word and frown for frown.
But now I see our lances are but straws,
Our strength as weak, our weakness past compare,
That seeming to be most which we indeed least are.
Then vail your stomachs, for it is no boot,
And place your hands below your husband's foot.
In token of which duty, if he please,
My hand is ready, may it do him ease.

(Act V, Scene ii)

This closing speech of submission is often seen (and delivered) as the expression of a woman now at peace with her husband and herself, a private communication between husband and wife. Countless actors and actresses alike following this tradition have grappled to come to terms with the unpalatable sentiment expressed therein, explaining away the immense distance between the overt sense and the latent subtext as Kate's discovery of her self-expression. But if, when Kate ultimately achieves the power of speech, the result appears to be that of a dog barking to order, what has Petrucio's brainwashing actually achieved? The speech, delivered to the assembled throng, is three times as long as any other in the play – embarrassingly long. The language of sub-servience is unending. It is embarrassing, not merely for its sentiments in a modern context but deliberately so on the part of Kate. You want excess? You can have it. The moon is the sun if you say it is. You want obedience? Well, get an earful of this. I'll obey so well you won't know what's hit you. It is inexorable. Insistent. If there is a spark of independence left in Kate (and of course there must be) then the speech is ironic. Anything rather than go through all that again. The subtext of the speech is an overt challenge to Petrucio's masculinity.

\* \* \*

Padua, where men come to wive it wilfully, where daughters are deemed 'a Prize' and are put up for auction, where women who step out of line are brutalised into submission, is a competitive grasping cynical city. A city where well-fed men slouch indolently over their port braying 'hear hear' when one of their number extracts a particularly ignominious confession of inferiority from his woman. A city where the sound of the hunting horn echoes symbolically over the walls. A city where a man as unscrupulously deadly as Sly / Petruchio is sure to thrive. But every action has its counter-action. It is to the new-found independence of Bianca and the Widow, finding the humiliation of Kate abhorrent, that we must look to understand the real nature of Sly's wish-fulfilment dream of revenge. The state of blind submission that Katherina finds herself in is how Sly would like his woman (and women) to be. The reality is something different. If there is a journey at all then it is Sly / Petruchio that has made it. As he collects his winnings (making him now even wealthier) and leads his wife back to her kennel at his heel, was that over-the-top speech something of an embarrassment to him? What has he ended up with? Is this what he wanted? But the dream is over and as the Tapster accompanies Sly to his home, we await the sequel, as yet unwritten, as Sly tries to put into action what he has discovered in his dream. Now that would be funny.

# Histories

# Introduction

The world of Shakespeare is one of a continual power struggle – action versus inaction. The power of the imagination versus *real politik*. The pragmatic versus the creative. From beginning to end Shakespeare was obsessed with the discrepancy between the thought of action and the act itself. The power of the mind to conceive of systems, universes, utopias, versus the gulf that exists between these dreams and the reality of coping with the environmental, cultural and economic disaster that is engulfing the world at this moment with ever greater rapidity. Greed, avarice, war, aggression, slaughter in God's name. Richmond in *Richard III* – God give me strength in my right arm [*sic*], to kill as many of my enemies as possible. It takes a butcher to beat a butcher. Bolingbroke's dying advice to Hal – 'Busy giddy minds with foreign quarrels'. Get out there, son, and deflect the country's attention away from the problems of unemployment, taxation, homelessness, with a 'just' war, trumped up by the Church against the French. Nearly six hundred years later Thatcher triumphed domestically the same way, the Archbishop blessing the troops at Plymouth as they left for the Falklands. Richard III, the man who says, 'That's what I'm going to do', and does it. Claudius and Hamlet, two men caught midway between the thought of action and the act itself. The one starting as man of action, the other finishing. In the middle, meeting in indeterminate indecision. Prospero, the man for whom it all happens in his head. He may conceive of overturning the natural order, reverse the laws of the universe, plan revolutionary systems, humble and humiliate his enemies, but at the end of it all, he will wake up, get up from his café table, pay for his croissant and his coffee and wander off down the street, exactly the same as when he started.

How to rule without being a ruthless pragmatist? Is it possible? Why can good government not encompass imagination and humanity? Why must it always consist of inhuman decisions to combat inhuman situations? As Alcibiades says in *Timon of Athens* when he comes storming in (another usurper) – 'I shall use the olive with the sword'. The problem is, how much olive, how much sword? Once force is used, where does it stop? Violent ends and violent means. The lessons of history continually unlearnt, as the West is finding to its cost in Afghanistan and Iraq.

Shakespeare poses a status quo, one against which he pits a protagonist. This protagonist usually smashes him or herself to pieces on the rock of the state, temporarily turning the turtle over on its back, before the turtle rights itself again and rumbles on its reactionary way. The tentacles of state bind protectively round the body of society, Rosencrantz and Guildenstern's 'massey wheel'. What lessons have been learnt? What has changed? The pyramid of power remains intact. The territorial imperative is exercised once again in the name of justice, divine right, necessity of state, etc. . . . Pragmatism. *Real politik*. As Bolingbroke says in *Henry IV, Part 1*, 'If these things be necessities, let us treat them like necessities'. Blair should play the part. What am I talking about? He already does. Which brings me to The Wars of the Roses.

* * *

In Spring 1986, Michael Pennington and I sat in a coffee bar around the corner from the Arts Council of Great Britain in Piccadilly and plotted the downfall of the acceptable face of British theatre. Our plan was to launch a radical alternative to the Royal Shakespeare Company by producing highly politicised versions of *Henry IV, Parts 1* and *2*, and *Henry V* with a company of twenty five actors, and tour them all round Britain, performing all three plays every Saturday. We called the project 'The Henrys.' The Arts Council jumped at the idea.

The following year, going for broke, (in all senses) we added *Richard*

*II*, the three *Henry VI*s condensed into two parts – entitled The House of Lancaster and The House of York – and *Richard III*, and toured world wide for two years under the banner of 'The Wars of the Roses'. On numerous occasions we played all seven in a week-end – *Richard II* on Friday night, *The Henry IV*s and *Henry V* on Saturday, The *Henry VI*s and *Richard III* on Sunday – a total of twenty four hours of Shakespeare out of fifty two. A plan to perform them all consecutively with only an hour and a half between each play never came to fruition.

How did it all come about?

I had been doing mediocre work at The Royal National Theatre where I was an Associate Director from 1980 – 1988. After an initial burst of success (and controversy with *The Romans in Britain*), I was unable to break a run of productions that seemed indistinguishable from A Thousand and One Anonymous Nights that (dis)graced the English stage. A limited success with Alfred de Musset's *Lorenzaccio* (which actually looks much better now from a distance); an interesting revenge figure in *The Spanish Tragedy* (its re-run brilliantly scheduled to play twelve performances in flaming July); an *Uncle Vanya* of which I had high hopes but which crashed on the first night – although I got an Olivier nomination for it; *You Can't Take It With You* – funny previews, unfunny critics. Something in the building was stifling me. I was seeking desperately a way of rebuilding my energy and enthusiasm and challenging myself to break with the repertoire system. Peter Hall posited a series of new companies. I put forward an idea for a touring unit. It would initiate projects outside the building – co-productions – tour them, bring them into The National. A link with the country, an attempt to make The National truly national. I would have my own Administrator, Production Unit, Stage Management team. The grant to The National Theatre that year was some 8% below inflation. The NT was short £1 million. Peter closed The Cottesloe Theatre. My plans went up in smoke. I was *very* grumpy.

I was also burning with anger at the iniquity of the British electoral system. Eleven million people had voted for Thatcher, fourteen million against. Scotland, Wales and the North were almost totally Labour and only in the fat, green, get-rich-quick Yuppie haven of the South did the

Conservative Party hold sway. Moreover, Margaret Thatcher had rallied her troops around her with a senseless war of expediency, sailing twelve thousand miles to the Falklands to do battle for 'a little patch of ground that hath in it no profit but the name / To pay five ducats, five, I would not farm it.', (*Hamlet*).

The Grand Mechanism of the Polish critic, Jan Kott in *Shakespeare Our Contemporary* was in full sway, the escalator shuttling mice and men up to the top, where the golden crock of Imperialism shone brightly, waiting for the next attempt to snatch it from its podium. Victorian values, under the guise of initiative and incentive, masked the true goal of greed, avarice, exploitation and self. Westminster Rule. Centralisation. Censorship. Power to the City. Bleed the rest of the country dry. Boadicea was in the saddle. The 'rotten parchment bonds' of the fourteenth century were being drawn up again as Britain went into hock, selling herself to any and all who had the money to buy a stake in her and fill the coffers of the fortunate few.

> This land . . .
> Is now leased out . . .
> Like to a tenement or pelting farm:
> That England, that was wont to conquer others,
> Hath made a shameful conquest of itself.
>
> (*Richard II*, Act II, Scene i)

Carta Mandua, Queen of the Brigantes, did a deal with the Romans while they were sorting out the Welsh. Sold her country for three hundred and fifty years for a few pieces of plate. Maybe the desire to plunder this few hundred square miles of rock and fields runs deep in the psyche of all those who hold power in their hands. (Then again, Marcos, Ceausescu, Noriega, Milosovitch, Mugabe, Hussein all testify that the latter half of the last century hasn't gone down as the greatest example of universal love.) What price humanity, compassion, equality and freedom? Doors were slammed firmly shut on the sixties. The media were belaboured with a censorship stick.

A conspiracy of silence and complicity surrounded shuffles, resignations, rise and fall, crash and takeover – the desperate feeling of manipulation and manoeuvre in the air. One's life controlled by secret forces and the watching eye. Boardrooms may have replaced the Palace at Westminster, Chairpersons (mainly men) replaced monarchs, but the rules were the same. So what has changed twenty years later I hear you cry?

So. Armed with £100,000 from the Arts Council of Great Britain, similar amounts from the Allied Irish Bank and Canadian philanthropists, Ed and David Mervish, off we trotted to form the English Shakespeare Company and tackle The Henrys. The parallels were plain. Shakespeare's *Henrys* were plays for today; the Irish problem still with us (still); the Scots clamouring for devolution and the desire to assert their own distinctive culture; the Welsh beleaguered in their welcoming hillsides, fighting a rearguard action to save their language, a million people speaking Welsh; the North laid waste by speculative bulldozers and lack of investment; urban decay hastened by the plethora of concrete car parks and high-rise, high-rent office blocks. Nothing had changed in six hundred years, save the means.

From the moment when an *Ur*-production of *Romeo and Juliet*, set in Renaissance Verona, went down the tubes in Leicester in 1976, my work with Shakespeare had been exclusively modern dress. Each production was successively an attempt to relate and clarify the language and open the plays out for new, young audiences. It was the working out of years of bafflement and frustration as I wrestled desperately with my own incomprehension when presented with obscure, effete, literary productions hailed by the critics as 'masterly re-evaluations'.

However, it was clear to me that total modern dress for *The Henrys* was out. Obvious to anyone, you might say. 'Not so my Lord.' There was no way round the fifth act in *Henry IV Part 1* – the battle scenes and the fight between Hal and Hotspur. Arm wrestling would not do, knives were too mini, a chess match inactive, and omitting it in favour of a newspaper report out of the question. There had to be a final, proper confrontation. After ten years of working exclusively in modern dress, I was about to break the stranglehold it had on me.

The last time I faced the problem was in a previous *Richard III* at The Young Vic Theatre in London in 1979. I cut the fight between Richard and Richmond, substituting a metaphor of Richmond (the butcher) splitting open a real pig's head (representing Richard the Boar) with an axe. Rather good, I thought (until the bills started coming in for dry cleaning from a blood-spattered front row). I couldn't quite bring myself to cut the most famous line in the play (the one about the horse) which was relayed inaudibly from off stage. Milton Shulman, critic of *The Evening Standard*, in one of his wittier moments, wrote, 'in this production, the least said about Richard's mode of transport, the better.'

So – Elizabethan? Medieval? An option. I was put off, however, by the memory of Trevor Nunn's attempt on *Henry IV Part 1* for the opening of The Barbican (the first night impression dominated by the sight of Gerard Murphy as Hal, his armour accidentally reversed on his arms, elbows on the inside, flailing like a demented windmill). Trevor appeared to have submerged both story and politics in an emblematic depiction of medieval pageantry and protocol. The plays seemed hollow.

*The Henrys* cut a huge swathe across the path of English life at the beginning of the fifteenth century. Yet, of course, the plays are also Elizabethan. Shakespeare analysed the political and social quick-sands of his own time, reflecting what he saw as iniquitous and scurrilous in the make up of the contemporary *moeurs* and *mores* in the mirror of centuries earlier. Or in the mythical lands of Illyria. Or shifting the ground to Athens, Rome, Verona – he was a wily old bird – there was too much at stake to get himself locked up like some of his contemporaries. In a perceptive book, *Political Shakespeare*, edited by Jonathan Dollimore and Alan Sinfield, the contributors analyse the underlying radical political subversion contained in Shakespeare's work, a subversion that is important to hold in mind, for example, in attempting to scrape off the cloying mud of Olivier's propaganda *Henry V*, a film that involved drastic cutting in order to make the jingoistic cap fit.

For some reason I had stick and cloth in my head. I was seeing some combination of tunic, greensward and canvas. Tents, drapes, poles, carpets, curtains. It was a throw-back to an early production of *Sir Gawain and the Green Knight* at the Newcastle Playhouse in 1971. Chris Dyer, the designer, drew some sketches; a combination of the medieval and the modern. Those quick sketches for The Boar's Head Tavern, Glendower's Castle, the Rebel Camp, actually formed the basis for the final production, The Boar's Head looking uncannily like the drawing, even though the stick and cloth idea was soon abandoned. The obvious was staring us in the face, but we had, or I had, avoided facing up to it.

There is a school of thought that believes Shakespeare should be performed in traditional dress and as Shakespeare 'intended'. Oh yes? What *did* Shakespeare intend? Who knows? Nobody and everybody. It is sometimes hard enough with a living author sitting by your side to know what she / he intends. Many a discussion, argument, alteration to a new play is the result of the spoken word often conveying a different meaning from the intention of the written word. I once heard Harold Pinter shouted down at a university drama festival in Bristol because the students did not believe that Pinter understood his own play. It could be. Writing is a mysterious force. The interpretation of combinations of words is an industry in itself. And, of course, finally the responsibility is taken out of the writers' and directors' hands. Actors can change the meaning of a line, a scene, a play, merely with an inflection. The old drama school exercise of a number of ways to say 'To be or not to be'. Interpretation. 'What Shakespeare really meant was . . . ' Who knows? Thank goodness interpretation is subjective. In the final analysis, a combination of words speaks to one person, in one way only. One only has to read widely differing accounts of an actor's performance on the same evening to know that this is a truism. With Shakespeare, due to the volume of received opinion, we are prejudiced before we begin. Nevertheless, there are, in any story, a set of objective circumstances, linked to time and place, that are constant no matter when that story is told. Characters exist in a social and political environment. What gives them their interest is *how* and *why* they relate to each other, given this set of objective circumstances.

The traditional-dress school of thought does not take into consideration that Shakespeare himself often performed the plays in modern dress. Thomas Platter noted in 1599: 'It is the English usage for eminent Lords or Knights at their decease to bequeath and leave almost the best of their clothes to their serving men, which it is unseemly for the latter to wear, so that they offer them then for sale for a small sum to the actors.' A handful of props, a cloak, a crown. When a specific costume is called for, it is usually mentioned in a list of special requirements. That *Julius Caesar* was played completely in togas or *A Midsummer Night's Dream* in short skirts is inconceivable. Soldiers' uniforms were worn with little concern for historical accuracy, if Henry Peacham's drawing of a scene from *Titus Andronicus*, made in about 1595, is any indication. In the drawing the leading character is in some form of Roman dress approximating a toga, while the men flanking him are clearly dressed as Elizabethan soldiers, doublet, hose, pikes and all. 'Traditional dress' is already a nonsense, because in so saying, we certainly do not mean uniformly Elizabethan costume for those plays. True, the Histories would have involved, two hundred years after the event, armour, heraldic surplices, etc., but almost certainly Elizabethan, not authentic medieval, ware.

It was this eclectic theatre of expediency as practised by the Elizabethans that provided the first clue as to how to set, first, *The Henrys* and then continue the style with *The Wars of the Roses*. We would provide a space that would allow the plays to range over the centuries in imagery. We would free our, and the audience's, imaginations by allowing an eclectic mix of costumes and props, choosing a time and a place that was most appropriate for a character or a scene. Modern dress at one moment, medieval, Victorian or Elizabethan the next. We would use a kit of props – chairs, tables, a trolley (we thumbed endless catalogues), a ladder, ammunition boxes, kit bags, a collection of large canvas cloths, suitcases, etc, and we would use them in all combinations possible. The kit, as far as was practicable, would remain on stage. The means of transformation from one scene to the next would remain visible. No tricks up our sleeves (until needed). We would create a style that was essentially rough theatre, but would add, where necessary, a degree of sophistication. It was stick and cloth brought up to date. A stick is a stick, is a stick, until it is a flute, a paddle, a pneumatic drill, a bow and arrow. A trolley is a trolley, until it is a cart, a Land Rover, a carriage. How many ways can you use a British Rail trolley? . . . Answers, please on a postcard to . . . in all this, I should add that there was a degree of expediency – the whole budget for props and furniture was only £10,000. This figure loomed large (or small) in all our discussions.

The setting, we decided, should also reflect the raw approach. We would create a steel structure that would provide a theatre within a theatre, the audience able to see the mechanics of flying, the lighting bridge, the iron-clad framework of the walls of a stage. The bridge should be able to go up and down and operate at several levels. Two sections of the framework should be moveable towers to provide upper levels. In those days we dreamed of fights and chases up and down the towers. We would hang curtains on the struts, and provide a colourful framework for The Boar's Head. The structure and the floor were black. We added a white border to the floor and a back projection screen with a door to the back. The slatted motif of the back projection framework had the feel of a Tudor rose, and the screen had a large, sliding, centre entrance. We added pulleys and ropes to haul canvases up and down. We thought then that the productions would be self-contained, with our own lighting, sound and flying systems, and could therefore play in unconventional spaces

*Henry IV, Parts 1* and *2* were looking good, but there was something not working for us in *Henry V*. The eclecticism made us uneasy. Our ingrained modernity was asserting itself. *Henry V*, with its war of expediency, ruthless manipulation, bribery and corruption, palpable pacifism, the French superior in numbers but beaten by superior technology, felt modern. It should be modern.

In his review at The Old Vic the following spring, Guardian critic Michael Billington, tilting with Tillyard, wrote: 'I find Bogdanov's interpretation of England's National Epic wilful, vain and historically dubious. I take Shakespeare's three plays to be complex, ambiguous works about the education of a king; about Hal's immersion in the life of his country in order to become an ideal governor . . . Mr Bogdanov often seems to be overlaying Shakespeare with a play of his own invention . . . *Henry V* also looks forward to the Tudor world in proving that kingliness can be achieved . . . dynastic succession vindicated . . . But my real objection is to the bias that constantly emphasises Hal's ruthlessness at the expense of his humanity.' (*The Guardian* April 1987) Billington must have been thinking of another Henry. Kissinger perhaps?

I had looked again, as part of my preparation, at the masterly Orson

Welles portrayal of Falstaff in *Chimes at Midnight* (Norman Rodway as Hotspur in a bath tub. An idea I half pinched, setting the same scene with Hotspur shaving). I think the version one of the best Shakespeare films made. Welles edits the two parts of *Henry IV* together, takes some of the dialogue and ideas from *Henry V*, then reshuffles text and story to come up with some extraordinary insights into the character. The film smells of sweat, dirt and war in a way I was never able to capture on stage. I started on too jokey a level with Falstaff's recruiting scene in *Henry IV, Part 2*, for example, and was never able to pull it back. One Wellesian link in particular I seized on. Welles reverses the two parts of the last scene of *Henry IV, Part 1* to leave Hal still at odds with his father. The king patently believes Falstaff has killed Hotspur and that Hal's claim to have done so is a lie. Obvious. And brilliant. Shakespeare finishes with an apparent reconciliation between father and son at the end of *Part 1*. But then, at the beginning of *Part 2*, they are estranged again, although it is only shortly after the Battle of Shrewsbury. The problem is that he wrote the second part some time after the first. It is possible, though unlikely, that, (a), on completing *Part 1* he didn't know he would write *Part 2* and, (b), taking *Part 1* complete in itself the story had to have a resolution. For us, *Part 2* following *Part 1* on Saturdays one hour later, the effect of finishing *Part 1* with the reversal was electric. It left the story wide open, with the audience buzzing with excitement to know what followed. It involved no text alterations. Many a member of the audience came back in the afternoon to find out how the story resolved itself, and then couldn't resist staying for the evening as well – stories of baby-sitting rows, spouses refusing to leave cars behind, emergency arrangements to get home – or stay the night – filtered back every week. Of course, there were always the silly ones who couldn't bear the reversed ending (they should be so lucky to know the text so well in the first place). Thus John Peter in *The Sunday Times*: apart from finding some of the comic business 'coarse beyond belief' and that I suffer from 'dogged attempts' to be 'contemporary', and that 'this sort of rabble-rousing rubbish distorts and vulgarises Shakespeare's cool tough line on power politics', he concludes that I feel that Shakespeare needs my helping hand: ' . . . he switches round the last two scenes of

*Part 1* for the sake of what he fondly imagines is a psychological insight.' And then *The Toronto Star*: 'It's all very interesting but it simply isn't Shakespeare. Just by transposing a couple of scenes, director Michael Bogdanov has turned a brilliantly constructed and unified work of art into something that is completely unsatisfying. He could not have said 'to be continued' more clearly if he had had a couple of pom-pom girls parade a banner across the stage.' *Quod erat demonstrandum*. As the story was indeed continued some seventy-five minutes later, I took this intended criticism as a compliment. Something about Shakespeare always brings out the worst in people. The transposition made total sense. Thank you, Orson.

The final rehearsals for the opening in Plymouth took place at the Headquarters of RAF Mountbatten, in a gigantic disused hangar on the sea front and real helicopters took off and landed during rehearsals of the battle sequences in *Henry V*. The Theatre Royal had rigged up our set, lights and sound in this vast, cavernous, corrugated and concrete space, where we had to prepare technically and dress-rehearse the three shows prior to opening cold, with virtually no time on stage, on a Monday night. In the parlous state of the Arts now as then, a theatre cannot afford to lose income being 'dark'.

We were in a hangar, on the sea front. The rain lashed, the wind howled, the blow heaters blew, the company performed heroically. Crucial decisions were taken. I decided to start the cycle with all our kit on stage at the beginning of *Henry IV, Part 1*, so that audiences could see how clever we were in using it all. To understand the set up at the beginning, I decided to re-cap the story of *Richard II* in folk ballad form, a traditional and popular way of telling a story, speaking information. The troubadour tradition.

Taking as its title Hal's name for himself when in disguise on the eve of the battle of Agincourt as he wanders through the camp, that little known Elizabethan / Victorian / contemporary folk ballad 'Harry Le Roy' was unearthed from the dusty back reaches of Michael Pennington's and my imagination, telling the complete story of *Richard II* in four verses.[1] In America the ballad has been the subject of numerous doctorates. We have always refused to divulge our sources.

I alternated all-night sessions on lights with Chris Ellis, lighting designer, with all-night sessions trying to sort out the music. The extracts that I chose were as eclectic as the costumes, sometimes commenting on the action, sometimes complementing it. Schubert, Berg, Mozart, Handel, The Chieftains, Vaughan Williams, Status Quo's *In the Army Now*, No 1 at the time, seemed to fit perfectly the mood at the end of *Henry IV, Part 2*. Elgar, Purcell, Jarre, Bach. Many pieces I chose were used to stir religious and patriotic memories. Functional 'classic' excerpts, *Zadok the Priest, Jerusalem, Pomp and Circumstance*. Expediency mainly, culled from various collections to hand.

Bits of old curtain and chenille table cloths were cut up to add a splash of colour to The Boar's Head. Skips and skips and skips of costumes, on loan and eventually hired from The National Theatre, were sifted through, tried on, accepted, rejected, as we attempted to fit characters, scene and mood. John Woodvine as Falstaff for the first time in gigantic white pudding padding, more like Michelin Man than Falstaff. The uniforms didn't work with the kit of bentwood chairs and the collapsible tables. Rough theatre was foundering on the rock of sophistication. Our splash of colour needed a splash of props to go with it. The sandbags leaked. The sliding screen . . . didn't. The white cloths wouldn't billow, pillow, create snowy landscapes. More a case of the Hesperus crossed with a St Moritz thaw. The tank, collapsible, used for the siege of Harfleur, was divided into two parts. At some venues it had to come from two separate entrances because of space. It was a real wobbly old Heath Robinson affair, the framework held together with pins. Michael leapt on it, staggered each time, regained his balance and began 'Once more unto the breach . . .' with smoke billowing around him, obscuring both face and voice. The tank fell apart on numerous occasions, finally to disappear from the production altogether halfway through the second year, much to my, but nobody elses, regret. I got my own back in, 2004, in a documentary for BBCTV, *The Welsh in Shakespeare*, where Michael Sheen declaimed the speech from a real helicopter before soaring high over Carreg Cennen.

It was cold, it was wet, it was windy. It was November. It was chaos. The sea-spray and gales lashed against the corrugated sides of the hangar.

In no time, the props and costumes were filthy as they lay on the floor. The screens jammed, broke, tore, didn't close, warped. Made of wood, made on the cheap. Costumes and props went AWOL and no let-up in the afternoon or evening. No breaks for anyone from 8 am till midnight. An acrimonious battle was fought amongst us all to get the production ready in time. With the funds exhausted, Michael and I put our hands in our pockets (not for the last time) to the tune of £5,000 apiece to help the production get there. A desperate air of panic set in among the wardrobe staff and Chris Dyer and I were hardly communicating any more as we wrestled with great white canvas cloths that didn't do any of the things I wanted.

And yet somehow we moved to the theatre to open with *Henry IV, Part 1* on Monday night with a full rehearsal of each of the plays behind us. Wednesday was *Henry IV, Part 2*, Friday *Henry V* and then on Saturday – with no chance of a dry run, the plays unprepared technically – all three.

It is extraordinary that those of us who work in theatre never seem able to understand the process of it. I long ago gave up judging productions at an early stage. Too many shows turn round from one performance to the next. 'I wouldn't go and see it if I were you, it runs for four hours.' 'What? Don't be silly. It's two hours and no interval.' Theatre for me, now, is always work in progress. Just get on with it and try and get it better. And yet how many people in the theatre profession leave a theatre after a preview thinking they have seen a definitive version? 'A funny thing happened on the way from Stratford to London', a certain *Guardian* critic has written on many an occasion. Nothing funny has happened at all. A show has merely played some eighty performances since the first night and is a different production.

As the cheers rang out on that Saturday night, we stood on stage and thought – how stupid can you get? The next three years would show us.

Michael and I jointly pasted up a version of the *Henry VIs*, condensing the three parts into two. The plays sprawl and brawl and they are clearly early works. It is conceivable that the three parts were written in the wrong order. They are probably the result of impro-visation and have been tampered with, edited, and the best writing is in

*Part 2*. We called our two parts *House of Lancaster* and *House of York*, the first being dominated by the former, the second featuring the rise of the latter. We decided to wrap up the rather rambling Joan of Arc story in the first half of *Lancaster*. It is clear that the original story is weighed down with a fair amount of sixteenth-century English patriotic propaganda, Shakespeare's or otherwise, and we took a crucial decision here to balance the English belief in her as a witch with the French (and her own) as a divinely inspired saviour.

The second half of *Lancaster* would begin with Henry meeting Margaret for the first time and would finish at the death of Suffolk, (Act IV, Scene 1 of Shakespeare's *Part 2*). *House of York* would begin with the Duke of York's return from Ireland and the Jack Cade Rebellion; we would condense the battles and finish the first half of this play with the famous 'Son who killed his father, father who killed his son' scene. The second half would see the rise of Richard Duke of Gloucester leading to his accession as Richard III in the play to follow. We wrote linking lines and passages where necessary to clarify the story and straighten up the loose ends (of which there were many). This became known as 'Bogspeare' although I probably provided only about two thirds of the four hundred-odd lines that were re-written.

It is worth noting that the Peter Hall-John Barton *Wars of the Roses* for The Royal Shakespeare Company included some 1,500 new lines, so we were quite modest really. Our work included such gems as:

**KING EDWARD IV:** We'll drive the quondam queen into the sea,
And make her swim the long way back to France.

and:

**SUFFOLK:** Fret not yourself my Lord for such reverse.

**SOMERSET:** Fear you not that, I will not brook this sneap.

and:

**WARWICK:** Let Richard be restored to his blood,
So shall his father's wrongs be recompensed.

**SOMERSET:** His father was a foul ignoble traitor.
Shall he reap honour from his father's shame?

The question of adapting the design style was now vexing us. The rear screen was rebuilt (to work, this time, we hoped), and the flying bridge reconstructed to go down to ground level, which up till then it had been unable to do.

We custom-built the scaffold 'zip-up' towers in lightweight steel to make them easier to negotiate (and more stable). Two sets of steps for ground-level access to the bridge were wheeled on from off-stage. And I introduced a white (grey, actually) circle motif to the glazed floor for *York* and *Lancaster*, reduced the lines of mobile sandbags from two to one and, sadness of sadness, lost the tank. We had started eclectically with the costumes and yet there *was* a sort of chronology to be found. Stephanie proposed that we begin *Richard II* in the Regency period, which would then allow us, with the advent of Bolingbroke as King Henry IV, to retain our Victorian frock coats and scarlet tunics for his court. The *Henry VIs* would progress through the Edwardian period, the First World War, the twenties and thirties, the Second World War, until we arrived at *Richard III* which I wanted modern and technological. This left *Henry V* as something of an anomaly, as we had already used modern dress in the original production. Accordingly, the suits were replaced with late Victorian frock-coats. The political arena of the plays thus spanned a period of roughly one hundred and fifty years. Street life, battles, etc, retained their eclecticism, though *Henry IV, Parts 1* and *2* remained the best examples of this. I concluded the *Roses* cycle with a conceptual stylistic juxtaposition: switching from modern battle fatigues, the fight between Richmond and Richard III took place in full medieval armour and with long-swords. Two dinosaurs battling for possession. This was followed immediately by Richmond's address to the nation in pin-stripe suit from a TV studio (living proof that there is no quick change in the world that cannot be achieved in thirty seconds). The cycle thus spanned six hundred years stylistically. From the point where territorial aggression is resolved by a one-to-one combat for the ruling of a country, to where it is currently at – the media recording events live as they occur in the Balkans, Afghanistan, Iraq.

The Regency style, Beau Brummell dandyism, suited our purposes; a profligate, dilettante Richard II. I suspect that were I to embark on a one-off production of the play this is not the period I would ideally choose – don't ask me which – I don't know, never having thought about it any other way. Michael and I decided that we wanted Richard surrounded by music and artists, a contrast to the puritan austerity of Bolingbroke Rule. The 1960s to 1980s? It would be colourful before turning dark and Victorian. Attempting a setting for this sumptuous scenario within the framework of our steely black structure was a poser; I added three sets of net curtains – all we could afford – sprayed the back set purple and left the two front sets white. We 'rouched' them. This allowed for a certain amount of softness when properly arranged, but did not quite match the velveteened volumes of the imagination, great swathes of silk and satin festooned liberally in the great hall surrounded by gilded oils and Louis Quinze. What we *did* have was our (my) bits of chenille tablecloth that we had used to dress the tavern in the Boar's Head. They would have to do. I draped the throne (symbol of misuse), an easel, the card table, three chairs and a cushion. Later we bought a few off-cuts of velvet. It did. Just.

Our versions of the *Henry VI*s were greeted with enthusiasm although the originals were soon brought out as the company culled stricken couplets from their folders with, 'There's a couple of lines here that you've left out and I'm not sure why . . . ' The deal was – anything could be re-inserted provided an actor was prepared to lose the same amount in exchange. To be fair, most of the company adhered to this side of the bargain. Although there were themes to follow as in *The Henrys*, it was naturally far harder to rehearse seven plays all at once and to keep the strands in one's head, and *House of Lancaster* and *House of York* were, in effect, two new texts started from scratch.

The *Henry VI* rehearsals were fast and furious. Discuss a scene, improvise it, set it. If satisfied, send it away with Assistant Directors Stella Bond and Sue Best to be worked on. And so many fights. There is always a problem with suspension of disbelief in staging medieval fights involving large numbers. Mostly, elephantine cavorting in suits of armour, wielding balls and chains and swords too heavy to lift, makes me laugh. In this frame of mind I had no wish to be hoist by my own petard.

Finally, I condensed all the big battles into ones of single combat, the sole remaining large one, known as 'the *York* rumble', finding its way into performance before being cut on our return from Australia, in late autumn 1988. However, there was still quite a lot of running on and off stage and obligatory smoke.

The choices of music were mainly from earlier periods with a few exceptions. Harsh, atonal bars from Berg's Violin Concerto introduced the rose-picking Temple Garden scene in the *House of Lancaster*, an indication of future disintegration; a jagged electronic theme from an unknown horror movie helped decapitate Suffolk. Henry VI's piety was emphasised by the use of a solo choir boy singing Psalm 121: 'I will lift up mine eyes unto the Lord'; a Gregorian chant accompanied Henry V's funeral and the deaths of Mortimer, Lancaster and Beaufort. All the battle scenes echoed to cannon fire and Byrd's *Mass for Four Voices*, emphasising the religious justification voiced by the participants. Live accordion music for the French victory at Orleans, and Henry VI's Coronation in France was introduced with Mozart's *Coronation Mass*. His wedding to Margaret was celebrated with Handel's *Music for the Royal Fireworks*. Various other court scenes in England were accompanied by Monteverdi's *Vespers* and Pergolesi's *Stabat Mater*. The same themes were used yet again in House of York but became more modern with *Glassworks* by Philip Glass and Louis Armstrong's *Alligator Crawl* which was used as background for Edward IV's Cocktail Party, beginning the second half. The long-sword / armour fight between Richmond and Richard was fought out to the strains of Samuel Barber's *Adagio for Strings*. It was a trick picked up from the film *Platoon*. Yes, Michael Coveney, Samuel Barber, *not* Mahler's Eighth.[2]

Believing in the divinity of Joan of Arc was proving a problem, and Mary Rutherford and I worked on the mysterious ethereal aspect; difficult, given the lack of text to do it with. I don't think I helped by loading down her supernatural powers with Peruvian pipes reminiscent of the film *Picnic at Hanging Rock*.

Louis Potter later wrote in *The Times Literary Supplement* (in a review otherwise extremely complimentary): 'The one failure to confront the text is the treatment of Joan of Arc . . . No devils appear to her. La Pucelle is played as the dazed recipient of an incomprehensible magic;

the music that accompanies her throughout her success suggests fairy land, and when it abandons her, the effect is of a performance of *Peter Pan* where no one claps in order to save Tinkerbell.' It *was* kitsch, though liked by many.

In fact I was struggling altogether to find depth in *House of Lancaster*. The downfall of Gloucester hinges on witchcraft. His wife dabbles in the occult in an attempt to find out whether her husband will be king or not. The predictions of the medium come true, in point of fact. The trap is to burden this scene down with a lot of comic mumbo jumbo. I fell right in. As with the Gads Hill fight in *Henry IV, Part 1* and the Recruiting Scene in *Henry IV, Part 2*, so far in that it was difficult to pull the scene back. The séance table won the Naff Prop prize for the tour. An empty goblet was to spill and run blood, a knife was to up end itself suddenly and sink into the table, an empty glass to fill with water. Passing through the surface was a network of tubes, wires and strings, leading to squeezy bottles . . . . Derek Scriminger, Stage Manager, the tallest of tall, for some reason elected to crouch under the table and work it all and succeeded only in soaking himself with water and diluted ketchup. Ditto the stage crew – our attempt at ectoplasm resulted in Barry Stanton as Bolingbroke the Conjurer winding his head and arms in white bandage like some Frankenstein emerging from his operation. The thunder and lightning emphasised the silliness of it all. Impossible after all this to take seriously the Hawking Scene that follows, where a blind man has to have his sight restored and then recovers the use of his leg by another 'miracle'. The problem with rehearsing such scenes so fast is that it leads to easy options, humour being the road of least resistance. It is easier to invent comic business quickly and leave the actors to develop it on their own, than to painstakingly (and painfully) build up the truth and reality of such skimpily written situations. Nevertheless, when so much 'real' action depends on the consequences, time must be taken. I didn't, and the result was always an uphill struggle to make the plot hang together in the second half of *House of Lancaster*. That we did, on occasions, succeed, given no time to re-conceive or re-rehearse, is a testimony to the actors' belief that they had to sacrifice the laughs in the service of the story.

Another road of least resistance, I suppose, was the developing of the hooligan, National Front theme in *House of York* in the form of the Cade Rebellion. Could one believe that this drink-sodden, totem-twirling, Union Jack brigade of Doc Martened bovver boys could ever take over the running of the country?

Michael Pennington turned Jack Cade into a machete-twirling tornado, with spiky red hair and a Union Jack vest. The chant of 'you're gonna get your fuckin' heads kicked in' rang out weekly on stage as pitched battles raged on sea ferries to the same cries and the Heysel Stadium collapsed. Europe certainly doesn't believe such groups could never take over the country.

In week six, tragedy struck. On Saturday afternoon I had been rehearsing with John Price. He had a fight call with Malcolm and Ian Burford on the York-Clifford duel in *House of York* and then we proceeded to have a marvellous Bolingbroke rehearsal. We also worked on an idea for a Dave Allen-style introduction to the whole cycle. Before the beginning of *Richard II*, we would set a table, a glass, John sitting there casually, a cigarette, lights down, then: 'Edward III, my Lord, had seven sons – are you with me so far?' and then he would go through the whole rigmarole of the royal succession, taken from the second part of *Henry VI*. John was in great form. We laughed and joked and finished at six o'clock with John enthusing about the idea and taking it away to develop it.

I was never to find out if it was a good idea or not. The following day I had a call to say that John had slipped and fallen while in the bathroom, had knocked himself unconscious and was in hospital. The next day was to reveal that in fact John had suffered a stroke. At that stage there was no cause for alarm but, as the days passed and John showed no signs of recovering consciousness, the awful truth of the situation began to dawn on us. When the news came that the doctors had switched off John's life support system, the tears flowed unrestrainedly. He had come into my life as an actor only one year before. We had fought, argued, discussed, laughed and enthused together and had become the firmest of friends professionally and personally. He was like a wolf – lean, lank, dark, gangling. But friendly, benign, his soft brown eyes quizzical, questioning. Hal's Angel.

With a critically short rehearsal period, we were now in deep trouble. John Castle, with whom I had coincided at Trinity College, Dublin, agreed to take over the roles of Bolingbroke, Pistol and York. It would take him all his time to learn the words. How would I ever be able to fill in any detail for him? We both agreed that I was to carry on with my normal schedule and he would catch up as best he could.

The last week in November. We moved into our end phase, for technical rehearsals. This time, it was to what was laughingly called a 'studio' in Limehouse. It was an old storage warehouse, barely large enough, measuring some fifty foot by seventy. One end had a huge entrance, obviously for container lorries, and no doors. It would have to be blocked up. So would the holes in the roof, the holes in the walls. It had been the mildest of autumns but, as luck would have it, the weather turned nasty for the two weeks that we were there. Rain, wind, snow, sleet, we had everything the Thames, ten yards away, could throw at us. We had underestimated and under-budgeted the extras.

At that level, production management in London is a Mafia activity. Call in all sorts of favours, do deals, trade in one small job on one production against a big one on another. Grease palms, scratch backs, turn blind eyes, etc. Sometimes it's a very close wind-sailing job. Simon Opie was a master mediator.

True, we *did* overspend. Michael and I dipped into our pockets yet again. This time it was to supply the armour and video camera for the end of *Richard III*. As I had pointed out to Prue Skene, Administrator, there wasn't anything else in *Richard III*. Just modern suits. The armour and video were the only real props and without them the production – indeed the whole cycle – had no climax.

And the same scramble on costumes as the year before.

We froze on. Coughs and colds notwithstanding, we managed to get some sort of a run of all seven plays. There was an awful lot to do in Bath. The pattern for the openings was –

| Tuesday 8th December: | *Richard II* |
| Wednesday 9th: | *Henry IV, Part 1* |
| Thursday 10th: | *Henry IV, Part 2* |
| Friday 11th: | *Henry V* |

| Saturday 12th: | *Richard II and Henry IV, Parts 1 and 2* |
| Monday 14th: | *Henry VI, House of Lancaster* |
| Tuesday 15th: | *Henry VI, House of York* |
| Wednesday 16th: | *Richard III* |

I don't suppose we can claim a world record, but opening seven shows, twenty four hours of Shakespeare in nine days is not bad going. Don't boast, don't complain. Why bother? What's the point? What are you trying to prove? A familiar argument ran: 'If the circumstances are so rushed, and the compromise so great, what's the point of it all? Why fuck up a great set of plays just to show you can get them on? Anyone can do shoddy, ill-prepared, technically unsound work.' It *was* an achievement just to get them on. But the reasons for doing it ran much deeper. Despite all the obvious drawbacks, there was paradoxically one great advantage.

Artistic freedom. Even if the compromises at times seemed unending, in another way the line was straight and true. The release of the language, the quality of the story-telling, at its best, was exhilarating. Nobody can get a production right. As a director, you do one good one, one bad one, one medium. You spend your time trying to eliminate the bad one. Then with one good and two medium, you're pretty good. With two good and one medium, you're world class. And here we were with seven on offer. It's a very simple equation really. If you get 90% of a production right (what is right?) you are a world beater. At 75% it is a great production and about the most that any self-respecting director can hope for. The problem with getting even 75% of *The Wars of the Roses* right, however, is that while out of twenty four hours eighteen might be passable, that still leaves six whole hours that are naff! That's two whole plays! Which two? I hear you cry. Opinions vary. And if Bath Theatre Royal was too small the year before, this time it was pretty catastrophic. We knew the routine, however. Build a platform out the back for the lights, to store the props, etc. The weather in December that year was mercifully mild, no repeat of the previous year's audience deep freeze. For some unfathomable reason, known only to the gods of theatre statistics, the year before, the turnover had been sensational. This time the public, if not exactly staying away, were not exactly besieging the box office either. From being one of the most successful venues, Bath turned out to be almost our worst. Why? It was the same time of year, the weather better, four new plays on offer. Was it an omen? *Richard II*, the first one in, was certainly pretty shaky. Very long, the first performance, three and a half hours – amazing the number of people who, having seen that opening night, were to say two years later, 'Funny, it's changed beyond all recognition.'

Really none of the shows was up to much, and *House of York* and *Lancaster* were very messy. Each of them contained twenty four fast-moving scenes. They needed tightening. The best was *Richard III*. It was clear that Andy was going to deliver all that he had promised in rehearsal, and the two scenes at the end were sensational. Andy's armour only just arrived in time for the Bath opening, and when he donned it we discovered to our horror that the hump had been built on the wrong side of his back. In a series of frantic phone calls, we ascertained that there was just enough time to get it changed. Straps and buckles were to break, and bits fly off – one of the penalties of tight budgets. The 'quick changes' in and out of costume on that first performance took an eternity. *Richard III* ran four hours. I had written *à la* Jan Kott a staged introduction to the central characters. The company was split as to its necessity, and to the end opinion was divided. I thought that maybe it was necessary for single performances, but for trilogies and cycles . . . Barry Stanton had not had time to learn it and carried a folder as if he were a 'Miss World / Come Dancing' compère.

This Introduction, effected in elegant thirties cream outfits to the background of a cool modern jazz number played by the company, went down sensationally. Not that the laughter was all intentional. As when John Darrell stepped forward, bass guitar strapped to his white suit, to be announced as Earl Rivers . . . 'And there you have it, the Woodvilles, the Plantagenets, the Politicians, the Ladies.'

We filmed the whole cycle in the very last week of our three year marathon at the Grand Theatre Swansea. Live. One a night. With eight cameras and a camera team who had never seen the shows before . . . The Wars of the Roses – the Nightmare Continues. The videos (now available on DVD) are, as you would expect, rough. They do, however, despite the blemishes and tired, uneven performances, give some idea of the extraordinary achievement of a company that dared.

These essays are an attempt to give some further insight into the thinking behind those productions and why collectively the Histories form such a monumental part of our dramatic heritage, painting as they do an incisive picture of our nation, the colours as vivid today as four or six hundred years ago.

If there are a few too many references to the Iraq war – *tant pis*. As Brecht said, the theatre should always be mindful of the needs of its time and our time, and has been dominated by the consequences of that Bush/Blair folly. I have always believed that theatre should have both an umbilical cord to the street and reflect the day's headlines. Were I to direct the Wars of the Roses today . . .

**Michael Bogdanov, April 2005[3]**

**Notes**

1. See Appendix II.
2. *Financial Times*, 21st January 1989.
3. This Introduction is adapted from *The English Shakespeare Company*, *The Story of The Wars of the Roses 1986–1989* by Michael Bogdanov and Michael Pennington, Nick Hern Books, 1989, (www.nickhernbooks.co.uk).

# Richard II

## The skipping King

*Richard II* is the only Shakespeare play that is written entirely in verse and in a good deal of rhyming couplets at that. There is an almost relentless hammering of what in any other playwright would be doggerel. Yet the play manages to be one of his most lyrical and despite what seems to be a constraint of style, the writing is positively elegiac.

The figure of Richard himself starts on an almost superficial level, his casual way of ruling, alienating the audience and focusing attention and sympathy on his victims. Yet as the play progresses, Shakespeare manages to turn the tide and as our compassion for this wayward, selfish king grows, so does our mistrust of Bolingbroke and his cronies. As with many of Shakespeare's protagonists, we lament the passing of colour and greet the era of conformity with suspicion.

The problem of pre-history in Richard II is immediately apparent in the very first scene that opens the play. In fact, the whole History cycle is a Pandora's box of onions that peel away, *Peer Gynt*-like, to nothing. The subject is the murder of the Duke of Gloucester, Thomas of Woodstock which has taken place before the play starts.

Bolingbroke accuses Mowbray of being responsible of Woodstock's death, thereby indirectly accusing Richard, on whose orders Mowbray was acting, thus sparking off a challenge to a duel. Mowbray covers up for Richard – *this time*.

What does Richard do? If Bolingbroke wins, as is likely, he becomes all powerful, proved right. His next tilt could be at the King himself – in fact, it is. He has to go.

In the unlikely event of Mowbray winning, he has a strong hold over Richard. He *definitely* has to go – for ever. You cannot have a courtier hanging around with grounds for blackmail, though Mowbray has grounds to be miffed inasmuch as he gets life, whereas Bolingbroke, the initiator of the challenge, only gets seven years.

A miscalculation on Richard's part – the first of many. The duel is not the answer, and Richard knows it. He can't risk a winner. But he plays the game. Why? Probably just enjoys the thrill of power. Ever the actor, he lets the duel go ahead, with ritual, pomp and pageantry, all the way right up to the moment of truth when, with a theatrical flourish, he stops the action.

> **LORD MARSHAL: Sound, trumpets; and set forward, combatants!**
> *A charge sounded. King Richard throws his warder into the lists*
> **Stay! The King hath thrown his warder down.**
>
> **KING RICHARD: Let them lay by their helmets and their spears**
> **And both return back to their chairs again.**
> (*To his counsellors*)
> **Withdraw with us, and let the trumpets sound**
> **While we return these dukes what we decree.**
>
> (Act I, Scene iii)

Our understanding of all this hinges therefore on our recognition of what lies behind Bolingbroke's challenge to Mowbray, and what appears to be Richard's whim in prematurely interrupting the duel.

How to make all this clear? Even an old play, *Thomas of Woodstock* (anonymous), dealing with the murder, isn't much help, focusing as it does on the deed without implicating Richard. There's nothing really for a director to lift that would make the situation more accessible and I suspect the answer lies in creating a pre-scene showing the murder and those involved, as one would do on film. Olivier, in both *Henry V* and *Richard III*, created pre-scenes explaining past events.

In the second scene, the Duchess of Gloucester, Thomas of Woodstock's widow, pleads with John of Gaunt, Woodstock's brother, to do something about her husband's murder. John of Gaunt refuses.

> JOHN OF GAUNT: God's is the quarrel; for God's substitute,
> His deputy anointed in His sight,
> Hath caused his death; the which if wrongfully,
> Let heaven revenge, for I may never lift
> An angry arm against His minister.

Clear as daylight. As long as you know that he's talking about Richard. The language is complex, the references oblique. Neither the Duchess nor John of Gaunt ever mentions Richard by name, yet knowledge of the king's participation in the crime is crucial to our understanding of why Richard has to get rid of both Mowbray and Bolingbroke. He doesn't effectively do either for exiling Bolingbroke was no solution; back he comes, a usurper, grabs the throne and does for Richard.

For this is where it all begins. The Wars of the Roses. A hundred years of dynastical slaughter and mayhem because, for those who believe in it, the order of history has been disturbed:

> KING RICHARD: . . . Not all the water in the rough rude sea
> Can wash the balm off from an anointed king.
> The breath of worldly men cannot depose
> The deputy elected by the Lord.
>
> (Act III, Scene ii)

There is a natural order to the universe; everything has its place, and divine right is part of that order. Provided, of course, that it's a Tudor king. (Don't question too closely who first decreed that – you might come up with the right answer).

As proof of Shakespeare's belief in the *status quo*, conservatives are often wont to quote, completely out of context, Ulysses' speech from *Troilus and Cressida* outlining this natural order.

> O, when degree is shaked,
> Which is the ladder to all high designs,
> The enterprise is sick. How could communities,
> Degrees in schools, and brotherhoods in cities,
> Peaceful commerce from dividable shores,
> The primogenitive and due of birth,
> Prerogative of age, crowns, sceptres, laurels,

> But by degree, stand in authentic place?
> Take but degree away, untune that string,
> And hark what discord follows!
>
> *(Troilus and Cressida* Act I, Scene iii)

Don't rock the boat, let sleeping dogs lie, anything for an easy life, we've always done it this way so why change? This may do for some, but I'm damned if it did for Shakespeare.

\* \* \*

Shakespeare drew practically all his material for *Richard II* from Rafael Holinshed's *Chronicles of England, Scotland and Ireland*, which was first published in 1577. Probably he used the second edition of 1587, since the portent of the withering of the bay trees in Act II.ii is not recorded in the first. Here, the Welsh captain sees this and other manifestations as omens and, having waited for Richard to arrive from Ireland for over a week, the Welsh soldiers disperse.[1] It is one of those Thomas Hardy-esque ironies that if Richard had arrived a day earlier he would have had the support of an army and Bolingbroke might never have succeeded in imprisoning him in Flint Castle.

> CAPTAIN: . . . We will not stay.
> The bay trees in our country are all withered,
> And meteors fright the fixèd stars of heaven.
> The pale-faced moon looks bloody on the earth,
> And lean-looked prophets whisper fearful change.
> Rich men look sad, and ruffians dance and leap –
> The one in fear to lose what they enjoy,
> The other to enjoy by rage and war.
> These signs forerun the death or fall of kings.
> Farewell. Our countrymen are gone and fled,
> As well assured Richard their king is dead.
>
> (Act II, Scene iv)

Scenes that are not in the original Holinshed are some of the most moving and lyrical in the play: Gaunt and the widowed Duchess of Gloucester; Gaunt's death; the gardeners at York; Richard's abdication;

the parting of the deposed king and his queen; the story of the groom – these are Shakespeare's own, and throughout, a giant unseen presence looms over the play. An inanimate character who nonetheless lives, breathes, expands, contracts, laughs, cries and generally hovers over the action as an anxious guardian angel.

It is England. This England. 'This royal throne of kings'. 'This blessed plot, this earth, this realm' is a fertile garden, a manor house, a fortress. Those who inhabit it only do so courtesy of her grace. The people do not own it, it is loaned to them. But England has a problem. He's called Richard II. He is destroying this England. He is abusing the trust that has been invested in him and England is bleeding to death in his care.

Richard is politically incompetent and unpopular: The Earl of Northumberland accuses him of gross abuse of the public purse and of being 'basely led / By flatterers'; Ross laments the 'grievous taxes' he has levied to pay for the Irish wars and his own wild extravagance; Willoughby complains that 'daily new exactions are devised'. In Richard's desperate search to fill his coffers to maintain his lifestyle, England itself is being auctioned off. Close to death at the start of Act II, John of Gaunt gives voice to the criticism piling up around Richard's head:

> Now he that made me knows I see thee ill;
> Ill in myself to see, and in thee seeing ill.
> Thy deathbed is no lesser than thy land,
> Wherein thou liest in reputation sick;
> And thou, too careless patient as thou art,
> Committest thy anointed body to the cure
> Of those 'physicians' that first wounded thee.
> A thousand flatterers sit within thy crown,
> Whose compass is no bigger than thy head,
> . . .
> Landlord of England art thou now, not king.
> Thy state of law is bondslave to the law,
> And thou –
>
> (Act II, Scene i)

and Richard, bored, rudely interrupts:

> RICHARD: – a lunatic lean-witted fool,
> Presuming on an ague's privilege,

> Darest with thy frozen admonition
> Make pale our cheek, chasing the royal blood
> With fury from his native residence.
> Now by my seat's right royal majesty,
> Wert thou not brother to great Edward's son,
> This tongue that runs so roundly in thy head
> Should run thy head from thy unreverent shoulders.

Shakespeare seems intent on making the man as unlikeable as possible. When he first hears of Gaunt's illness he flippantly remarks,

> Forget, forgive, conclude and be agreed;
> Our doctors say this is no month to bleed.
>
> (Act I, Scene i)

This deepens into a speech of contemptuous and shocking callousness on the news that Gaunt is close to death:

> Now put it, God, in the physician's mind
> To help him to his grave immediately!
> The lining of his coffers shall make coats
> To deck our soldiers for these Irish wars.
> Come, gentlemen, let's all go visit him.
> Pray God we may make haste and come too late!
>
> (Act I, Scene iv)

The comparison here is with Richard III, but whereas we are intrigued and amused at the brazen effrontery of Richard III's scurrility, here there is something distasteful and offensive. Now close to death, John of Gaunt gives us his view of an ideal England that is being decimated. With the prescience of a clairvoyant, he prefigures Henry VI when he says:

> Methinks I am a prophet new-inspired,
> And thus, expiring, do foretell of him:
> His rash fierce blaze of riot cannot last;
> For violent fires soon burn out themselves.
> Small showers last long, but sudden storms are short.
>
> (Act II, Scene i)

Predicting that the king's vanity will ruin him, he suddenly launches off into a prophesy of England's imminent destruction. John of Gaunt's love of his country stands diametrically opposed to the contemptuous mishandling of its sacred qualities by Richard in God's name.

> This royal throne of kings, this sceptred isle,
> This earth of majesty, this seat of Mars,
> This other Eden – demi-paradise –
> This fortress built by Nature for herself
> Against infection and the hand of war,
> This happy breed of men, this little world,
> This precious stone set in the silver sea,
> Which serves it in the office of a wall,
> Or as a moat defensive to a house
> Against the envy of less happier lands;
> This blessèd plot, this earth, this realm, this England . . .

> > (Act II, Scene i)

Gaunt predicates everything that England should be under Richard's rule but patently isn't. The nation is:

> This nurse, this teeming womb of royal kings,
> Feared by their breed, and famous by their birth,
> Renownèd for their deeds as far from home
> For Christian service and true chivalry
> As is the sepulchre in stubborn Jewry
> Of the world's ransom, blessèd Mary's son;
> This land of such dear souls, this dear dear land,
> Dear for her reputation through the world,
> Is now leased out – I die pronouncing it –
> Like to a tenement or pelting farm.
> England, bound in with the triumphant sea,
> Whose rocky shore beats back the envious siege
> Of watery Neptune, is now bound in with shame . . .
> That England that was wont to conquer others
> Hath made a shameful conquest of itself.

> > (Act II, Scene i)

Richard's betrayal of England is compounded by a further demonstration of personal contempt for individual life and feeling. Just moments after Gaunt's death, the king cynically announces that he will seize his 'plate, coin, revenues, and movables' in order to fund the Irish wars – in effect dispossessing Gaunt's banished son, Bolingbroke, of his inheritance and thereby triggering the events that will end in Richard's abdication. Ignoring York's eloquent plea to honour the life of dedication that John of Gaunt has given to his country and the crown, Richard coolly repeats, 'Think what you will: we seize into our hands/His plate, his goods, his money, and his lands.' What has changed? Today, in hock to big business, globalisation, and our 'special' relationship, Britain is once again leased out, a 'landlord' in charge, not a ruler.

Gardens are everywhere in the play, but 'This other Eden' of John of Gaunt's has been over-farmed, transformed from a green, colourful, luxurious and verdant source of nourishment into a barren wasteland of overworked fields, disappearing hedgerows and endangered wildlife. Pesticides have decimated indigenous plants and the soil lies poisoned and polluted. It is badly in need of resuscitation – a great deal of suckling, nurturing and TLC. The gardeners put it succinctly in Act III.iv:

GARDENER: (*to one man*)
Go, bind thou up young dangling apricocks
Which, like unruly children, make their sire
Stoop with oppression of their prodigal weight.
Give some supportance to the bending twigs.
(*To the other*)
Go thou, like an executioner
Cut off the heads of too fast-growing sprays
That look too lofty in our commonwealth.
All must be even in our government.
You thus employed, I will go root away
The noisome weeds which without profit suck
The soil's fertility from wholesome flowers.

FIRST MAN: Why should we, in the compass of a pale,
Keep law and form and due proportion,
Showing as in a model our firm estate,
When our sea-wallèd garden, the whole land,
Is full of weeds, her fairest flowers choked up,

Her fruit trees all unpruned, her hedges ruined,
Her knots disordered, and her wholesome herbs
Swarming with caterpillars?

The gardeners lament the fact that Richard has not tended his garden and reluctantly admit the need for a wholesale clearout of the weeds that are choking the earth. That means getting rid of Richard and chums, and accepting the rule of Bolingbroke. There is a feeling of regret for the passing of such a colourful character. If only Richard had done what they do:

GARDENER: . . . O, what a pity is it
That he had not so trimmed and dressed his land
As we this garden! We at time of year
Do wound the bark, the skin of our fruit trees,
Lest being overproud in sap and blood
With too much riches it confound itself.
Had he done so to great and growing men
They might have lived to bear, and he to taste
Their fruits of duty. Superfluous branches
We lop away that bearing boughs may live.
Had he done so, himself and borne the crown
Which waste of idle hours hath quite thrown down.

The gardeners are at one with John of Gaunt's vision. From both ends of the spectrum the picture of England is one of devastating neglect. A rich, fecund land suffering under the yoke of tyranny. Richard had to go. But why must the pendulum always swing so violently back the other way? Would you want a Bolingbroke to marry your sister?

In fact Richard's reign sounds rather exciting – music and dance, fun and games, lots of stand-up. Arts and sport and plenty of partying. Problem is, he pushed it all a bit too far and when the money ran out . . . well, so did his friends. Shades of Timon of Athens.

KING HENRY: . . . The skipping King, he ambled up and down,
With shallow jesters, and rash bavin wits,
Soon kindled and soon burnt, carded his state,
Mingled his royalty with capering fools,
Had his great name profanèd with their scorns,

And gave his countenance against his name
To laugh at gibing boys, and stand the push
Of every beardless vain comparative,
Grew a companion to the common streets,
Enfeoffed himself to popularity,
That, being daily swallowed by men's eyes,
They surfeited with honey, and began
To loathe the taste of sweetness, whereof a little
More than a little is by much too much.
So, when he had occasion to be seen,
He was but as the cuckoo is in June,
Heard, not regarded . . .

(Henry IV, Part 1, Act III, Scene ii)

Do we believe this description of Richard from a man who was so patently biased? Who continually convinces himself that tomorrow is the day he'll go on that pilgrimage to the Holy Land? He really will. Our advantage as an audience watching the plays chronologically is that we've already seen Richard II in action and can measure Bolingbroke's view of him against what we have seen. It provides a fascinating duality of choice in the story-telling. To confound or not to confound the audience's expectations.

Bolingbroke naturally fancies himself as the antithesis of all this, his view of himself shot through with the prim Puritanism of an austere recluse. A self-appointed arbiter of public morality: A one-man Viewers and Listeners Association.

KING HENRY: . . . Had I so lavish of my presence been,
So common-hackneyed in the eyes of men,
So stale and cheap to vulgar company,
Opinion, that did help me to the crown,
Had still kept loyal to possession,
And left me in reputeless banishment,
A fellow of no mark nor likelihood.
By being seldom seen, I could not stir
But like a comet I was wondered at,
That men would tell their children, 'This is he!'
Others would say, 'Where, which is Bolingbroke?'

And then I stole all courtesy from heaven,
And dressed myself in such humility
That I did pluck allegiance from men's hearts,
Loud shouts and salutations from their mouths,
Even in the presence of the crownèd King.
Thus did I keep my person fresh and new,
My presence, like a robe pontifical,
Ne'er seen but wondered at, and so my state,
Seldom, but sumptuous, showed like a feast,
And won by rareness such solemnity.

*(Henry IV, Part 1*, Act III, Scene ii)

What Bolingbroke neglects to say is that he nicked the crown in the first place. And herein lies the difference in the two regimes. The one artistic, insouciant, profligate – the other devious, austere, philistine. Thatcher after the 60s, suits instead of flares.

Richard II is not merely de-throned, he is hurled into the abyss and with him the structure of the feudal world. The fire of the sun-king is doused, the glass is smashed, the natural order is disturbed, and Richard is no longer a king but a mere mortal. The problem with thinking (and believing) that you are the Lord's anointed is that you end up on the plus side of arrogant. Humility and listening are not qualities synonymous with those who believe themselves untouchable. Not that Richard was a Medieval Bagwan, but the seeds of his downfall are in his contempt for anything that smacks of the democratic process. He has abused and violated his position and, in trying to invoke the divine mystique of kingship, all he is capable of is hollow rhetoric:

For every man that Bolingbroke hath pressed
To lift shrewd steel against our golden crown,
God for his Richard hath in heavenly pay
A glorious angel. Then if angels fight,
Weak men must fall; for heaven still guards the right.
*Enter Salisbury*
Welcome, my lord. How far off lies your power?

(Act III, Scene ii)

Wonderful. While purporting to believe that his divinity is hedged, his immediate problem is the number of soldiers he's got to protect him. Fantasy and reality collide, with reality the winner. And the reality is that he is a weak, self-indulgent wastrel who hastens his own downfall with a streak of paranoid defeatism. It is easier to wallow in a slough of despond than find the will to act positively in his own defence. It is also more satisfying, more exciting, and in trying to keep control of his own ruin, Richard falls faster than anyone can push him, hastening his own mixed metaphor demise by being one jump ahead:

> **RICHARD: What must the king do now?**
> **. . . Must he lose**
> **The name of king? A God's name, let it go.**
>
> (Act III, Scene iii)

Here lies the principal contrast between the 'skipping king' and the 'vile politician'. Bolingbroke stakes out the territory carefully, moving forward slowly, sweeping the ground for hidden mines, his true purpose, that of taking the crown, veiled until he is absolutely sure of support for his aim. Paradoxically it is Richard who forces the pace and flushes Bolingbroke's real motives out into the open. Richard who finally gets under Bolingbroke's skin, forcing an admission of his true purpose:

> **RICHARD: . . . Set on towards London, cousin, is it so?**

(ie, the Tower).

> **BOLINGBROKE: Yea, my good lord.**
> **RICHARD: Then I must not say no.**

London, the seat of power, where power changes hands. But Richard is not going to go quietly. Oh, no. The actor in him ensures that he will cause Bolingbroke the maximum embarrassment. He leads him to believe that the hand-over will be easy.

> **BOLINGBROKE: Fetch hither Richard, that in common view**
> **He may surrender. So we shall proceed**
> **Without suspicion.**
>
> (Act IV, Scene i)

Ever cautious, Bolingbroke needs this public display of surrender to avoid the accusation of a behind-doors *putsch*. It's called covering your arse. Richard, however, despite what appeared earlier to be meek compliance, has other ideas. A public platform? Perfect for a consummate drama queen: ·

**RICHARD: . . . To what service am I sent for hither?**

Shocked pause. Wait a minute, it wasn't supposed to happen like this. The very office of kingship is degraded by that word 'service'. Chauffeur? Head cook and bottle washer?

**BOLINGBROKE: I thought you had been willing to resign.**

That's it. The word is out in the open. Richard's cue for a display of theatrical fireworks. The prosaic Bolingbroke can now only be a helpless bystander as the process of handing over the crown becomes an humiliating farce.

**RICHARD: Give me the crown.**
**Here, cousin – seize the crown. Here, cousin –**
**On this side, my hand; and on that side, thine.**
**Now is this golden crown like a deep well**
**That owes two buckets, filling one another,**
**The emptier ever dancing in the air,**
**The other down, unseen, and full of water.**
**That bucket down and full of tears am I,**
**Drinking my griefs whilst you mount up on high.**

(Act IV, Scene i)

Two grown men, the most powerful in the land, like two dogs fighting over a piece of meat clenched between their teeth. Both have their hand on the crown, neither wearing it; a pathetic tug of war, one of the most disturbing moments of Roses history, rivalling Queen Margaret wiping the Duke of York's face with a cloth steeped in the blood of his murdered son in *Henry VI, Part 3*.

Richard suddenly switches his mode of speech, formality replacing his earlier insouciance. He turns the coronation ceremony upside down, contemptuously demonstrating that he knew what the sanctity of kingship really is about all along. He tears up the rule book in a grotesque parody of that ceremony:

> . . . Now, mark me how I will undo myself.
> I give this heavy weight from off my head,
> And this unwieldy sceptre from my hand,
> The pride of kingly sway from out my heart.
> With mine own tears I wash away my balm,
> With mine own hands I give away my crown,
> With mine own tongue deny my sacred state,
> With mine own breath release all duteous oaths.
> All pomp and majesty I do forswear.
> My manors, rents, revenues, I forgo.
> My acts, decrees, and statutes I deny.
> God pardon all oaths that are broke to me;
> God keep all vows unbroken are made to thee;

Richard is the judge, jury and presiding officer at his own downfall, and in a storming finale, creates for himself and the onlookers a mock ritual for the handing-over ceremony, deliberately pointing up the absurdity of the deposition:

> . . . God save the King! Will no one say Amen?
> Am I both priest and clerk? Well then, Amen.

The actor takes centre stage for a dying soliloquy that to the on-lookers seems endless. They can only stand helpless with embarrassment as Richard uncrowns himself. What does he gain from his theatrical antics? In the final analysis, he merely prolongs the agony for himself of handing over power to Bolingbroke.

In real life, the reign of Richard II was bedevilled by popular revolt and aristocratic punch-ups and he was thrown off the throne, not once, but twice. Four plays about the king, including Shakespeare's, appeared on the London stage during his lifetime, all dwelling on his incompetence, cronyism and the responsibility for the murder of his uncle, Thomas of Woodstock, the Duke of Gloucester.

But it was Shakespeare's play that got under the skin of Elizabeth I, for the parallels were plain for all to see. She, too, was accused of being misled by her favourites and flatterers, and Elizabeth immediately recognised the resemblance to herself. In her later years she faced both rebellion and dissent and is quoted as saying, 'I am Richard the Second, know ye not that?' and complained that 'a tragedy' of the king had been 'played forty times in open streets and houses'. The night before his attempted *putsch* in 1601, supporters of the Earl of Essex paid the Company of the Lord Chamberlain's Men to revive a play about 'the deposing and killing of Richard the Second' at The Globe Theatre. The performance took place as arranged, but Essex's attempted coup the following day was a cock-up and he was taken prisoner and beheaded. The parallels between Richard II and Elizabeth were so overt that the deposition scene was cut by the censors. For seven years performances of Richard II were given without its central and most riveting scene and it was only restored by James I and VI in 1608 after Elizabeth's death. It made for a strange play.

What do you call an uncrowned king? He is a king and not a king. 'God save King Henry? Unking'd Richard says'. And with the crown goes his very identity:

. . . I have no name, no title –
No, not that name was given me at the font –
But 'tis usurped. Alack the heavy day,
That I have worn so many winters out
And know not now what name to call myself!

(Act IV, Scene i)

No name or not, you can't have an ex-king hanging around for too long. You never know who's going to suddenly get sentimental about the good old days. Enter Exton. Yet another fall guy to do the dirty work and keep the boss's hands clean.

Like a dog proudly bringing back a stick thrown by its master, Exton lays the body of Richard before Bolingbroke:

EXTON: Great King, within this coffin I present
Thy buried fear. Herein all breathless lies
The mightiest of thy greatest enemies,
Richard of Bordeaux, by me hither brought.

KING HENRY: Exton, I thank thee not; for thou has wrought
A deed of slander with thy fatal hand
Upon my head and all this famous land.

EXTON: From your own mouth, my lord, did I this deed.

KING HENRY: They love not poison that do poison need;
Nor do I thee. Though I did wish him dead,
I hate the murderer, love him murderèd.
The guilt of conscience take thou for thy labour,
But neither my good word nor princely favour.
With Cain go wander thorough shades of night,
And never show thy head by day nor light.

(Act V, Scene vi)

It's one thing to give the order, it's another to see the victim of that order gaping up at you. The king is appalled at being confronted with Richard's cadavre and launches immediately into a typical piece of Bolingbrokean back-sliding and evasion. It is significant that he changed his mind about imprisoning Richard in the Tower, diverting him to Pomfret when already on route to London. Better not to have him anywhere near the capital if an 'accident' happens, in case tongues wag. Better to be a long way away. . . . We've seen it before: the indirect accusation of Richard over Thomas of Woodstock's death, which led to Bolingbroke challenging Mowbray to a duel, Later, in *Henry IV, Part 1*, we will see him avoid confrontation with Hotspur with an overt lie in order to bring him to heel. Now, we get another lie, a total denial of his involvement in the order to kill Richard. He looks Exton straight in the eye – 'They love not poison that do poison need.' If he were a rugby player, Bolingbroke would be continually penalised for coming in from the side. A vile politician indeed.

*Thomas of Woodstock*, is a valuable source of material for the characters of Bushy, Bagot and Green, notoriously under-written in *Richard II*, yet held by John of Gaunt, Bolingbroke and others to be the authors of Richard's being led astray, and his concomitant misuse of power. Bolingbroke has two of them executed. The problem is that these 'caterpillars of the Commonwealth' are so sketchily drawn that there is very little evidence of their crimes against the state on which to pin a convincing death penalty. Hence, there is a very peremptory trial with a number of accusations not borne out by the text, and off they are marched into history.

> BOLINGBROKE: . . . You have misled a prince, a royal king,
> A happy gentleman in blood and lineaments,
> By you unhappied and disfigured clean.
> You have in manner with your sinful hours
> Made a divorce betwixt his Queen and him,
> Broke the possession of a royal bed,
> And stained the beauty of a fair queen's cheeks
> With tears drawn from her eyes by your foul wrongs.
> Myself – a prince by fortune of my birth,
> Near to the King in blood, and near in love
> Till you did make him misinterpret me –
> Have stooped my neck under your injuries,
> And sighed my English breath in foreign clouds,
> Eating the bitter bread of banishment
> Whilst you have fed upon my signories,
> Disparked my parks, and felled my forest woods,
> From my own windows torn my household coat,
> Razed out my imprese, leaving me no sign
> Save men's opinions and my living blood
> To show the world I am a gentleman.
> This and much more, much more than twice all this,
> Condemns you to the death. See them delivered over
> To execution and the hand of death.
>
> (Act III, Scene i)

Oh, dear! They've messed up his lawn, spoilt his hunting and kicked a ball through his favourite window. An ASBO, maybe, but beheading? Nor is the accusation that they've come between the queen and Richard borne out by the text. Quite the opposite. And as for giving Bolingbroke a bad name by loud-mouthing him to Richard with whom he professes to be bosom buddies, well . . . we have known such people who delude themselves as to the real nature of the truth; who believe something to be implicitly true at the moment that they say it simply *because* they say it. Falstaff springs to mind. When Bolingbroke wants something, any old excuse will do. It's a shame that we don't see more of Bushy, Bagot and Green. They disappear after Act II, Scene ii, paradoxically having aroused our sympathy. But if they are a problem so is Aumerle.

The scenes containing the Aumerle sub-plot., coming as they do right at the end of the play in Act V – between Richard on his way to the Tower and his murder – are palpably a dramatic device to hold the audience in suspense while waiting for the dénouement. The problem is asking us onlookers suddenly, at that stage in the play, to involve and interest ourselves in characters who only play supporting roles, merely to demonstrate a conspiracy against Bolingbroke. This is hardly balanced by having the chance to see the Duke of York willing to sacrifice his son Aumerle, as a traitor, thereby giving Bolingbroke the opportunity to demonstrate clemency. It's easy when the danger is so insignificant and the boy is so young. With the other conspirators, as with Bushey, Bagot and Green, Henry Bolingbroke is somewhat less than merciful. Dramatically, the incident is the calm before the storm, for immediately he orders the arrests of Aumerle's co-conspirators:

> KING HENRY: But for our trusty brother-in-law and the Abbot,
> With all the rest of that consorted crew,
> Destruction straight shall dog them at the heels.
> Good uncle, help to order several powers
> To Oxford, or where'er these traitors are.
> They shall not live within this world, I swear,
> But I will have them if I once know where.
>
> (Act V, Scene iii)

Then, in the next scene, he's killing Richard and banishing Exton. After all that, is it any wonder that he wants to go on a pilgrimage?

By the conclusion, Shakespeare has achieved something of a miracle in completely turning the tables on our feelings for Richard. He transforms him from a distasteful, selfish waster into someone for whom we have heartfelt sympathy. Or do we? Once a pig, always a pig. The trouble is, by the side of machiavellian Bolingbroke, Richard now looks positively angelic: the paradox of many of Shakespeare's falling tyrants is that they have a great deal more poetry in their souls than their conquerors: compare Macbeth and Malcolm. This aching gap between the pragmatism needed to rule and the power of the imagination to transcend earthly concerns is one which preoccupied Shakespeare, constantly baffling him. Man's inability to combine passion, poetry and humanity with the daily grind of taxation, unemployment, homelessness. Put like that, the difficulty seems obvious enough. 'If these things be necessities, let us treat them like necessities'. And so *real politik* rules and our hearts are left behind in the left luggage locker.

Towards the end of Richard's reign, it is impossible not to think of Richard's weaknesses somehow as strengths. In adversity, he cuts a much more humane figure than when he was king, his mind now unfettered and freed from those same problems of taxation and war. His downfall is orchestrated with impressive skill and, stripped of all office, he has time to confront his life and its shortcomings in some of the most intensely poetic passages of this most intensely lyrical play. In his final, long, last speech he muses on his misuse of his life. 'I did waste time, and now doth time waste me'.

> . . . For now hath time made me his numbering clock.
> My thoughts are minutes, and with sighs they jar
> Their watches on unto mine eyes, the outward watch
> Whereto my finger, like a dial's point,
> Is pointing still in cleansing them from tears.
> Now, sir, the sound that tells what hour it is
> Are clamorous groans which strike upon my heart,
> Which is the bell. So sighs, and tears, and groans
> Show minutes, times, and hours. But my time
> Runs posting on in Bolingbroke's proud joy,
> While I stand fooling here, his jack of the clock.

(Act V, Scene v)

He is now far from being 'glistering Phaeton', a sun King. He is not only down, he is out.

> Down, down I come like glistering Phaeton,
> Wanting the manage of unruly jades.
> In the base court – base-court, where kings grow base
> To come at traitors' calls, and do them grace.

In the base-court. Come down – down court, down King,
For night owls shriek where mounting larks should sing.

(Act III, Scene iii)

Richard's God has deserted him; all that is left behind is an impotent fool. Richard's dying words 'Exton, thy fierce hand / Hath with the king's blood stained the king's own land' are an ironic echo of the guilt with which Bolingbroke is left:

KING HENRY: . . . Lords, I protest, my soul is full of woe
That blood should sprinkle me to make me grow.
. . . I'll make a voyage to the Holy Land
To wash this blood off from my guilty hand.

(Act V, Scene vi)

Both Richard and King Henry, as he now is, are soaked in blood, blood which Henry will attempt to use to fertilise Gaunt's garden and make it grow again 'They love not poison that do poison need'. Bolingbroke needed it all right, as he will need it again. It was the only route to becoming unequivocally king. But the guilt is now a monkey on his shoulder and the battle lines are drawn. For the next hundred years, far from healing England's wounds, Bolingbroke has set in motion a train of events that will lead to a surfeit of civil and internecine butchery as the ambition of two families turns Britain into the killing fields.

### Notes

1. Probably the same actor played Owen Glendower in *Henry IV, Part 1*. There is even a similarity of language.

# The Henry IVs
## I know you all

*Of a man who was mighty but wild as a boy,*
*O list to the ballad of Harry Le Roy*

I don't buy Hal. He's a little shit. Sure, he makes some great war speeches but so did Churchill. When you're trying to persuade folks to get themselves killed to keep you in Mars Bars, it's amazing how the rhetoric flows. This 'star of England' embodies perfectly the dichotomy that Shakespeare finds in all rulers. The balancing act that they have to perform on the tight-rope of *real politik* and idealism; expediency wins out every time. Hal, unlike Macbeth, Richard III, Brutus, *et al*, doesn't let his imagination get a grip on him. He neatly sidesteps the pitfalls of ego and religion to emerge triumphantly at the end of *Henry V* with his reputation intact and France dangling at the end of his sword. How does he pull it all off without being rumbled?

There are two kinds of suspense drama. One where we are on the edge of our seats right until the last moment, waiting to find out whodunit. The other where we know the guilty party up front – either through a flash-back to the crime or through a self-confession. The *Henry IVs* fall into this latter category.

PRINCE HAL: I know you all, and will awhile uphold
The unyoked humour of your idleness.
Yet herein will I imitate the sun,
Who doth permit the base contagious clouds
To smother up his beauty from the world,

That when he please again to be himself,
Being wanted, he may be more wondered at
By breaking through the foul and ugly mists
Of vapours that did seem to strangle him.
If all the year were playing holidays,
To sport would be as tedious as to work;
But when they seldom come, they wished-for come,
And nothing pleaseth but rare accidents.
So when this loose behaviour I throw off,
And pay the debt I never promisèd,
By how much better than my word I am,
By so much shall I falsify men's hopes.
And like bright metal on a sullen ground,
My reformation, glittering o'er my fault,
Shall show more goodly, and attract more eyes
Than that which hath no foil to set it off.
I'll so offend, to make offence a skill,
Redeeming time when men think least I will.

(*Part 1*, Act I, Scene ii)

There it is, up front, a statement of intent. True or false? Is Hal the blagger of all time, wool-pulling over his and our eyes, a Mitty-esque figure fantasising about reforming his nature? There is no sense of irony in the speech, no petulant defiance, immaturity (though of course an actor could bring out all three of these characteristics). No – there is only the simple 'I know you all' – an objective appraisal of the intrinsic falsehood of the life he is leading and that at some point he will have to abandon. The gap year. Bumming it in Thailand. The losers will be his companions, those who are conned into believing that they have captured the ear of the future king and who will, at a Caligula-like stroke, fill positions in the law courts and treasury, instigate a Cade-like land where the pissing conduit will run with claret. Some hope.

Hal plays a long game. For close to eight hours we wait for the pay off. It comes at the conclusion of *Henry IV, Part 2* as the newly-crowned king, Henry V, chucks Falstaff out of his kingdom with the cursory couplet – 'I know thee not, old man. Fall to thy prayers.', Act V.v.

We search every moment of Hal's exploits with Falstaff, Poins, Pistol,

Bardolph, and Peto for double meanings or a hidden agenda, forewarned with the knowledge that it's all a game; fascinated to see how he will pull it all off – will he/won't he? Is he just a loud-mouthed no-hoper? But because we know what's going on we look for the clues. At the climax at the Boar's Head Tavern charade where Hal and Falstaff take turns to act out King and vassal (*Part 1*, Act II.iv), Falstaff says, 'Banish plump Jack, and banish all the world'. Hal replies 'I do, I will'. The signal for uncontrolled mirth and hilarity at the absurd proposition that when Hal is king he will get rid of his roistering companion in drink and sex? Or a chilly, prophetic indication of what *will* happen? No one in the bar knows. But we do.

Dodging, ducking, diving, weaving, Hal shimmies past desperate tackles, slips through outstretched arms to triumphantly touch down between the posts, leaving behind a trail of wrecked lives and the deaths of those with whom he purported to be friends; the rejection of a class of which he purported to be the champion, and whom he treats with contempt. Falstaff? Banish the fat slug. Bardolph? Hang him. 'We would have all such offenders so cut off'. Poins? Marry his sister? In yer dreams. 'Well, thus we play the fools with the time, and the spirits of the wise sit in the clouds and mock us.' Francis the drawer? Take the piss mercilessly, cruelly:

PRINCE HAL: . . . hark you, Francis, for the sugar thou gavest me, 'twas a pennyworth, was it not?

FRANCIS: O Lord, I would it had been two!

PRINCE HAL: I will give thee for it a thousand pound – ask me when thou wilt, and thou shalt have it.

POINS: (*within*) Francis!

FRANCIS: Anon, anon.

PRINCE HAL: Anon, Francis? No, Francis, but tomorrow, Francis. Or Francis, a-Thursday. Or indeed Francis, when thou wilt. But Francis!

FRANCIS: My lord?

PRINCE HAL: Wilt thou rob this leathern-jerkin, crystal-button, not-pated, agate-ring, puke-stocking, caddis-garter, smooth-tongue Spanish pouch?

FRANCIS: O Lord, sir, who do you mean?

PRINCE HAL: Why then your brown bastard is your only drink. For look you, Francis, your white canvas doublet will sully. In Barbary, sir, it cannot come to so much.

FRANCIS: What, sir?

POINS: (*within*) Francis!

PRINCE HAL: Away, you rogue, dost thou not hear them call?

(*Part 1*, Act II, Scene iv)

Ho, ho, a bundle of laughs. It's enough to make you ban hunting, not because of the fox but because of the hunter. A cruel exercise in class power. What on earth has the poor lad done to deserve such callous treatment? Quickly? Doll? Beat 'em up. Throw 'em in gaol. 'O God, that might should thus overcome right.' Williams? Humiliate him. Take no prisoners. In fact, if you do, kill 'em. Subjugate Kate. Crush France. No, I don't buy Hal.

Only Warwick (*Part 2*, Act IV.iv) seems to have grasped Hal's tactics but his speech smacks as much of good hoodie psychoanalysis – the path of Marxist rebel to conservative billionaire – as of blinding insight into Hal's brat-pack behaviour. Maybe Bolingbroke / Henry IV was a bit too close to the wood:

KING HENRY IV: Most subject is the fattest soil to weeds,
And he, the noble image of my youth,
Is overspread with them . . .
The blood weeps from my heart when I do shape
In forms imaginary th'unguided days
And rotten times that you shall look upon
When I am sleeping with my ancestors.
For when this headstrong riot hath no curb,
When rage and hot blood are his counsellors,
When means and lavish manners meet together,
O, with what wings shall his affections fly
Towards fronting peril and opposed decay!

WARWICK : My gracious lord, you look beyond him quite.
The Prince but studies his companions

Like a strange tongue, wherein, to gain the language,
'Tis needful that the most immodest word
Be looked upon and learnt, which, once attained,
Your highness knows, comes to no further use
But to be known and hated. So, like gross terms,
The Prince will, in the perfectness of time,
Cast off his followers, and their memory
Shall as a pattern or a measure live
By which his grace must mete the lives of other,
Turning past evils to advantages.

*(Part 2*, Act IV, Scene iv)

His speech repeats thought-for-thought Hal's opening soliloquy of almost two plays earlier, proof that when Will is up against it, a bit of recycling is in order.

Thus the path of Hal to the throne is a pre-meditated detour through the highways and by-ways of profligacy – one eye on the impression he makes on his yob companions, and the other a calculated assault on the rigid code of royal conduct that allows him to cock a snook at king and country while knowing that it will all end in conformity (now where have we seen all that before?)

'Let the end try the man'. 'Thus we play the fool with the time.', *Part 1*, Act IV.ii. In *Henry IV, Part 2*, Act II.iv, he is caught with his pants down. It costs nothing to play while the cat's away. But when the cat's at home . . .

PRINCE HENRY: Peto, how now, what news?

PETO: The King your father is at Westminster,
And there are twenty weak and wearied posts
Come from the north; and as I came along
I met and overtook a dozen captains,
Bare-headed, sweating, knocking at the taverns,
And asking every one for Sir John Falstaff.

PRINCE HENRY: By heaven, Poins, I feel me much to blame,
So idly to profane the precious time
When tempest of commotion, like the south
Borne with black vapour, doth begin to melt

And drop upon our bare unarmèd heads.
Give me my sword and cloak. Falstaff, good night.

And when the time is right he'll spring the surprise . . . obviously not after the Battle of Shrewsbury, where Falstaff claims to have killed Hotspur in Hal's place:

PRINCE HAL: Why, Percy I killed myself, and saw thee dead.

FALSTAFF: Didst thou? Lord, Lord, how this world is given to lying! I grant you I was down, and out of breath, and so was he, but we rose both at an instant, and fought a long hour by Shrewsbury clock. If I may be believed, so. If not, let them that should reward valour bear the sin upon their own heads. I'll take it upon my death, I gave him this wound in the thigh. If the man were alive, and would deny it, zounds, I would make him eat a piece of my sword.

LANCASTER: This is the strangest tale that I ever heard.

PRINCE HAL: This is the strangest fellow, brother John.

(*Part 1*, Act V, Scene iv)

Brother John is sceptically standing by. Better to wait for a more opportune moment. Watch your back, Falstaff . . .

\* \* \*

Who is Falstaff? What does he represent? Whether or not he is modelled on the real-life figure of Sir John Oldcastle, as the latter's family believed, thus occasioning a change of name for the character, Falstaff has come to embody all that is attractive in the Lord of Misrule. For a character who towers over the *Henry IVs* and who, even in death, casts a huge shadow over *Henry V*, he is a decidedly un-English character. His facility with language, colourful imagination and flights of wonderful fantasy, pissed or quasi-sober, are more reminiscent of Celts one has known. A Dylan Thomas or a Brendan Behan of an earlier Elizabethan era. But do you trust him? Charm and companionship ooze from him as he relieves you of your last fiver but you willingly stand him another pint merely to prise another story from his fertile imagination. How much of it was Shakespeare? Falstaff is akin to a stand-up routine, Burbage engaging, toying with, and confronting an audience with an improvised analysis of what motivates human behaviour. A one-on-one conversation that often rambles on beyond its time. Certainly, Shakespeare would not have written down everything that Falstaff says. There must have been an agreement between himself and Dick as to what the general gist of a soliloquy would be about and then Burbage would pick up the ball and run with it. A colloquy between a great writer and a great performer. But I bet Will had the last word.

Because underneath the lightness of the banter is a scurrilous villain whose behaviour is contemptible. It is no wonder that Hal, while ostensibly encouraging his antics, distances himself from the ultimate consequences while admitting to himself the attraction of such an opposite. There is no surprise in the demise of the fat fool, only the *frisson* of satisfaction in seeing the puffed-up, fantasising, self-aggrandising conman and coward get his comeuppance. Orson Welles captured perfectly the mean, sly, calculating quality of the character in *Chimes at Midnight*, the steel beyond the laughing eyes, the knife that wings its way towards your back, even as you share a glass. He robs and pillages and sends men to their graves without a second thought:

PRINCE HAL: . . . But tell me, Jack, whose fellows are these that come after?

FALSTAFF: Mine, Hal, mine.

PRINCE HAL: I did never see such pitiful rascals.

FALSTAFF: Tut, tut, good enough to toss, food for powder, food for powder, they'll fill a pit as well as better. Tush, man, mortal men, mortal men.

(*Part 1*, Act IV, Scene ii)

He recruits only the weak, the defenceless, the poor, the vulnerable, allowing the fit and strong to buy their way out of conscription.

SHALLOW: Come, Sir John, which four will you have?

FALSTAFF: Do you choose for me.

SHALLOW: Marry, then, Mouldy, Bullcalf, Feeble, and Shadow.

FALSTAFF: Mouldy and Bullcalf: for you, Mouldy, stay at home till you are past service; and for your part, Bullcalf, grow till you come unto it. I will none of you.

SHALLOW: Sir John, Sir John, do not yourself wrong; they are your likeliest men, and I would have you served with the best.

FALSTAFF: Will you tell me, Master Shallow, how to choose a man? Care I for the limb, the thews, the stature, bulk, and big assemblance of a man? Give me the spirit, Master Shallow. Here's Wart; you see what a ragged appearance it is. 'A shall charge you, and discharge you, with the motion of a pewterer's hammer, come off and on swifter than he that gibbets on the brewer's bucket. And this same half-faced fellow Shadow; give me this man; he presents no mark to the enemy – the foeman may with as great aim level at the edge of a penknife. And for a retreat, how swiftly will this Feeble the woman's tailor run off! O, give me the spare men, and spare me the great ones.

*(Part 2*, Act III, Scene ii)*

Hospitality and friendship are mercilessly abused:

FALSTAFF: Master Shallow, I owe you a thousand pound.

SHALLOW: Yea marry, Sir John, which I beseech you to let me have home with me.

FALSTAFF: That can hardly be, Master Shallow. Do not you grieve at this.

And his credo is summed up in the great Honour speech:

FALSTAFF: . . . honour pricks me on. Yea, but how if honour prick me off when I come on, how then? Can honour set to a leg? No. Or an arm? No. Or take away the grief of a wound? No. Honour hath no skill in surgery then? No. What is honour? A word. What is in that word honour? What is that honour? Air. A trim reckoning! Who hath it? He that died a'Wednesday. Doth he feel it? No. Doth he hear it? No. 'Tis insensible, then? Yea, to the dead. But will it not live with the living? No. Why? Detraction will not suffer it. Therefore I'll none of it. Honour is a mere scutcheon – and so ends my catechism.

*(Part 1*, Act V, Scene i)*

The apparent truth of this pacifist statement marks the real truth behind its sentiment. That of the abject coward who achieves glory by slashing a wound in a dead man's thigh and claims the victory as his.

The better part of valour is discretion, in the which better part I have saved my life. Zounds, I am afraid of this gunpowder Percy, though he be dead. How if he should counterfeit too and rise? By my faith, I am afraid he would prove the better counterfeit. Therefore I'll make him sure, yea, and I'll swear I killed him. Why may not he rise as well as I? Nothing confutes me but eyes, and nobody sees me. Therefore, sirrah (*stabbing him*), with a new wound in your thigh, come you along with me.

(*Part 1*, Act V, Scene iv)

No. No matter which way you turn him, Falstaff is, despite his snake-like fascination, a deeply unattractive character.

* * *

*Henry IV, Parts 1* and *2* follow a similar structural pattern in alternating court and low-life scenes, and together they form the most complete State of the British Nation picture in dramatic history, capable as they are of a myriad of mirror images of UK life at any point in the last six hundred years. Understandably, *Henry IV, Part 1* is more performed, studied and popular than *Henry IV, Part 2*. Logical, really – nobody goes to just see Part Two of anything, but with Part One you are in at the beginning of the story. I studied Part One for 'O' Level, and played Poins in a school production. We went to see a rival version performed by Alleyn's School and were shocked at the sight of boys in dresses humping on a table in the Boar's Head Tavern. The fifties were a time of Hank Jansen under the bedclothes, measuring each other behind the bicycle sheds, Health and Efficiency in a brown wrapper. Overt sexuality was embarrassing. Yet the *Henrys* are riddled with raunch and can be studied today in a way that was closed to us then, callow, smutty schoolboys that we were. Similarly, we are no longer impaled on a gung ho imperial spike that refuses to countenance anything other than royalty as deity. My Country Right or Wrong. Do or Die. The immediate post-war period was a monarchist's heaven.

How wild exactly was Henry? The problem is that despite numerous reports about his behaviour, we do not actually see him do anything. No binge drinking, mugging, joy-riding. Not all hoodies are criminals, it's just being one of the boys. His misdemeanours – apart from the 'vile company' he keeps – rest on one incident only. In the anonymous *The Famous Victories of Henry V*, written in about 1580, he has a punch-up with the Lord Chief Justice.

The action covers both Henry's wild youth, in which he is a very boisterous madcap prince indeed, and the famous victories of the title, culminating in the wooing of Princess Katherine of France.

Shakespeare chose not to show the scene from the *Famous Victories* when, in defence of a palpably guilty thief, Thomas Cutter, one of his servants, Hal fetches the Lord Chief Justice one about the ear in court, for refusing to release Cutter. For this, Hal is sent to prison and from such stuff legends grow. In *Henry IV, Part 2*, we get a reference only to this when the page announces the Lord Chief Justice's arrival with 'Here comes the nobleman that committed the Prince for striking him about Bardolph.', Act I.ii. Thus, Cutter mutates into Bardolph, seen throughout *Henry IV, Part 1* and at the beginning of *Henry IV, Part 2*, as something of Hal's servant. This prepares the way for Hal's brutal treatment of Bardolph in *Henry V*, where, in France, he has him hanged for stealing 'a pax of little price' from a church.

The Lord Chief Justice affair acts as a useful springboard for others to lament Hal's profligacy and add flesh to the wild legend. Twice, Bolingbroke / Henry IV lets off a diatribe against his son, comparing him unfavourably with the Earl of Northumberland's son, Hotspur, and on his deathbed he raises an apocalyptic vision of a Britain cursed with Hal's behaviour.

> KING HENRY IV: . . . What, canst thou not forbear me half
> an hour?
>
> Then get thee gone, and dig my grave thyself,
> And bid the merry bells ring to thine ear
> That thou art crownèd, not that I am dead.
> Let all the tears that should bedew my hearse
> Be drops of balm to sanctify they head;
> Only compound me with forgotten dust.
> Give that which gave thee life unto the worms.
> Pluck down my officers, break my decrees;
> For now a time is come to mock at form –
> Harry the Fifth is crowned! Up, vanity!

Down, royal state! All you sage counsellors, hence!
And to the English court assemble now,
From every region, apes of idleness!
Now, neighbour confines, purge you of your scum!
Have you a ruffian that will swear, drink, dance,
Revel the night, rob, murder, and commit
The oldest sins the newest kind of ways?
Be happy, he will trouble you no more.
England shall double gild his treble guilt;
England shall give him office, honour, might;
For the fifth Harry from curbed licence plucks
The muzzle of restraint, and the wild dog
Shall flesh his tooth on every innocent.
O my poor kingdom, sick with civil blows!
When that my care could not withhold thy riots,
What wilt thou do when riot is thy care?
O, thou wilt be a wilderness again,
Peopled with wolves, thy old inhabitants!

(*Part 2*, Act IV, Scene v)

But to what does Hal's behaviour in the plays *actually* amount? He refuses to take part in the Gad's Hill robbery, instead robbing Falstaff and the boys of their ill-gotten gains and returning the booty to the unfortunate pilgrims with a little bit of extra for their trouble ('The money shall be paid back again with advantage.', Act II.iv). We see him defy the Lord's Chief Justice when it costs him nothing (Act II.iv). We see him enjoying common company but we never see him drunk. There is no sense that he joins in the whoring and indeed, until Katherine at the end of *Henry V*, he doesn't go anywhere near a woman. I am still waiting for the first English gay Hal, as in the Dutch director Luc Percival's psychodrama productions, *Schlachten* at the Deutsche-schauspielhaus, Hamburg, in 2000. The timid, gentle, homosexual Hal is forced by his father through disparaging comparisons with the hot-headed, war-mongering butchness of Hotspur into a demonstration of hyper-masculinity. Roland Renner, a member of my Schauspielhaus company when I was Intendant (Chief Executive) for three years, played Falstaff as an ageing queen – more Danny La Rue than Orson Welles.

The relationship of an old man in love with a young boy was always going to end in tears. Cross-dressing and the sexual ambiguity contained therein have led us in the 21st century to mine the plays more openly for their homosexual content in ways that would have been taboo in past centuries. Jonathan Goldberg, in 'Hal's Desire, Shakespeare's Idaho'[1] is another to advance the theory of the 'bed-presser' Falstaff and Hal as lovers. It's a theory. But try as one will to inject fucking and fighting into the story a pure reading of the text comes up with Hal merely the observer of others' behaviour, summed up in *Henry IV, Part 2*, Act II.iv, where Hal and Poins dress up as tapsters in the Boars Head Tavern to overhear what Falstaff is saying about them (shades of Diana and Fergy in police outfits, blagging their way undetected into a night club). This is the perfect image of Hal's projection of himself as a member of the lower orders. His mind can never get beyond the sense of himself playing a part, standing outside the class to which he has loaned his body if not his mind. Every act, every statement, must be disguised. He can never be himself. The true Hal is only revealed in instinctive flashes, where his guard drops and the ruthless cynic is revealed. A pragmatic chip off the old Bolingbroke block. 'If these things be necessities, then let us treat them like necessities'. For Hal, the necessity is to pretend to be wild until the black crow turns into an exotic bird of paradise.

I also don't buy into the idea that Hal's behaviour is the typical adolescent phase of a teenager rebelling against his father whilst serving an apprenticeship for the crown. This is a Tillyard inherited view[2], still peddled by those who studied under or are influenced by his disciples. Hence Michael Billington in *The Guardian* (April 2005) reviewing Nick Hytner's productions of *Henry IV, Parts 1* and *2* at The Royal National Theatre:

> . . . a story of the education of a prince . . . in Hynter's hands . . . a study of a son, desperate to engage his father's love.

It would be, if we didn't have that calculated speech up front to tell us otherwise. Take Claudius' confession speech out of *Hamlet*, 'O my offence is rank', and you would never know whether he had committed the murder or not. Interesting. Nevertheless, the situation is complicated by Hal's relationship with his father – Henry Bolingbroke, Henry IV – which is founded on the quintessential parental disappointment in what appears to be an under-achieving elder son. Hal didn't make the First XI, not like Hotspur.

> KING HENRY: . . . there thou makest me sad, and makest me sin
> In envy that my Lord Northumberland
> Should be the father to so blest a son:
> A son who is the theme of honour's tongue,
> Amongst a grove the very straightest plant,
> Who is sweet Fortune's minion and her pride –
> Whilst I by looking on the praise of him
> See riot and dishonour stain the brow
> Of my young Harry. O that it could be proved
> That some night-tripping fairy had exchanged
> In cradle-clothes our children where they lay,
> And called mine Percy, his Plantagenet!
> Then would I have his Harry, and he mine.

*(Part 1*, Act I, Scene i)

And then later:

> Why, Harry, do I tell thee of my foes,
> Which art my nearest and dearest enemy?
> Thou art like enough, through vassal fear,
> Base inclination, and the start of spleen,
> To fight against me under Percy's pay,
> To dog his heels, and curtsy at his frowns,
> To show how much thou art degenerate.

*(Part 1*, Act III, Scene ii)

Push a boy too hard in one direction and the chances are he'll charge off in the other. Chess, cricket and philosophy? Nah – sex, drugs and rock 'n' roll. But I'll surprise you, says Hal in an echo of his first soliloquy, when you least expect it. I'll sort it out:

> Do not think it so, you shall not find it so;
> And God forgive them that so much have swayed
> Your majesty's good thoughts away from me!

> I will redeem all this on Percy's head,
> And in the closing of some glorious day
> Be bold to tell you that I am your son . . .
> If not, the end of life cancels all bonds,
> And I will die a hundred thousand deaths
> Ere break the smallest parcel of this vow.
>
> (*Part 1*, Act III, Scene ii)

If there is a trace of historical fact left in the plays of the legend of the wild prince, it may be in the relationship with his father. In reality, Hal was much closer to the decision-making process of the court than the plays depict. The impression that he spent all his days whooping it up are a false one and as King Henry became increasingly ill, Hal – Prince Henry – took more and more control of the council, packing it with associates and chums of his own – a situation that mirrored Richard II, and one of the very reasons why Bolingbroke usurped the crown in the first place. Prince Henry became so powerful that it was even mooted that the king abdicate in favour of his son. Henry's reaction to this suggestion was characteristically swift and decisive, when without warning he peremptorily dismissed Hal and his pals from the council. Hal's brother, Thomas of Clarence, was installed in his place and there remains a reference to this incident in *Henry IV, Part I*, Act III.ii, when in the midst of giving Hal a bollocking for his behaviour the king says, 'Thy place in Council thou has rudely lost, / Which by thy younger brother is supplied'. Shakespeare's change in emphasis from the historical is that the dismissal is attributed to Hal's wildness rather than his political ambition, the sense of which is non-existent outside his opening soliloquy.

Historically, Hal was only sixteen at the time of the Battle of Tewkesbury, and, needing no ID card to prove his age, was already into a binge-drinking culture in a way that today's youth would have envied. Such a charismatic young heir apparent to the throne with a penchant for painting the town red naturally would have attracted much attention and a group of companions would have grown up around him. Whether these would have included a surrogate father-figure in a Falstaff is another matter, but certainly a bunch of hangers-on who were the antithesis of the sober king and his courtiers. Holinshed, the source of the father / son relationship has two stories concerning the estrangement of Hal and Henry and their ultimate reconciliation. The first is the story where Hal, mistakenly thinking his father dead, takes the crown from his pillow and tries it on for size:

> ... My gracious lord! My father!
> This sleep is sound indeed; this is a sleep
> That from this golden rigol hath divorced
> So many English kings. Thy due from me
> Is tears and heavy sorrows of the blood,
> Which nature, love, and filial tenderness
> Shall, O dear father, pay thee plenteously.
> My due from thee is this imperial crown,
> Which, as immediate from thy place and blood,
> Deserves itself to me.
> *He puts the crown on his head.*
> Lo, where it sits,
> Which God shall guard, and put the world's whole strength
> Into one giant arm, it shall not force
> This lineal honour from me. This from thee
> Will I to mine leave, as 'tis left to me.
>
> (*Part 2*, Act IV, Scene v)

The second story which appears in *The Famous Victories* and which surprisingly Shakespeare did not use is one of Hal's appearance before his father in the midst of Council with a group of followers, all dressed in 'strange apparell'. Drawing a knife and proffering it to Bolingbroke à la Richard III and Anne, he asks the king to kill him if he suspects him of being disloyal: 'The king moved herewith, cast from him the dagger, and embracing the prince kissed him, and with shedding tears confessed, that in deed he had him partlie in suspicion, though now (as he perceived) not with just cause, and therefore from thenceefoorth no misreport should cause him to have him in mistrust'[3]. We get a suggestion of this when, at Henry's accusation that Hal is intending to join with the rebels and fight on Harry Percy's side, Hal throws up his hands in horror and says, 'Do not think it so, you shall not find it so;

And God forgive them that so much have swayed / Your majesty's good thoughts away from me!', Act III.ii. He calls these gossips 'smiling pickthanks and base newsmongers'. The fact remains, though, that to Henry it looks as if Hal has been caught with his pants down, red-handedly appropriating the crown. Hal must convince his father of the genuineness of his tears. He gives the crown back:

> . . . There is your crown,
> And He that wears the crown immortally
> Long guard it yours! If I affect it more
> Than as your honour and as your renown,
> Let me no more from this obedience rise . . .
>
> (Act IV, Scene v)

Thus king and son are reconciled for a second time – the first a temporary moment when he saves the king's life at the hands of the Douglas at the Battle of Shrewsbury, a moment undermined by Falstaff claiming victory over Hotspur, thus leaving the way open for the estrangement in Part Two. The fact that as long ago as *Richard II*, we have learnt that Bolingbroke hasn't seen his son for some time – 'Can no man tell me of my unthrifty son? 'Tis full some time since I did see him last' – only serves to underline the gulf that has grown between them and the theatrical neglect of Hal's courtly duties that Shakespeare has inserted into the story.

What father would not want a son like Hotspur? Brave, blunt, forthright, honest. But could he lead a country? It's the old Shakespeare dichotomy. You may want the Harry Percys to be in charge but the place would soon be in chaos. Too many risks taken, the heart ruling the head; too much nose off-cutting for face-spiting. No, you need a cool pragmatist weighing up the options. A 'vile politician'. A Bolingbroke. A Hal. . . . It's superficially attractive to have a valiant warrior who fights fair, believes in a chivalric code, particularly when your back is to the wall. But fairness never won wars. A Macbeth to save a Duncan. A Macduff to do the dirty work. And in times of peace? No. Hotspur is a rebel, sometimes with, sometimes without, a cause and there is an argument for believing that Hal is able to defeat him because where, for

Hotspur, the duel is a trial of fighting skill, for Hal to win is a psychological imperative. His determination is stronger, his need is greater:

> And God forgive them that so much have swayed
> Your majesty's good thoughts away from me!
> I will redeem all this on Percy's head,
> And in the closing of some glorious day
> Be bold to tell you that I am your son,
> When I will wear a garment all of blood,
> And stain my favours in a bloody mask,
> Which, washed away, shall scour my shame with it.
> And that shall be the day, whene'er it lights,
> That this same child of honour and renown,
> This gallant Hotspur, this all-praisèd knight,
> And your unthought-of Harry chance to meet.
> For every honour sitting on his helm,
> Would they were multitudes, and on my head
> My shames redoubled. For the time will come
> That I shall make this northern youth exchange
> His glorious deeds for my indignities.
> Percy is but my factor, good my lord,
> To engross up glorious deeds on my behalf,
> And I will call him to so strict account
> That he shall render every glory up,
> Yea, even the slightest worship of his time,
> Or I will tear the reckoning from his heart.
> This in the name of God I promise here,
> The which if He be pleased I shall perform,
> I do beseech your majesty may salve
> The long-grown wounds of my intemperance.
> If not, the end of life cancels all bonds,
> And I will die a hundred thousand deaths
> Ere break the smallest parcel of this vow.
>
> *(Part 1*, Act III, Scene ii)

And he does exactly that.

\* \* \*

Three male characters dominate the eight-play cycle. Bolingbroke / Henry IV, whose spurt for the tape begins the whole cycle in *Richard II*, before dying at the end of *Henry IV, Part 2*, passing the baton onto his son: Hal / Henry V, who runs through three plays and is heard about in the fourth (*Richard III*) and Richard of Gloucester / Richard III, who starts his ascent in *Henry VI, Part 2*. We may add to this trio a female fourth – Queen Margaret / Margaret of Anjou, whose formidable march through the plays parallels Richard's, interlocking and interweaving her fate with his, a nemesis figure, a fury, whose chorus-like prophesies are fulfilled in a way reminiscent of the witches in *Macbeth*.

Bolingbroke is the cautious counterpart to Richard III, marking out his territory, sweeping the ground for mines and only advancing when he is sure of his position. But the burden of guilt that he feels is one that he carries with him throughout his reign, even as he commits more crimes to keep him on the throne.

> . . . God knows, my son,
> By what by-paths and indirect crooked ways
> I met this crown . . .
>
> (*Part 2*, Act IV, Scene v)

Acquiring the crown illegitimately and then getting rid of Richard II has given him such a deep-rooted complex that he feels that the only way he can atone is to go on a crusade to fight the infidel. As if that will make it all right. The lasting legacy of the crusades is the schism today that exists between Christianity and Islam – the seemingly irreconcilable differences stemming from this abject period of our colonial history. *Henry IV, Part 1* begins immediately with Bolingbroke's stated intention:

> . . . Therefore friends,
> As far as to the sepulchre of Christ –
> Whose soldier now, under whose blessed cross
> We are impressèd and engaged to fight –
> Forthwith a power of English shall we levy,
> Whose arms were moulded in their mother's womb
> To chase these pagans in those holy fields
> Over whose acres walked those blessèd feet,

> Which fourteen hundred years ago were nailed
> For our advantage on the bitter cross.

*(Part 1, Act I, Scene i)*

Two plays later, on his deathbed, he is still trying to get there. But his purpose is clear. It was all a ruse to divert attention from problems at home. A trip to the Holy Land is just an excuse to mask his insecurity and keep his critics and opponents quiet. So watch yourself, he says to Hal, and take a leaf out of my book. His dying advice to Hal sums up as succinctly as anything he says the way his mind never ceases to operate on the political level.

> Yet thou standest more sure than I could do,
> Thou art not firm enough, since griefs are green;
> And all my friends, which thou must make thy friends,
> Have but their stings and teeth newly ta'en out,
> By whose fell working I was first advanced,
> And by whose power I well might lodge a fear
> To be again displaced; which to avoid,
> I cut them off, and had a purpose now
> To lead out many to the Holy Land,
> Lest rest and lying still might make them look
> Too near unto my state. Therefore, my Harry,
> Be it thy course to busy giddy minds
> With foreign quarrels, that action hence borne out . . .

*(Part 2, Act IV, Scene v)*

Divert your enemies away from the problems at home with a trumped-up war of expediency. And Hal does just that. His old dad's advice holds good.

Rally the country round the flag – it's amazing what it will do for your popularity. It seems that this bellicose jingoistic streak runs deep in the British psyche, for six hundred years later Thatcher triumphed in exactly the same way. Heading for disaster in the polls, she headed for The Falklands and returned to win a resounding victory in the following election. Blair tried the same trick and despite ferocious opposition stirred up by the illegitimacy of the war in Iraq, around half of the population were nevertheless in favour of aggressively toppling Sadaam

Hussein. Despite being severely economical with the truth, Blair still managed to win an unprecedented third term of government for the Labour party. What is it about war that brings out the worst? Sanguine, rational people succumb to the rush of adrenalin that the sound of drum and shell stir in the blood, losing all sense of proportion. And they kid themselves that a particular cause is just, flying in the teeth of incontrovertible evidence. 'Busy giddy minds with foreign quarrels'. Bolingbroke was there six hundred years ago. But he never did get to the Holy Land. He was conned by some tea leaf reader into thinking that was where he'd meet his maker, but like Birnham Wood, it was a trick. He died in the Jerusalem Room of the Palace.

\* \* \*

There was at least one Welshman in Shakespeare's company of actors – on occasions, two, and a father and son who were Welsh-speaking. It is possible to trace the paths of these players through the thirty seven plays – from *Henry IV, Part 1* right through to *Cymbeline*, one of his last plays, and examine both the stereotypes and the prejudices. Voluble, emotional and given to saying 'Look you', nevertheless there is an appreciation of the Welsh and Welsh culture that belies the reputation of later centuries. It is clear that in the Tudor court the Welsh had great standing and with such a champion as Shakespeare to defend them it is a mystery as to why the people of this small country have, until very recently, endured racial ridicule and suffered the suppression of their language, one of the oldest in Europe.

In the midst of the Machiavellian mayhem of the rebels, Northumberland and Glendower dividing England into three parts comes one of the most heart-rending and beautiful scenes in the whole of the canon. Edmund Mortimer, an heir to the throne, whose persona Shakespeare condenses from two characters of the same name, has been taken prisoner by Owen Glendower. There he falls in love with Glendower's daughter and marries her. Only one problem – she can speak no English, he no Welsh:

> MORTIMER: This is the deadly spite that angers me,
> My wife can speak no English, I no Welsh.

And then Glendower translates what Lady Mortimer says:

**GLENDOWER: My daughter weeps, she will not part with you,
She'll be a soldier too, she'll to the wars.**

**MORTIMER: Good father, tell her that she and my aunt Percy
Shall follow in your conduct speedily.**

*Glendower speaks to her in Welsh, and she answers him in the same.*

**GLENDOWER: She is desperate here, a peevish self-willed harlotry,
one that no persuasion can do good upon.**

*The lady speaks in Welsh.*

(*Part 1*, Act III, Scene i)

It is noticeable that the Welsh has not survived the transposition into the quarto or the folio editions – a non Welsh-speaking stage manager. Not uncommon outside of Wales. All we have is a series of stage directions: *'The lady speaks in Welsh'*. *'The lady speaks again in Welsh'*. *'Here, the lady sings a Welsh song'*. Obviously, there was a whole scene in which both she and her father, Glendower, speak in Welsh with each other, which has been lost to us but which probably the actor playing Glendower composed. Any production worth its salt has to invent such a scene.[4] Mortimer can only look on impotently:

**MORTIMER: I understand thy looks, that pretty Welsh
Which thou pourest down from these swelling heavens
I am too perfect in and, but for shame
In such a parley should I answer thee.**

*The lady speaks again in Welsh.*

**I understand thy kisses, and thou mine,
And that's a feeling disputation,
But I will never be a truant, love,
Till I have learnt thy language, for thy tongue
Makes Welsh as sweet as ditties highly penned,
Sung by a fair queen in a summer's bower
With ravishing division to her lute.**

**GLENDOWER: Nay, if you melt, then will she run mad.**

*The lady speaks again in Welsh.*

**MORTIMER: O, I am ignorance itself in this!**
*(Part 1*, Act III, Scene i)

Here, in one short scene, is the proof of Shakespeare's extraordinary all-embracing humanity and tolerance. The language is beautiful, Mortimer will learn it. No matter that English is the language spoken by the majority. The young Welsh-speaking boy who played the role of Glendower's daughter found himself in one of the theatre's earliest and most quintessential pleas for racial, linguistic and cultural tolerance. A man who could write such a scene and with such an understanding of cultural difference can never be accused of anti-semitism in the writing of *The Merchant of Venice*, or chauvinistic misogyny in *The Taming of the Shrew*. Once a humanist, always a humanist. Four centuries later, Brian Friel repeated the situation in *Translations*, a play about the love of a British soldier and a young Irish-speaking peasant girl.

The bardic figure of Owen Glendower, his language fired with myth and poetic imagination, has traditionally been the butt of much ridicule, mocked and jeered at for his bombast and portentousness, an early Welsh windbag. But Shakespeare is not dealing here in stereotypes. We only have to look at his treatment of the English in the same scene. Glendower is confronted by the more prosaic and down-to-earth scepticism of the Geordie Hotspur. The cultural eloquence of the Welsh versus the linguistic philistinism of the English – a polarisation of the two cultures that exists to this day. Was Shakespeare's tongue planted firmly in his cheek?

**MORTIMER: Fie, cousin Percy, how you cross my father!**

**HOTSPUR: I cannot choose. Sometime he angers me**
**With telling me of the moldwarp and the ant,**
**Or the dreamer Merlin and his prophecies,**
**And of a dragon and a finless fish,**
**A clip-winged griffin and a moulten raven,**
**A couching lion and a ramping cat,**
**And such a deal of skimble-skamble stuff**
**As puts me from my faith. I tell you what –**
**He held me last night at least nine hours**
**In reckoning up the several devils' names**

That were his lackeys. I cried 'Hum', and 'Well, go to!'
But marked him not a word. O, he is as tedious
As a tired horse, a railing wife,
Worse than a smoky house. I had rather live
With cheese and garlic in a windmill, far,
Than feed on cates and have him talk to me
In any summer house in Christendom.

(*Part 1*, Act III, Scene i)

A direct clash – Anglo-Saxon versus Celt. Lady Mortimer sings a song in Welsh (see Appendix II):

GLENDOWER: She bids you on the wanton rushes lay you down,
And rest your gentle head upon her lap,
And she will sing the song that pleaseth you,
And on your eyelids crown the god of sleep . . .

Hotspur, immediately jealous of Lady Mortimer's talent, makes a series of crude sexual jokes full of double meaning, using his wife as a butt:

HOTSPUR: Come, Kate, thou art perfect in lying down.
Come, quick, quick, that I may lay my head in thy lap.
LADY PERCY: Go, ye giddy goose.

And it gets worse:

LADY PERCY: . . . Lie still, ye thief, and hear the lady sing in Welsh.
HOTSPUR: I had rather hear Lady my brach howl in Irish.
LADY PERCY: Wouldst thou have thy head broken?
HOTSPUR: No.
LADY PERCY: Then be still.
HOTSPUR: Neither, 'tis a woman's fault.
LADY PERCY: Now, God help thee!
HOTSPUR: To the Welsh lady's bed.
LADY PERCY: What's that?
HOTSPUR: Peace, she sings.
*Here the lady sings a Welsh song.*

What is he doing? Why won't he keep still? Is he trying to burrow under Lady Percy's skirt? Hotspur immediately wishes to offer up his wife in competition. He's had enough of this Celtic mysticism and what he sees as effete cultural affectation. And as his resentment grows so the positions become even more polarised. The Hotspur that defied Bolingbroke because he took a dislike to his effete envoy because he was:

> . . . perfumèd like a milliner,
> And 'twixt his finger and his thumb he held
> A pouncet-box, which ever and anon
> He gave his nose, and took it away again . . .
>
> *(Part 1*, Act I, Scene iii)

now turns his Philistine guns on the Glendower household:

HOTSPUR: . . . Come, Kate, I'll have your song too.

LADY PERCY: Not mine, in good sooth.

HOTSPUR: Not yours, in good sooth! Heart, you swear like a comfit-maker's wife – 'Not you, in good sooth!', and 'As true as I live!', and 'As God shall mend me!', and 'As sure as day!' –
And givest such sarcenet surety for thy oaths
As if thou never walkest further than Finsbury.
Swear me, Kate, like a lady as thou art,
A good mouth-filling oath, and leave 'In sooth',
And such protest of pepper-gingerbread,
To velvet-guards, and Sunday citizens.
Come, sing.

LADY PERCY: I will not sing.

> *(Part 1*, Act III, Scene i)

Language should be short, blunt and not more than two syllables and preferably contain an oath every other word. Hotspur would have been at home in today's dumbed-down yob culture, where 'fuck' has become a *de rigeur* appendage to every descriptive epithet. He digs a linguistic hole for himself, out of which he is unable to climb with dignity. All this amidst the medieval equivalent of Potsdam.

Geoffrey of Monmouth, in his *Histories of the Kings of Britain*, recounts the story of the division of Britain into three parts during the reign of *Lir*. This becomes the springboard both for Shakespeare's play *King Lear* and for the defeat of the rebels in *Henry IV, Part 1*.

GLENDOWER: Come, here is the map, shall we divide our right
According to our threefold order taken?

MORTIMER: The Archdeacon hath divided it
Into three limits very equally.
England, from Trent and Severn hitherto,
By south and east is to my part assigned.
All westward, Wales beyond the Severn shore,
And all the fertile land within that bound,
To Owen Glendower. And, dear coz, to you
The remnant northward, lying off from Trent . . .

HOTSPUR: Methinks my moiety, north from Burton here,
In quantity equals not one of yours.
See how this river comes me cranking in,
And cuts me from the best of all my land
A huge half-moon, a monstrous cantle out.
I'll have the current in this place damm'd up,
And here the smug and silver Trent shall run
In a new channel, fair and evenly.
It shall not wind with such a deep indent,
To rob me of so rich a bottom here.

GLENDOWER: Not wind? It shall, it must – you see it doth.
. . .

HOTSPUR: I'll have it so, a little charge will do it.

GLENDOWER: I'll not have it altered.

HOTSPUR: Will not you?

GLENDOWER: No, nor you shall not.

HOTSPUR: Who shall say me nay?

GLENDOWER: Why, that will I.

HOTSPUR: Let me not understand you, then, speak it in Welsh.

GLENDOWER: I can speak English, lord, as well as you,
For I was trained up in the English court,
Where, being but young, I framèd to the harp

Many an English ditty lovely well,
And gave the tongue a helpful ornament –
A virtue that was never seen in you.

HOTSPUR: . . . I had rather hear a brazen candle-stick turned,
Or a dry wheel grate on the axle-tree,
And that would set my teeth nothing on edge,
Nothing so much as mincing poetry.
'Tis like the forced gait of a shuffling nag.

GLENDOWER: Come, you shall have Trent turned.

(*Part 1*, Act III, Scene i)

The attempt founders on that old rock of dispute, national bound-aries. West Bank, Alsace-Lorraine, Poland partition, Cyprus, Uganda, Rwanda, the Congo, Somalia – in fact, anywhere in Africa – the farmer's fence encroaching one metre into the neighbour's meadow, the overhanging tree . . . history is littered with the corpses of shattered agreements, victims of greed and avarice, the territorial imperative. Have Trent turned? Patently ridiculous. But the failure of Percy, Glendower and Mortimer to amicably resolve the frightening division of the land into three parts leads irrevocably to disarray and defeat as first Northumberland and then Glendower fail to turn up for the match. Wisely, it would appear, for where in *Henry IV, Part 1* civil dispute at Shrewsbury is resolved in the traditional battle of armies in a one-to-one combat culminating in the ultimate contest of leader against leader for the glory of the crown, here in *Henry IV, Part 2* the Battle of Tewkesbury is won without a single shot being fired. Prince John, a true younger chip off the old Bolingbroke block, outwits the rebels with a false promise of peace, arrests them when their armies disperse and then has them beheaded. A masterly piece of *real politik* heralding the onset of pragmatic rule and the death of the chivalric code embodied in the heroics of Hotspur:

ARCHBISHOP: Will you thus break your faith?
PRINCE JOHN: I pawned thee none.
I promised you redress of these same grievances
Whereof you did complain, which, by mine honour,

I will perform with a most Christian care.
But, for you rebels, look to taste the due
Meet for rebellion and such acts as yours.
Most shallowly did you these arms commence,
Fondly brought here, and foolishly sent hence.
Strike up our drums, pursue the scattered stray;
God, and not we, hath safely fought today.
Some guard these traitors to the block of death,
Treason's true bed and yielder-up of breath.

(*Part 2*, Act IV, Scene ii)

However much Bolingbroke may have longed for a *soupçon* of Percy
in Hal, it is surely John's tactics that he admired most. We catch a
glimpse of this family trait, which Hal is to exploit so ruthlessly when
he comes to the throne, in Bolingbroke's first encounter with Hotspur,
where he outrageously and perfidiously denies Hotspur's claims to keep
his prisoners.

HOTSPUR: Revolted Mortimer!
He never did fall off, my sovereign liege,
But by the chance of war. To prove that true
Needs no more but one tongue for all those wounds,
Those mouthèd wounds, which valiantly he took,
When on the gentle Severn's sedgy bank,
In single opposition hand to hand,
He did confound the best part of an hour
In changing hardiment with great Glendower.
Three times they breathed, and three times did they drink
Upon agreement of swift Severn's flood,
Who then affrighted with their bloody looks
Ran fearfully among the trembling reeds,
And hid his crisp head in the hollow bank,
Bloodstainèd with these valiant combatants.
Never did bare and rotten policy
Colour her working with such deadly wounds,
Nor never could the noble Mortimer
Receive so many, and all willingly.
Then let him not him be slandered with revolt.

> **KING HENRY:** Thou dost belie him, Percy, thou dost belie him,
> He never did encounter with Glendower.
> I tell thee, he durst as well have met the devil alone
> As Owen Glendower for an enemy.
> Art thou not ashamed? But sirrah, henceforth
> Let me not hear you speak of Mortimer.
>
> *(Part 1*, Act I, Scene iii)

With so admired a son, a role model for the English youth, why does Northumberland betray Harry Percy, refusing to turn up for the match at Shrewsbury, leaving the team a key striker short? He must know that he is condemning him to probable death.

> **Fain would I go to meet the Archbishop,**
> **But many thousand reasons hold me back.**
>
> *(Part 2*, Act II, Scene iii)

Maybe as Hal's behaviour is a reaction against his father's parenting methods, so Hotspur's bravery is an instinctive reaction against his father's cowardice. Both sons defy their fathers and represent as they do the two faces of the same coin.

What sort of land would it have been if the rebels had succeeded? Probably a land that would pretty soon have descended into chaos as rival factions fought with each other over possession and splinter groups formed radical movements to out-manoeuvre each other. An Anglo-Saxon equivalent of a medieval Italy – fiefdoms everywhere, back to the feuding era of the Celtic tribes. It's a good job that the rebels behaved like squabbling war lords, Britain would have been changed irrevocably. (Wales might have thrived though). Britain today is *en route* to federalism, devolution achieving peacefully what six hundred years ago was attempted by force. Even so, it is amazing how many of the old grievances and attitudes are still prevalent. The Scots, the Welsh and the Northern Irish find it hard to erase the memory of six hundred years of English oppression, their countries still, when the chips are down, under Westminster rule.

## Notes

1. *Theory and Practice*, ed. Nigel Wood, OUP, 1995.
2. *The Elizabethan World Picture*, E.M.W. Tillyard, Chatto & Windsor, 1943.
3. *Sources of Shakespeare* Vol. IV, Geoffrey Bullough, Columbia UP, 1962.
4. I offer up a possible example in Appendix I.

# Henry V

## This star of England

Henry V, a charismatic chameleon. Charming but ruthless. Coldness behind the eyes, one aspect that Olivier got right. Does he change from the character we meet in the *Henry IV*s, or is his apparent transformation into the heroic talisman of England's glory days merely a development of characteristics of which we have had evidence throughout? One thing is for sure: he'd have made your Top Ten Favourite Actors of All Time.

Unfortunately, this has led (and leads) the play to be interpreted in a variety of ways: as a romantic celebration of the unification of England and France, through the ultimate coupling of a golden pair; as an ironic satire on the futility of war; as a hymn to a latter-day Greek god of heroism; xenophobic jingoism, subversive pacifism – you pays your money and you takes your choice. But because it is capable of having the subjective bias of its interpreters thrust upon it – almost more than any other play in the canon – it has yielded wildly swinging versions in performance and polarised views in print. A play 'which men of action have been wont silently to admire . . . and literary men volubly to condemn' (The Cambridge Dover Wilson *Shakespeare, Henry V*).

Hazlitt begins it in 1817. Post Waterloo, filled with anger at the restoration of the Bourbons in France, he fired off a republican salvo at England's favourite play and its military hero. 'Henry because he did not know how to govern his own kingdom determined to make war upon his neighbours. Because his own title to the crown was doubtful he laid claim to that of France. Because he did not know how to exercise the enormous power which had just dropped into his hands to any one good purpose he immediately undertook (a cheap and obvious resource of sovereignty) to do all the mischief he could.'[1] The Irish Unionist Edward Dowden went into a paroxysm of orgasmic ecstasy over Henry as 'Shakespeare's ideal of manhood in the sphere of practical achievement':

**Henry's freedom from egoism, his modesty, his integrity, his joyous humour, his practical piety, his habit of judging things by natural and not artificial standards all these are various developments of the central elements of his character, his noble realisation of fact.[2]**

A closer examination of the text, however, reveals the play to be one of the best examples of Stephen Greenblatt's invisible bullet theory,[3] a play riddled with subversion but also one demonstrating Shakespeare's ability to bob and duck and dive and weave away from any suggestion that he is unpatriotic. Rather like Bertolt Brecht's defence during the McCarthy Communist witch-hunt of the '50s in America. Yet a modern reading of the play cannot fail to come down on the side of pacifism and see how a war of political expediency was won more by luck than judgement, and, historically, through the superior fire-power of the long bow – 'which every schoolboy know'. Bolingbroke's dying injunction 'to busy giddy minds with foreign quarrels' is here taken up in France with a vengeance.

Holinshed, the main source for the play, concludes with the following tribute to Henry:

**This Henrie was a king, of life without spot, a prince whome all men loved, and of none disdained, a capteine against whome fortune never frowned, nor mischance once spurned, whose people him so severe a justicer both loved and obeid (and so humane withall) that he left no offence unpunished, nor freendship unrewarded; a terrour to rebels, and supressour of sedition, his virtues notable, his qualities most praiseworthy.[4]**

The above has been taken by many to be the definitive judgement that history makes on Henry, but this is to ignore the small print further down. Here, there is a piece of Henry's bullshit on his death-bed, protesting the purity of his motives for invading France.

**And herewith he protested unto them, that neither the ambitious desire to enlarge his dominions, neither to purchase vain renowne and worldlie fame, nor anie other consideration had moved him to take the warrs in hand; but onelie that in prosecuting his just title, he might in the end attaine to a perfect peace, and come to enjoy those peeces of his inheritance, which to him of right belonged: and that before the beginning of the same warres, he was fullie persuaded by men both wise and of great holiness of life, that upon such intent he might and ought both begin the same warres, and follow them, till he have brought them to an end justlie and rightlie, and that without all danger of God's displeasure or perill of soul.**

A more succinct description of Bush / Blair and their motives for invading Iraq cannot be found. And for WMD, in *Henry V* read Salic law.

Salic law is the tortuous route whereby the Church attempts to prove Henry's right to the throne of France through the female line. Holinshed describes the practice as 'sharp invention' and this is the line taken up by Shakespeare. We meet the Archbishop of Canterbury and the Bishop of Ely discussing a new law passed by the Commons, stripping the Church of a large part of its possessions and putting the proceeds to such ungodly uses as the relief of the poor, aged and sick. Oh, yes, and for Henry's own personal use. They work on Henry, who is not only 'a true lover of the Holy Church', but who has received from them massive support for his war chest for the war against France. They have given him

**. . . a greater sum**
**Than ever at one time the clergy yet**
**Did . . . part withal.**

(Act I, Scene i)

– a massive bribe, in other words, to keep his hands off Church wealth, and deliberately egging him on to pursue those 'foreign quarrels'. (Note that Henry is not loth to follow his father's advice; a standing army is already in position for that war, without the need for an excuse to legitimise it. Salic law is the icing.)

The two bishops, working a pincer movement on Henry, sound more like two conniving politicians indulging in a bit of brown envelope business than men of the cloth. Corruption never worse than when at the top. It was ever thus:

CANTERBURY: My lord, I'll tell you. That self bill is urged
Which in th'eleventh year of the last King's reign
Was like, and had indeed against us passed,
But that the scambling and unquiet time
Did push it out of farther question.

ELY: But how, my lord, shall we resist it now?

CANTERBURY: It must be thought on. If it pass against us,
We lose the better half of our possession;
For all the temporal lands which men devout
By testament have given to the Church
Would they strip from us; being valued thus –
As much as would maintain, to the King's honour,
Full fifteen earls, and fifteen hundred knights,
Six thousand and two hundred good esquires;
And, to relief of lazars and weak age,
Of indigent faint souls past corporal toil,
A hundred almshouses right well supplied;
And, to the coffers of the King beside,
A thousand pounds by th'year. Thus runs the bill.

ELY: This would drink deep.

CANTERBURY: 'Twould drink the cup and all.

ELY: But what prevention?

and

ELY: But, my good lord,
How now for mitigation of this bill
Urged by the Commons? Doth his majesty
Incline to it, or no?

CANTERBURY: He seems indifferent,
Or rather swaying more upon our part
Than cherishing th'exhibiters against us;
For I have made an offer to his majesty –
Upon our spiritual Convocation,
And in regard of causes now in hand,
Which I have opened to his grace at large
As touching France – to give a greater sum

> Than ever at one time the clergy yet
> Did to his predecessors part withal.

(Act I, Scene i)

It is to deflect this Bill, then, that the boys vigorously persuade Henry of his claim to the French crown. And thus begins the long-winded, convoluted, pedantic explanation of the family tree that proves his lineage. A taste:

> CANTERBURY: . . . King Pepin, which deposèd Childeric,
> Did, as heir general, being descended
> Of Blithild, which was daughter to King Clothair,
> Make claim and title to the crown of France.
> Hugh Capet also – who usurped the crown
> Of Charles the Duke of Lorraine, sole heir male
> Of the true line and stock of Charles the Great –
> To find his title with some shows of truth,
> Though in pure truth it was corrupt and naught,
> Conveyed himself as th'heir to th'Lady Lingare,
> Daughter to Charlemain, who was the son
> To Lewis the Emperor, and Lewis the son
> Of Charles the Great. Also King Lewis the Tenth,
> Who was sole heir to the usurper Capet,
> Could not keep quiet in his conscience,
> Wearing the crown of France, till satisfied
> That fair Queen Isabel, his grandmother,
> Was lineal of the Lady Ermengare,
> Daughter to Charles the foresaid Duke of Lorraine . . .

(Act I, Scene ii)

And so on and so on, finishing with a line that, however it is played, is bound to get a laugh:

> So that, as clear as is the summer's sun,

(pause for laughter to subside)

> King Pepin's title, and Hugh Capet's claim,
> King Lewis his satisfaction, all appear
> To hold in right and title of the female . . .

Amidst all this we mustn't lose sight of the fact that what is on offer here is a dossier of dodgy proof providing a trumped-up excuse to invade France. Familiar or what? The wish is always father to the deed where extension of wealth and power are concerned. Despite the Duke of Exeter, Henry's uncle, asserting to the French king that the claim has not been 'picked from the wormholes of long vanished days', it is strange to say the least that nobody has ever mentioned this spurious claim before, so it can hardly have been a cornerstone of English foreign policy. And where have we heard *that* before?

> . . . That you may know
> 'Tis no sinister nor no awkward claim
> Picked from the worm-holes of long-vanished days,
> Nor from the dust of old oblivion raked,
> He sends you this most memorable line,
> In every branch truly demonstrative,
> Willing you overlook this pedigree;
> And when you find him evenly derived
> From his most famed of famous ancestors,
> Edward the Third, he bids you then resign
> Your crown and kingdom, indirectly held
> From him, the native and true challenger.

> (Act II, Scene iv)

Egged on by the clergy, who would rather see him destroy France than lose any of their land and possessions, Henry buys this load of political bollocks proving his hereditary right through the female line. The claim is ruthlessly prosecuted and the demand to hand over his throne is put to the French king with an army already in France. Henry was clearly predetermined to invade and uses the Salic law merely as a pretext. With God on his side who can blame him? 'May I with right with conscience make this claim?' says Henry and the Archbishop of Canterbury replies, 'The sin upon my head, dread sovereign!' It bothered Henry not a jot that his own claim to the throne, achieved only by the deposition of Richard II by his father Henry Bolingbroke, was illegitimate and that in England the female line was debarred from inheriting. No. 'Salic law', the equivalent of UN Resolution 43, legitimised the war. God has said there are WMD, so WMD we will find. And France? Like Iraq, no joy, only devastation:

> BURGUNDY: . . . let it not disgrace me
> If I demand, before this royal view,
> What rub or what impediment there is
> Why that the naked, poor, and mangled peace,
> Dear nurse of arts, plenties, and joyful births,
> Should not in this best garden of the world,
> Our fertile France, put up her lovely visage?
> Alas, she hath from France too long been chased,
> And all her husbandry doth lie on heaps,
> Corrupting in it own fertility.
> Her vine, the merry cheerer of the heart,
> Unprunèd dies; her hedges even-pleached,
> Like prisoners wildly overgrown with hair,
> Put forth disordered twigs; her fallow leas
> The darnel, hemlock, and rank fumitory
> Doth root upon, while that the coulter rusts
> That should deracinate such savagery.
> The even mead, that erst brought sweetly forth
> The freckled cowslip, burnet and green clover,
> Wanting the scythe, all uncorrected, rank,
> Conceives by idleness, and nothing teems
> But hateful docks, rough thistles, kecksies, burs,
> Losing both beauty and utility;
> And as our vineyards, fallows, meads, and hedges,
> Defective in their natures, grow to wildness,
> Even so our houses and ourselves and children
> Have lost, or do not learn for want of time,
> The sciences that should become our country,
> But grow like savages – as soldiers will
> That nothing do but meditate on blood –
> To swearing and stern looks, diffused attire,
> And everything that seems unnatural.

(Act V, Scene ii)

The disordered garden in *Richard II* has now become a picture painted by Burgundy of devastation covering the land and the people.

Henry has put the garden of England in order and, with the arrests of the traitors Scroop, Grey and Cambridge at Southampton, given it some judicious pruning. But in so doing he has ruined the garden of France. Burgundy's sober speech casts a cloud over the English victory celebrations, reminding us that Henry's war has decimated a land, a people and its culture. Shades again of Iraq.

\* \* \*

Henry is ruthless in eliminating any who get in his way. The treachery of the conspirators Cambridge, Scrope and Grey came to light on the night before Henry's departure for Calais, yet Shakespeare begins his scene, Act II.ii, by suggesting that their treachery is clear long before this moment:

> **BEDFORD: For God his grace is bold to trust these traitors.**
> **EXETER: They shall be apprehended by and by.**

The plan is already in place to trap them with an admission of their guilt. The treachery of the conspirators consists, according to Exeter, simply of the intention to murder Henry for foreign cash. A contract killing set up by France. Henry, obviously well informed of this, his intelligence system working well, tricks the conspirators into signing their own death warrants. They confess that their motive was greed; but one of them, Richard Earl of Cambridge, hints at a deeper motive:

> **For me the gold of France did not seduce,**
> **Although I did admit it as a motive**
> **The sooner to affect what I intended.**

The three traitors, Richard Plantagenet, Henry Scrope and Sir Thomas Grey, actually represent, as Shakespeare well knew, the cause of the deposed Richard II. This is one of those moments where Shakespeare hints darkly at a sub-text, a hidden bullet leaving us to consider its impact. Henry has succeeded in boiling down all political problems to a question of loyalty. If Englishmen are not wholeheartedly with Henry, they are against him – and that means complicity with France. The idea of a totalitarian state completely purged of all internal opposition, all dissent suppressed and complete loyalty guaranteed, is an illusion, perpetrated by a leader determined to leave his mark on history as the perfect ruler. Blair was obviously carrying his copy of *Henry V* around in his back pocket when he steamrollered over the dissident voices of Cook, Galloway and the chorus of disapproval.

The ruthlessness shown domestically is but a taste of the chilling pragmatism shown in war. Though Holinshed describes the atrocities that actually took place at the siege of Harfleur, Shakespeare is content merely to let Henry utter the threat of violence, leaving us in no doubt through the graphic detail, that he would have no compunction at all in letting loose his dogs of war on the citizens of Harfleur if it became necessary. He says to the Mayor,

> If I begin the battery once again,
> I will not leave the half-achievèd Harfleur
> Till in her ashes she lie burièd.
> . . . Therefore, you men of Harfleur,
> Take pity of your town and of your people
> Whiles yet my solders are in my command . . .
> If not, why, in a moment look to see
> The blind and bloody soldier with foul hand
> Defile the locks of your shrill-shrieking daughters;
> Your fathers taken by the silver beards,
> And their most reverend heads dashed to the walls;
> Your naked infants spitted upon pikes,
> Whiles the mad mothers with their howls confused
> Do break the clouds, as did the wives of Jewry
> At Herod's bloody-hunting slaughtermen.
>
> (Act III, Scene iii)

This is the streak of ruthlessness, witnessed at the banishment of Falstaff, which now finds its apotheosis in this war with France. Bardolph, his erstwhile servant and supposed friend, is summarily executed without a backward glance. A terse injunction 'to kill all the prisoners', flying in the face of combat procedure, is a pragmatic decision taken in the face of possible defeat. Down in numbers? Release those soldiers whose duty it is to guard the prisoners in order to have more in the front line.

Consequence? Too bad – the prisoners must die. In retaliation, the French kill the boys guarding the luggage. 'I was not angry till I came to France/Until this instant' says Henry. 'Kill all the boys and the luggage? It's expressly against the law of arms!' says Fluellen (Act IV.vii) Not a word about killing prisoners being against the law of arms. Not only that, but Gower attributes Henry's act to revenge for the above and that it is therefore just. This ignores the fact that the order to kill the prisoners was given before the action of the French. 'Wherefore the king most worthily hath ordered every soldier to cut his prisoner's throat. O, 'tis a gallant king!'

This gallant, Welsh king does not even know that he has won the battle and has to be told by the French envoy, Mountjoy (Act IV.vii). When informed that some ten thousand French had died and only twenty nine English, he reads out the names of four noblemen and says, 'None else of name; and of all other men/But five and twenty' (Act IV.viii). Presumably, these were commoners and not worthy of being read out. He does not even bother to see if Court and Bates, with whom he had personal contact the night before, are on the list. (We know the exact numbers and names of British and American dead in Iraq, but Iraqis? 10,000? 150,000? Who cares.) 'O God, thy arm was here!/And not to us but to thy arm alone' – or rather the arms of the Welsh archers. It's a good job God was somewhere. He certainly wasn't with the French. Or the Iraqis. 'We few, we happy few, we band of brothers . . .'

\* \* \*

The ironic and subversive is most evident in the Chorus. After apologising to us for not having hydraulics at his disposal, thus preparing us for the massive suspension of disbelief as epic words are matched by puny action, he proceeds to pull the wool over our eyes as Henry pulls it over those of others. This has the effect of working on us as a kind of Brechtian alienation device, set the coconuts up to knock 'em down. The German poet, Heinrich Heine destroyed the Romantic Movement in Germany with 'Stimmungsbrechung' (1797–1856) – breaking the mood. He would finish a cloying description of a sunset with a line akin to 'and suddenly a feeling of nausea swept over me like a cup of cold sick'. The Chorus is a bit like that. Nothing is said that can be taken at face value. 'Now all the youth of England are on fire and silken dalliance in the wardrobe lies' (Act II.i). Who are these lads, these hearts, these 'culled and choice-drawn cavaliers'? None other than Pistol, Nym and Bardolph, whose mission is to go to France . . . 'like horse leeches my boys / to suck to suck the very blood to suck!' (Act II.iii). (In the very next scene, the French king remarks, 'Thus come the English upon us', creating an umbilical cord of irony between British imperialism and football hooligans.) And what are their exploits? Do we see brave heroics matching the Chorus's high-flown rhetoric of great deeds? No. We see them hiding from the action, being pistol-whipped into battle and the only deeds are those of theft, pillage and desecration; the stealing of crucifixes and fire shovels. The glory of the Battle of Agincourt? We see none of it. Only the decidedly unglamorous sight of Pistol kicking the shit out of a wounded Frenchman and bribed to hang on to him illegally instead of turning him over.

The Chorus' claim that the French 'Shake in their fear and with pale policy / Seek to divert the English purposes.', (Act II.Chorus), is obviously meant to prepare us for an easy victory. Far from quaking in their shoes, the French are making intelligent military preparation and indulging in over-confident boasting about the rival merits of their horses. The Chorus' announcements of what happens next are often at odds with the events. He leaves us totally unprepared for the first bishop scene, the first Eastcheap scene and the leek-eating scene, all of which come immediately after he has told us that the action is somewhere else. All this is an argument for re-ordering certain of the Chorus' passages to coincide with the action, though I have yet to find an editor with the temerity to do so. Leave that to insouciant directors. Or maybe Shakespeare was being deliberate in spreading structural confusion.

'A little touch of Harry in the night?'

> . . . O now, who will behold
> The royal Captain of this ruined band
> Walking from watch to watch, from tent to tent,
> Let him cry, 'Praise and glory on his head!'
> For forth he goes and visits all his host,

Bids them good morrow with a modest smile,
And calls them brothers, friends, and countrymen.
Upon his royal face there is no note
How dread an army hath enrounded him,
Nor doth he dedicate one jot of colour
Unto the weary and all-watchèd night,
But freshly looks, and overbears attaint
With cheerful semblance and sweet majesty;
That every wretch, pining and pale before,
Beholding him, plucks comfort from his looks.
A largess universal, like the sun,
His liberal eye doth give to every one,
Thawing cold fear, that mean and gentle all
Behold, as may unworthiness define,
A little touch of Harry in the night.

(Chorus IV)

Oh yes? We see none of this. Borrowing Sir Thomas Erpingham's cloak under the pretext of wishing solitude, Henry disguises himself and walks about the tents, on the eve of the Battle of Agincourt, eavesdropping to hear what is being said about him – the Welsh paranoia – (cf. *Richard III* on the eve of the Battle of Bosworth). Far from geeing up the troops with some comforting words, Henry gets into an argument with his soldiers about the justness of his cause, his frustration boiling over into petulance at his inability to reveal his true identity, and conceiving a vengeful plan to get his own back one day in his true persona.

This is the scene (Act IV.i) on which the central pacifist argument of the play rests. He falls into conversation with three soldiers – Bates, Court and Williams, shivering in the trenches, waiting for the dawn to rise that will herald the attack. The king's army is already on retreat, having suffered heavy losses and riddled with dysentery. Williams unknowingly engages the king in an argument on the nature of war, equality and the unbridgeable gap between subject and king. When is a war just? What's the king think of it all? The scene confounds all the jingoism associated with the play and puts the case for pacifism, humanity and democratic involvement in the consequences of decisions taken by leaders. Secure in his disguise (and his Welsh accent), Henry attempts to place the king on the same footing as these, his common soldiers. 'I think the king is but a man, as I am'. Bates is having none of it; he quickly gets under Henry's skin (would Henry's assumed accent slip under pressure?) *This* is how an ordinary man who is not a member of any aristocratic *elite* feels on the night before a battle.

> BATES: He may show what outward courage he will, but I believe, as cold a night as 'tis, he could wish himself in Thames up to the neck; and so I would he were, and I by him, at all adventures, so we were quit here.
>
> KING HENRY: By my troth, I will speak my conscience of the King: I think he would not wish himself anywhere but where he is.
>
> BATES: Then I would he were here alone; so should he be sure to be ransomed, and a many poor men's lives saved.
>
> KING HENRY: I dare say you love him not so ill to wish him here alone, howsoever you speak this to feel other men's minds. Methinks I could not die anywhere so contented as in the King's company, his cause being just and his quarrel honourable.
>
> WILLIAMS: That's more than we know.
>
> BATES: Ay, or more than we should seek after; for we know enough if we know we are the King's subjects. If his cause be wrong, our obedience to the King wipes the crime of it out of us.
>
> (Act IV, Scene i)

Bates challenging Henry's motives for prosecuting the war in the first place questions the whole moral justice of the king's expedition and the dubious political gain from a victory over France. The whole *raison d'être* is examined in the light of the blind obedience demanded of a compliant and willing fighting force, suggesting that, in an ideal democratic world, the people would have a say in whether they are going to give their lives to a dubious cause or not, and that kings (or Prime Ministers) should fight their own battles if they are so keen.

Williams continues the debate, placing Henry in the morally indefensible position of being responsible for death and injury, and for creating cripples, orphans and widows in pursuit of a selfish, unjust cause.

But if the cause be not good, the King himself hath a heavy reckoning to make, when all those legs, and arms, and heads, chopped off in a battle, shall join together at the latter day, and cry all, 'We died at such a place'; some swearing, some crying for a surgeon, some upon their wives left poor behind them, some upon the debts they owe, some upon their children rawly left. I am afeard there are few die well that die in a battle, for how can they charitably dispose of anything when blood is their argument? Now, if these men do not die well, it will be a black matter for the King that led them to it, who to disobey were against all proportion of subjection.

This is one of Shakespeare's most cogent arguments against the megalomaniac ambition of war-mongering tyrants sacrificing thousands of lives (millions) in pursuit of the territorial imperative. Williams insists that all the responsibility for the carnage of the war finally is the king's. Henry is completely wrong-footed, ducking out characteristically of the moral responsibility for his actions and his people, invoking duty to God and country as his principal argument. Williams in no way buys this, recognising the argument for what it is, a cop out. Henry finds himself backed into a corner at Williams' insistence that there is an unbridgeable gap of such inequality between subject and king that the abuse of that power is what has led to the situation in which they now find themselves. The argument is unanswerable and, petulantly, Henry seeks a way out that only serves to reinforce Williams' analysis of the essential difference between them. He picks a quarrel knowing that at some time in the future he will assert his authority over Williams in the only way he knows how – the imperial power of king over subject. Thou shalt obey.

WILLIAMS: 'Tis certain, every man that dies ill, the ill upon his own head – the King is not to answer it.

BATES: I do not desire he should answer for me, and yet I determine to fight lustily for him.

KING HENRY: I myself heard the King say he would not be ransomed.

WILLIAMS: Ay, he said so, to make us fight cheerfully: but when our throats are cut he may be ransomed, and we ne'er the wiser.

KING HENRY: If I live to see it, I will never trust his word after.

WILLIAMS: You pay him then! That's a perilous shot out of an elder-gun, that a poor and private displeasure can do against a monarch! You may as well go about to turn the sun to ice, with fanning in his face with a peacock's feather. You'll never trust his word after! Come, 'tis a foolish saying.

KING HENRY: Your reproof is something too round. I should be angry with you, if the time were convenient.

WILLIAMS: Let it be a quarrel between us, if you live.

KING HENRY: I embrace it.

WILLIAMS: How shall I know thee again?

KING HENRY: Give me any gage of thine, and I will wear it in my bonnet: then, if ever thou dar'st acknowledge it, I will make it my quarrel.

The question of responsibility touches a raw nerve in Henry throughout the play. The blame always falls elsewhere: on the Church for encouraging him to go to war; on the Dauphin for sending him tennis balls; on the French king for resisting his claim; to the citizens of Harfleur for having the temerity to defend their town (Act I.ii 18–28; Act I.ii 282–284; Act II.iv 105–109; Act III.iii 1–43). After the departure of the three soldiers, Henry is able to return, in soliloquy, to his royal identity and release his frustration (thank goodness he can now drop that accent). It's all so unfair! Kingship carries with it a heavy burden of responsibility:

Upon the King! Let us our lives, our souls,
Our debts, our careful wives,
Our children, and our sins, lay on the King!
We must bear all. O hard condition,
Twin-born with greatness, subject to the breath
Of every fool, whose sense no more can feel
But his own wringing! What infinite heart's ease
Must kings neglect that private men enjoy!

(Act IV, Scene i)

In the aftermath of the dispute, Henry reveals his true self, his contempt for the ordinary class, something we have been aware of from his early posturing days in The Boar's Head Tavern. The king's subjects are described by terms of aristocratic contempt – 'fool . . . wretch . . . slave . . . peasant':

> And but for ceremony, such a wretch,
> Winding up days with toil, and nights with sleep,
> Had the fore-hand and vantage of a king.
> The slave, a member of the country's peace,
> Enjoys it, but in gross brain little wots [knows]
> What watch the king keeps to maintain the peace,
> Whose hours the peasant best advantages.

(Act IV, Scene i)

His reference to Williams as a fool with a gross brain is bitter and unfair and his anger unreasonable and unjust. However, significantly at no time does he say that Williams is wrong, the worm of conscience gnawing at him as he wriggles on the hook.

So what are we to make of the methods of this 'star of England'? That he carries the guilt around with him of his father's usurpation is palpably obvious. Before Agincourt he prays:

> KING HENRY: . . . Not today, O Lord,
> O not today, think not upon the fault
> My father made in compassing the crown!
> I Richard's body have interrèd new,
> And on it have bestowed more contrite tears
> Than from it issued forcèd drops of blood.
> Five hundred poor I have in yearly pay,
> Who twice a day their withered hands hold up
> Toward heaven, to pardon blood; and I have built
> Two chantries where the sad and solemn priests
> Sing still for Richard's soul. More will I do,
> Though all that I can do is nothing worth,
> Since that my penitence comes after all,
> Imploring pardon.

(Act IV, Scene i)

He is paying five hundred extras a yearly sum to pray twice a day for his soul! And he's got a bunch of priests in two specially-built chantries singing to get him into Heaven. That's real abuse of the public purse – beats Charlie's helicopter any day.

\* \* \*

*'Il faut que j'apprenne a parler'.*[5] It is necessary that I learn English. Katherine does not have to learn English because she is a willing participant in a love match. No. It is the *'il faut'* that gives the game away. It is an imperative. There is compulsion. Unfortunately, if I am going to be given away against my wishes, then I've got to get my head round those awful flat vowel sounds.

Kate is Henry's 'capital demand'. She is goods, chattels. It is necessary that he conquer Katherine as he conquers France. His male pride demands it. And the moment that we see him win both is the moment that he plants a kiss on her lips (Act V.ii). We have been conditioned, particularly as a result of the Oliver and Branagh films, to believe that Henry's winning of Katherine is a love scene in which two stars of their respective countries become the Burton and Taylor, the Posh and Becks, of the Anglo-French alliance. The truth is that the wooing is a whirlwind five-minute job, while the rest of the court stand outside the door waiting for Henry to get a result:

> I am glad thou canst speak no better English; for if thou couldst, thou wouldst find me such a plain King that thou wouldst think I had sold my farm to buy my crown. I know no ways to mince it in love, but directly to say, 'I love you': then if you urge me farther than to say, 'Do you, in faith?' I wear out my suit. Give me your answer, i'faith, do; and so clap hands, and a bargain. How say you, lady?
>
> (Act V, Scene ii)

It is a scene between an arrogant showman and a recalcitrant young girl who knows there can be only one ending but is determined to put up a fight. Five minutes. Henry pulls out all the stops, tries every trick. It would seem that he has learnt his wooing technique at Hotspur's knee for there is more than the blunt, plain-speaking persona of Harry Percy in the way he protests his simplicity, honesty, lack of affectation, inability to dance, rhyme, play a musical instrument and above all pleading an almost dyslexic inarticulacy:

> KING HENRY: Marry, if you would put me to verses, or to dance for your sake, Kate, why, you undid me. For the one, I have neither words

nor measure; and for the other, I have no strength in measure, yet a reasonable measure in strength. If I could win a lady at leapfrog, or by vaulting into my saddle with my armour on my back, under the correction of bragging be it spoken, I should quickly leap into a wife. Or if I might buffet for my love, or bound my horse for her favours, I could lay on like a butcher, and sit like a jackanapes, never off. But, before God, Kate, I cannot look greenly, nor gasp out my eloquence, nor I have no cunning in protestation: only downright oaths, which I never use till urged, nor never break for urging.

(Act V, Scene ii)

Liar. From the moment we first meet Henry we have been aware of Hal / Henry's power of oratory and persuasion. Has he forgotten the breach? St Crispin's Day? Henry the actor. The protestations of a plain soldier don't cut it when set against the arrogance which he displays in his treatment of his erstwhile companions and in the aftermath of the argument with Bates, Court and Williams. His appellation and constant repetition of 'Kate' for 'Katherine' has the bluntness of Hotspur about it – an attempt to be down-to-earth and matey. I'm 'enry V, but you can call me 'al. Even in his disguised encounter with Pistol in the trenches he calls himself Harry Le Roy, banking on Pistol's ignorance of French not to know that *roi* is king.

If thou canst love a fellow of this temper, Kate, whose face is not worth sunburning, that never looks in his glass for love of anything he sees there, let thine eye be thy cook. I speak to thee plain soldier. If thou canst love me for this, take me; if not, to say to thee that I shall die is true – but for thy love, by the Lord, no – yet I love thee too. And while thou liv'st, dear Kate, take a fellow of plain and uncoined constancy; for he perforce must do thee right, because he hath not the gift to woo in other places. For these fellows of infinite tongue, that can rhyme themselves into ladies' favours, they do always reason themselves out again. What! A speaker is but a prater, a rhyme is but a ballad. A good leg will fall; a straight back will stoop; a black beard will turn white; a curled pate will grow bald; a fair face will wither; a full eye will wax hollow: but a good heart, Kate, is the sun and the moon – or rather, the sun, and not the moon; for it shines bright and never changes, but keeps his course truly. If thou would have such a one, take me; and take me, take a soldier; take a soldier, take a king. And what say'st thou then to my love? Speak, my fair, and fairly, I pray thee.

Henry's true motives become apparent in the very next speech:

KATHERINE: Is it possible dat I sould love de *ennemi* of *France*?

HENRY: No, it is not possible you should love the enemy of France, Kate; but in loving me you should love the friend of France, for I love France so well that I will not part with a village of it – I will have it all mine: and Kate, when France is mine, and I am yours, then yours is France, and you are mine.

I love France so well that I will not part with a village of it. Thus *la belle France* and the *belle* Katherine are synonymous. One is the other, love of land conquers all. Henry's dream of reviving the Crusade, another inheritance from his father, produces the sharpest irony of all:

Shall not thou and I, between Saint Dennis and Saint George, compound a boy, half French half English, that shall go to Constantinople and take the Turk by the beard?

(Act V, Scene ii)

Note that Henry does not offer to go on a crusade himself, offering up a putative future son in his place. But the boy they compounded was Henry VI, the coupling producing a child who will preside over disaster.

\* \* \*

At the siege of Harfleur, the Welsh and the Irish touch on the raw nerve of national identity:

FLUELLEN: Captain Macmorris, I think, look you, under your correction, there is not many of your nation –

MACMORRIS: Of my nation? What ish my nation? Ish a villain, and a bastard, and a knave, and a rascal. What ish my nation? Who talks of my nation?

(Act III, Scene ii)

Before the projected row over Celtic identity can flare into full-scale physical aggression, 'the town sounds a parley'. English, Scots, Welsh,

Irish are united once again in their desire to defeat the enemy across the water.

The question of nationhood is still with us, devolution in Scotland and Wales having raised as many problems as it has solved. The fact that the argument between Fluellen and Macmorris takes place during the heat of battle says much about the passion with which the Celts believe in an identity separate from that of the Anglo Saxon. The dispute today is carried on at both a political and a sporting level and, though of recent years an interloper, Italy, has come along to play with the ball, the heart of the yearly rugby fest in the Northern hemisphere is still the hundred years-old Five Nations tournament. It wasn't always so. This strange game with barbaric rules of engagement where big men grunt and groan and fight and push as they grab and grapple with each other, more often than not incurring black eyes, broken noses and bloody wounds from the studs of a stamping boot, was played as a 'friendly' tournament between the four nations of the UK. Then a fifth was admitted, a foreigner whose roads were cobbled and whose loos were holes in the ground. How on earth did they manage to cook so well in such circumstances? And this nation played a rugby that was as far from the biff and bash of this septic isle as is pole dancing from ballet. France was, as ever, the one to beat.

The ground has shifted, though, over the years, and Scotland, Ireland and Wales are united in their hunger to beat England and rejoice at a French win over the 'auld enemy'. The dispute is over a piece of leather whose shape defies all logic, an apt metaphor for what outsiders are unable to perceive as a problem, but which at home manifests itself in vast cultural differences of language, temperament and culture. What is my nation indeed? Shakespeare puts together an almost microcosmic, stereotypical group of representatives – a voluble philosophising Welshman, an aggressive Irishman with a short fuse, literally – his solution to ending the siege of Harfleur is to dynamite the lot – 'By my hand . . . the work·ish ill done . . . I would have blowed up the town, so Chrish save me, la! In an hour. O, 'tish ill done, 'tish ill done!'.

**FLUELLEN: Look you, if you take the matter otherwise than is meant, Captain Macmorris, peradventure I shall think you do not use me with**

that affability as in discretion you ought to use me, look you, being as good a man as yourself, both in the disciplines of war, and in the derivation of my birth, and in other particularities.

MACMORRIS: I do not know you so good a man as myself. So Chrish save me, I will cut off your head.

(Act III, Scene ii)

Here, the Englishman Captain Gower is the appeaser: 'Gentlemen both, you will mistake each other'. Fight the French rather than fight with each other.

What was it that Shakespeare spotted that made him prefigure the modern stereotype of the Irish as hard-drinking, bomb-toting and spoiling for a fight? In this scenario the quarrel is between the Welsh and the Irish, something that today only takes the form of friendly rivalry, a mutual appreciation of each other's culture uniting them rather than separating. After all, Cardiff is closer to Dublin than it is to London as the crow flies, give or take the Irish Sea in between, and the coast of Ireland can be seen from parts of Wales. The landscape of Ceredigion (Cardigan) merges seamlessly with that of Wicklow and as for the Highlands of Scotland, they are further from Westminster than is the coast of France. Is it any wonder that the resentment of hundreds of years of oppressive English rule still survives, not just under the surface but boils over into acts of violence? This dispute over nationhood will run and run until the North of Ireland is united with the South, the West Lothian question is settled in Scotland and the Welsh Assembly has devolved powers to match those of Edinburgh.

\* \* \*

For a play that has traditionally come to embody the great and glorious feats of English imperialism there are an awful lot of Welsh about. And more than any other play, with the exception of the Mortimer / Glendower / Lady Mortimer episode in *Henry IV, Part 1* (see the *Henry IV*s), *Henry V* reveals Shakespeare's appreciation of the people and culture of that small country, Wales. Not only does the character of the voluble Fluellen run right through the play, but his English companion, Captain Gower, has a Welsh name, as does Henry's protagonist, Williams. But the most interesting aspect of the Welshness of the play is Henry's insistence himself on his Welsh credentials:

FLUELLEN: Your grandfather of famous memory, an't please your majesty, and your great-uncle Edward the Black Prince of Wales, as I have read in the chronicles, fought a most prave pattle here in France.

KING HENRY: They did, Fluellen.

FLUELLEN: Your majesty says very true. If your majesties is remember of it, the Welshmen did good service in a garden where leeks did grow, wearing leeks in their Monmouth caps, which your majesty know to this hour is an honourable badge of the service; and I do believe your majesty takes no scorn to wear the leek upon Saint Tavy's day.

KING HENRY: I wear it for a memorable honour;
For I am Welsh, you know, good countryman.

FLUELLEN: All the water in Wye cannot wash your majesty's Welsh plood out of your pody, I can tell you that. God pless it and preserve it, as long as it pleases His grace, and His majesty too!

KING HENRY: Thanks, good my countryman.

FLUELLEN: By Jeshu, I am your majesty's countryman, I care not who know it; I will confess it to all the 'orld. I need not to be ashamed of your majesty, praised be God, so long as your majesty is an honest man.

KING HENRY: God keep me so!

(Act IV, Scene vii)

On the prowl round the camp on the eve of the Battle of Agincourt he encounters Pistol:

PISTOL: The King's a bawcock, and a heart of gold,
A lad of life, an imp of fame;
Of parents good, of fist most valiant.
I kiss his dirty shoe, and from heartstring
I love the lovely bully. What is thy name?

KING HENRY: Harry le Roy.

PISTOL: Le Roy? A Cornish name. Art thou of Cornish crew?

KING HENRY: No, I am a Welshman.

PISTOL: Know'st thou Fluellen?

KING HENRY: Yes.

PISTOL: Tell him I'll knock his leek about his pate
Upon Saint Davy's day.

KING HENRY: Do not you wear your dagger in your cap that day, lest he knock that about yours.

PISTOL: Art thou his friend?

KING HENRY: And his kinsman too.

PISTOL: The *figo* for thee then!

KING HENRY: I thank you. God be with you!

(Act IV, Scene i)

Welsh and proud of it. *En route* to the confrontation with Williams, Bates and Court, he overhears a conversation with the passing Fluellen and Gower:

KING HENRY: Though it appear a little out of fashion,
There is much care and valour in this Welshman.

Sympathy with a fellow Welshman. And it is for Fluellen that Shakespeare reserves the most cogent statement of his appreciation of Welsh culture. Earlier, the yob Pistol has sneered at Fluellen and derided his nationality. The Battle of Agincourt is over but the Battle of the Leek is about to begin.

FLUELLEN: . . . You called me yesterday mountain-squire, but I will make you today a squire of low degree. I pray you fall to – if you can mock a leek, you can eat a leek.

GOWER: Enough, Captain you have astonished him.

FLUELLEN: I say, I will make him eat some part of my leek, or I will peat his pate four days. Bite, I pray you, it is good for your green wound and your ploody coxcomb.

PISTOL: Must I bite?

FLUELLEN: Yes, certainly; and out of doubt, and out of question too, and ambiguities.

PISTOL: By this leek, I will most horribly revenge – I eat and eat, I swear –

FLUELLEN: Eat, I pray you; will you have some more sauce to you leek? There is not enough leek to swear by.

PISTOL: Quiet thy cudgel, thou dost see I eat.

FLUELLEN: Much good do you, scauld knave, heartily. Nay, pray you throw none away, the skin is good for your broken coxcomb. When you take occasions to see leeks hereafter, I pray you mock at 'em, that is all.

PISTOL: Good!

FLUELLEN: Ay, leeks is good. Hold you, there is a groat to heal your pate.

PISTOL: Me a groat?

FLUELLEN: Yes, verily and in truth you shall take it, or I have another leek in my pocket which you shall eat.

(Act V, Scene i)

And he produces a leek of Max Boycean proportions. However, it is left to the Englishman, Gower, to put the cultural boot in with a powerful plea for racial tolerance that goes beyond the local:

GOWER: Go, go, you are a counterfeit cowardly knave. Will you mock at an ancient tradition, begun upon an honourable respect, and worn as a memorable trophy of predeceased valour, and dare not avouch in your deeds any of your words? I have seen you gleeking and galling at this gentleman twice or thrice. You thought, because he could not speak English in the native garb, he could not therefore handle an English cudgel. You find it otherwise, and henceforth let a Welsh correction teach you a good English condition. Fare ye well.

(Act V, Scene i)

Apart from the odd excursion into French, German, Scots and Irish accents, nowhere else in Shakespeare do we find characters who consistently speak in the vernacular. Pastor Hugh Evans in *The Merry Wives of Windsor* and Fluellen, probably played by the same actor, both hold their style of language throughout the plays. It is strange that the compassion and understanding with which Shakespeare treated the Welsh has been consistently ignored by academics and critics alike. From a high point of respect during the reign of the Tudors, the prejudice gathered pace through the industrial revolution and has refused to go away. A language that was described by Shakespeare as 'that pretty Welsh' and 'as sweet as ditties penned, sung by a fair queen in a summers bower' was until recently suppressed and despised. No wonder the Welsh feel a constant need to affirm their identity. Where did Shakespeare get his knowledge of the Welsh? Certainly, the Welsh were held in high respect in the Tudor court, signifying a sea change in the attitude to what many had previously perceived as a barbaric land of mist and mountain. Did it come from his Welsh school master, Thomas Jenkins, at Stratford Upon Avon Grammar School? Or perhaps he learned the songs, myths and legends at the knee of his grandmother, Alys Griffin, a supposed descendant of the high kings of Wales. That would make Shakespeare Welsh . . .

## Notes

1. *Characters of Shakespeare's Plays,* Hazlitt, Wiley & Puttnam, 1945.
2. *Shakespeare: A Critical Study of His Mind and Art,* Edward Dowden. A course of lectures at Trinity College Dublin, 1875.
3. *Political Shakespeare,* ed Jonathon Dolimore and Alan Sinfield, MUP, 1985.
4. *Chronicles of England, Scotland and Ireland,* Holinshed.
5. In 1995 I was making a documentary in Ladywood, Birmingham, England, entitled *Shakespeare on the Estate* and I persuaded a duo drag act whom I met in a laundrette to perform the Katherine / Alice scene (III.iv) at a ladies' hen night in the back room of a pub. Alice teaches Katherine the parts of the body which Katherine attempts to memorise, going back to the beginning each time adding a new one and ending with the bawdy mispronunciations of 'le foot et le count'. The crowd cottoned on and began to enumerate the body parts with the performers, ending with a triumphant shout of 'le fuck et le cunt'. It was clear that the scene is so structured as to invite the participation from the pit in a manner that the reading of the text does not reveal, nor have I seen explored in any contemporary production. Something that The Globe, with its middle class pass at audience involvement would do well to take on board.

# The Henry VIs

A rose by any other name would smell . . .

The *Henry VI*s sprawl and brawl and run wildly up and down the field like a kid with a new pair of football boots that are too big. Tackling here, mis-kicking there, falling in the mud, skewing the ball out of play, diving headers and occasional flashes of brilliant ball control, dribbling past five defenders to plant the ball high in the top left-hand corner of the net. The physical metaphor is particularly apt, for in *Part 1* there are more than twenty-odd fights and on the diminutive stage of The Rose that would have been some feat. And we're not talking here of some slo-mo stylisation or pat-a-cake thrust and parry. We're talking real sword play, with real swords that would have enthused the lads and the half-time pundits would have taken apart. I was once sitting in the front row of a performance of *King John* in a small theatre in Shibuya in Tokyo. As is the Japanese wont, they had placed the theatre on the twenty-third floor of a department building. The stage was the size of a pocket hand-kerchief but the cast numbered about thirty. At one point suddenly all thirty of them erupted onto stage and beat the shit out of each other – and I really mean the shit. Japanese actors fight for real. It was terrifying. I cowered in my seat. It must have been a bit like that at The Rose.

'But this lumbering shapeless chronicle begins to make sense if we can see it as being framed by the death of a hero and the birth of a monster'.[1] Whatever technical and linguistic shortcomings there may be in the plays, the *Henry VI*s cemented Shakespeare's reputation as the coming dramatist of the Elizabethan stage, drawing jealous fire from his contemporaries Ben Jonson and Robert Greene – the latter calling him an 'upstart crow[2], beautified with our feathers' in the belief that Shakespeare had filched material from his play. They had reason to be jealous. The crowds loved these swashbuckling adventures, taking familiar historical figures, turning them inside out and stabbing them in the back – Elizabethan spaghetti westerns.

The overwhelming effect of these plays, despite their unevenness, is a vision of Man the political animal manipulating events and bending fear and superstition to the demands of his ambition. He is simultaneously the perpetrator and victim of his own *real politik* – an existential force that recognises the absurdity of any belief other than in oneself.

In *Part 1* the decline of Britain in the 15th century mirrors that of the 20th – the loss of influence as an international power, and the deterioration of the domestic situation at home; and in both instances, wars are to blame. Division and internal weakness erodes and corrupts government. The last fifty years have seen the collapse of Britain as a real international power as internecine squabbles have riven our two main political parties; the thrust has ceased to be the national interest and become instead the cult of the individual.

If there is a common theme that links the *Henry VIs* with today, it is the fractious rivalry and petty squabbling that has characterised the Conservative and Labour Parties as it did the Houses of York and Lancaster. The lack of belief in collective achievement paved the way for both Richard III and Margaret Thatcher. John of Gaunt's other Eden of long ago was indeed leased out 'as to a tenement farm', in hock to ruthless ambition that served individual interest and favoured the strong. The days of Henry V and the British Empire, of former national glories, became, in both instances, distant, sun-kissed memories lingering on only in heightened myth and Little England xenophobia. The common good sacrificed on the altar of self.

It might not have happened if the throne had not been in the care of a Protector – Humphrey, Duke of Gloucester, the situation complicated by the attempt of the various factions to gain control of the young king. In reality, Henry was only a child when attaining the throne; in the play he's already coming up to adulthood, giving more dramatic scope to the weakness of his reign. As Gloucester and Winchester, Somerset and Warwick struggle for ascendancy, Henry himself anticipates the consequences of such self obsession:

> O, what a scandal is it to our crown
> That two such noble peers as ye should jar!
> Believe me, lords, my tender years can tell
> Civil dissension is a viperous worm
> That gnaws the bowels of the commonwealth.

> *(Part 1*, Act III, Scene i)

But it is left to Exeter to set the in-fighting in context:

> But howsoe'er, no simple man that sees
> This jarring discord of nobility . . .
> But that it doth presage some ill event.
> 'Tis much when sceptres are in children's hands;
> But more when envy breeds unkind division.
> There comes the ruin, there begins confusion.

> *(Part 1*, Act IV, Scene i)

Although written after the *Henry VIs*, the death of Henry V – 'this star of England' – and the internecine strife that followed, is foreshadowed in the Chorus's final speech:

> Small time, but in that small most greatly lived
> This star of England. Fortune made his sword,
> By which the world's best garden he achieved,
> And of it left his son imperial lord.
> Henry the Sixth, in infant bands crown'd King
> Of France and England, did this king succeed,
> Whose state so many had the managing
> That they lost France and made his England bleed . . .

> *(Henry V*, Epilogue)

Henry is hardly cold in his coffin when the family squabbles start:

**WINCHESTER: He was a king blessed of the King of Kings.**
**Upon the French the dreadful Judgement Day**

So dreadful will not be as was his sight.
The battle of the Lord of Hosts he fought;
The Church's prayers made him so prosperous.

GLOUCESTER: The Church? Where is it? Had not churchmen prayed,
His thread of life had not so soon decayed.

(*Part 1*, Act I, Scene i)

And by *Part 2* France has gone with barely a flick of the eyebrow to acknowledge its passing:

KING: Welcome, Lord Somerset. What news from France?

SOMERSET: That all your interest in those territories
Is utterly bereft you; all is lost

KING: Cold news, Lord Somerset; but God's will be done!

YORK: (*aside*) Cold news for me; for I had hope of France
As firmly as I had hope for fertile England.

(*Part 2*, Act III, Scene i)

Thus the dramatic action of *Part 1* polarises into two conflicting interests – internecine squabbles at home and the war with France abroad. As the struggle rages around the weak king, the stage is set for the rise of Shakespeare's most engaging villain, the Duke of York's youngest son, Richard of Gloucester. Thus the plays encompass in their entire sweep the collapse of idealism and the onset of materialism as lost eras of chivalry and honour are mourned over, even as those mourning take pragmatic action to ensure that they never return. Romanticism morphs into brutal realism: Richard II to Bolingbroke; Hotspur to Hal and Prince John; Talbot and son into Margaret and Suffolk; all of them into Richard III. Falstaff's rejection of honour in *Henry IV, Part 1* stands at the door of this charnel house holding up a sign for all that enter to abandon God and principle.

Guarding the door is a soldier as popular and renowned in his time as Wellington, Nelson, Montgomery . . . Talbot stands four-square as the ideal heroic warrior, fighting by the book, upholding ancient chivalric codes of birth and fame – an ideal which the French violate:

. . . Base muleteers of France!

Like peasant footboys do they keep the walls
And dare not take up arms like gentlemen.

*(Part 1*, Act III, Scene ii)

Gentlemen fight with swords, not with guns, and with one arm behind the back.

Rather than fight and run away to live and fight another day, his son, John Talbot, inherits his father's romantic set of rules of engagement with the inevitable consequences. Beaten back by the French, outnumbered, Talbot pleads with son John to save himself.

TALBOT: If we both stay, we both are sure to die.

JOHN: Then let me stay, and, father, do you fly.
Upon my death the French can little boast;
In yours they will; in you all hopes are lost.
Flight cannot stain the honour you have won;

TALBOT: And leave my followers here to fight alone?
My age was never tainted with such shame.

JOHN: And shall my youth be guilty of such blame?
No more can I be severed from you side
Than can yourself yourself in twain divide.
Stay, go, do what you will – the like do I;
For live, I will not if my father die.

(Act IV, Scene vi)

As at the Somme, the American War of Independence, or the Valley of Death, so England is defeated by the intransigent stubbornness of a leader who fought by the book and eschewed tactics. In Act IV.iv, Somerset's is a lone voice raised against the wholesale adulation heaped on Talbot's life and death:

SOMERSET: This expedition was by York and Talbot
Too rashly plotted . . .
. . . The over-daring Talbot
Hath sullied all his gloss of former honour
By this unheedful, desperate, wild adventure.

(Act IV, Scene iv)

The French, a bunch of cads, have no such compunction about playing the game. Rouen is captured by soldiers disguised as peasants and at Orléans the English leaders are picked off by snipers. Rather than reading this as anti-French propaganda, it is better to look at it in the context of all's fair in war. If you want to win, there are no rules. The French won. No point looking down your nose. This is particularly true of the contrast between the two main protagonists – a bastard peasant girl versus an aristocratic nobleman; evasion and trickery versus old-fashioned heroics. And in contrast with John Talbot, Joan is ready to reject both her father and her family to save her neck. Even her name – *la Pucelle* – has in it implicit irony, the word meaning both virgin and whore. After her capture and burning at the stake, the marriage of Henry to Margaret of Anjou is greeted as an act of gross betrayal of the English cause and the concluding of an 'effeminate peace' something that degrades and dishonours the memory of the fallen. Richard is not alone when he displays disgust at the idea of Henry's French nuptials.

> **RICHARD: . . . After the slaughter of so many peers,**
> **So many captains, gentlemen and soldiers**
> **That in this quarrel have been overthrown**
> **And sold their bodies for their country's benefit . . .**

> (Act V, Scene iv)

This is Joan of Arc's posthumous revenge. Talbot, Salisbury and Bedford may represent an aristocratic Old Boys' club, but it is Joan and the French who embody the new political reality, setting Shakespeare's agenda for the rest of the canon. We await the growth of Richard III, passing through some pretty awesome Machiaveli on the way.

\* \* \*

The *Henry VI*s are notable for the emergence for the first time on stage of female power. Indeed, the plays have often been pressed into service to advance the cause of feminism. All three female characters in *Part 1* attempt to rule their menfolk – often by sorcery. This has been seen as proof that Shakespeare was a misogynist – a women-hater. This ignores the social context of a world where real power was invested solely in the hands of men. It is hardly surprising that women resorted to desperate measures in order to achieve some crumb of equality.

Two female figures dominate the action. If Joan of Arc – Joan la Pucelle – looms over *Henry VI, Part 1*, then Margaret of Anjou – Queen Margaret – emerges as a potent political force in *Henry VI, Parts 2* and *3*.

Trading on the audience's belief in the occult and the supernatural, Shakespeare allows the character of Joan to be the victim of a massive dollop of Elizabethan propaganda, investing her with the qualities of a witch – 'A disciple and limb of the Fiend . . . that used false enchantment and sorcery'. But it was not witchcraft that defeated the Dauphin but brilliant sword play, so it is hardly surprising that having faced down the entire English army the humiliated leaders believe that the only way they could have lost the battle was through sorcery. (Rather like Sir Clive Woodward explaining away the rugby annihilation in 2005 of the British Lions by the All Blacks as being due to the spear tackle on the captain, O'Driscoll in the first minute of the first test.) 'The holy maid' sees herself as something else – the saviour of France – and if no male is going to step up to the plate then a woman will. And Shakespeare gives her the power of oratory so to do. No sorcery there, only eloquent language, such as that used by Henry V to exhort his troops into one final push into the breach; language that convinces Burgundy not to fight on the side of the English but to return to the fold. 'Look on thy country, look on fertile France,' she begs.

> LA PUCELLE: . . . And see the cities and the towns defac'd
> By wasting ruin of the cruel foe;
> As looks the mother on her lowly babe
> When death doth close his tender dying eyes,
> See, see the pining malady of France;
> Behold the wounds, the most unnatural wounds,
> Which thou thyself has give her woeful breast.
>
> (*Part 1*, Act III, Scene v)

Burgundy is persuaded – 'Either she hath bewitch'd me with her words or nature makes me suddenly relent'. 'Done like a Frenchman,' Joan says and then adds an aside guaranteed to get a laugh from the groundlings but dangerous to attribute to Shakespeare rather than an actor looking for a cheap rise – 'Turn and turn again'.

Described at first as a shepherdess and a prophet, Joan is caricatured and parodied throughout the play as the converse of the English hero, Talbot (it is said that strong men wept at his death in Act IV). The two characters stand in apposition throughout the play, albeit stylistically from a totally different perspective. Where Talbot is treated with dignity and respect, Joan is pilloried and degraded. Having declared, 'I must not yield to any rites of love / For my professions sacred from above' (Act I.ii), she seduces the Dauphin (Act II.i). Where Talbot's death is heroic, Joan twists and lies in a desperate attempt to save her life. 'O, burn her, burn her: hanging is too good' (Act V.iv), says her father. Not exactly a leaf out of the Talbots' familial bonding book. She claims virginity, then pregnancy identifying some half dozen fathers; when all else fails, she curses. For her, as for Falstaff, honour is a mere scutcheon. What use is it if you're dead? Leave that to the Talbots. The brazenness of her fabrications to save her neck (and France) is refreshingly shameless. Better to be expedient. In war, idealism has no place. With or without the aid of the supernatural, there is still a battle to be fought where men will die for real. No point sitting on your fanny waiting for a miracle to happen. She is acutely aware of her mortality. As she says to the Dauphin:

> LA PUCELLE: At all times will you have my power alike?
> Sleeping or waking, must I still prevail,
> Or will you blame and lay the fault on me?
> Improvident soldiers! Had your watch been good
> This sudden mischief never could have fall'n.
>
> (Act II, Scene i)

No saint, but no witch either. More a tough, street-fighting girl for whom the realities of war demand a certain kind of behaviour. And if myth and magic help the cause so much the better. Instead, in a messy ending, the English defeat Joan by ganging up on her. But the triumph is shortlived. This was to be their last success in France.

Margaret of Anjou is another kettle of *poisson*. Sorcery and witchcraft of another kind. Acting the pimp, Suffolk wins her for Henry's hand with a titillating seductive litany of her qualities and then falls for her himself. Thus he becomes a power behind the weak throne, secure in the sexual favours of the queen, safe in the knowledge that the naïve, ineffectual Henry would suspect nothing. Margaret is a prototype Macbeth, a female counterpart of Richard of Gloucester, by whom she is outwitted but whom she outlives. York, no angel himself, rails against her:

> She wolf of France . . .
> O tiger's heart wrapped in a woman's hide!
> How couldst thou drain the life-blood of the child,
> To bid the father wipe his eyes withal,
> And yet be seen to bear a woman's face?
> Women are soft, mild, pitiful, and flexible;
> Thou stern, obdurate, flinty, rough, remorseless.
> Biddest thou me rage? Why, now thou hast thy wish;
> Wouldst have me weep? Why, now thou hast thy will;
> For raging wind blows up incessant showers,
> And when the rage allays, the rain begins.
>
> *(Part 3*, Act I, Scene iv)

As Margaret has just wiped his face with a napkin steeped in the blood of Rutland, his murdered son, York's rage is somewhat understandable; yet he himself has been guilty of callous acts in the course of his quest for the throne. His words are wild and whirling, the emotions running the gamut, the histrionic actor demonstrating the highs and lows of rhetorical passion. Margaret teaches York a lesson in brutal callousness. Waiting until his tirade is over and his passion spent in incoherent weeping, she says, 'And here's to right our gentle hearted king' and stabs him. And:

> Off with his head, and set it on York gates;
> So York may overlook the town of York.

* * *

If civil war is a domestic struggle to ascertain what kind of government the people desire for themselves, then anyone can play. Midway between the death of Gloucester and the start of the Wars of the Roses, the boys are joined by an unlikely figure from the common folk – Jack Cade. The original Cade Rebellion, born of genuine grievances, had the support of the landowners and gentry. In *Henry VI, Part 2* we are confronted by a man gathering to his standard the illiterate and uneducated under the pretence that he is the rightful heir to the throne. The measures that he would institute would warm the cockles of the New Brutalists. The lawyers would all be killed, there would be no more reading and writing, and henceforth the laws would all come out of his mouth. The Tories would have loved him. Home Secretary in no time. The only thing a bit *de trop* maybe, would be having the 'pissing conduit' run with red claret.

This dynamic trouble-maker from Kent has been enlisted by York to aid his cause by gathering around him a large contingent of peasants who are encouraged to revolt on the promise of plenty.

> CADE: Be brave, then, for your captain is brave, and vows reformation. There shall be in England seven halfpenny loaves sold for a penny; the three-hooped pot shall have ten hoops; and I will make it felony to drink small beer. All the realm shall be in common, and in Cheapside shall my palfrey go to grass. And when I am king, as king I will be –
>
> ALL: God save your majesty!
>
> CADE: I thank you, good people. There shall be no money; all shall eat and drink on my score; and I will apparel them all in one livery, that they may agree like brothers and worship me their lord.
>
> (*Henry VI, Part 2*, Act IV, Scene ii)

Shakespeare's portrait of the common people is hardly a flattering one. And his version of this Kentish rebellion is somewhat unbelievable. (There has always been a pocket of insurrection in this plummy heartland of English garden conservatism. In 1985 the Kent miners, all six thousand of them, were the last to capitulate). The people are dimwitted, fickle, destructive, galvanised into action at the thought of rich pickings but are cowed and give up easily when threatened.

The whole episode has the atmosphere of a demented carnival about it. York's description of Cade stuck full of weapons conjures up the image of a grotesque Morris dancer:

> . . . I have seen
> Him caper upright like a wild Morisco,
> Shaking the bloody darts as he his bells.

(*Part 2*, Act III, Scene i)

This frenzied carnival spirit runs right through the rebellion, giving Cade a wild anarchic power. There is something alluring in the mumbo-jumbo of his mixed-up philosophy, an appeal to popular grievances that would have found many takers in his audience – lower taxes, lower prices (inflation was a big Elizabethan issue), but most of all, power in the hands of the people. This pot pourri of communism, fascism, theocracy and free booze had an instant attraction about it. And the promise of direct action to cure all their ills rallied many of the poor to the cause. Who wouldn't thrill at the idea of setting 'London Bridge afire, and if you can the Tower too'? The grassroots rebellion, timed and linked as it is to a shady Yorkist cause, offers a picture of power at its most fluid and its most dangerous. Amidst all the absurdity of the affair is a serious threat to government and civil order. If not contained, then anarchy will rule and York and his followers would have been hard pushed to bring the rebels back into line once they'd tasted popular power. When the mob go on the rampage in *Julius Caesar*, the flames, fanned by Antony's oratory, send the fire out of control. The mob seek out the leaders responsible for Caesar's assassination. They come across Cinna, not the conspirator, but the poet. They kill him anyway, for his rotten poetry.

This same danger of indiscriminate retribution runs through the Cade revolt. The attack on Lord Say, sent to try and negotiate, is most chilling:

CADE: . . . Thou has most traitorously corrupted the youth of the realm in erecting a grammar school; and whereas, before, our forefathers had no other books but the score and the tally, thou hast caused printing to be used; and, contrary to the King, his crown, and dignity, thou hast built a paper-mill. It will be proved to thy face that thou hast men about thee that usually talk of a noun and a verb, and such abominable words as no Christian ear can endure to hear. Thou hast appointed justices of peace, to call poor men before them about matters they were not able to answer. Moreover, thou hast put them in prison; and because they could not read, thou hast hanged them; when, indeed, only for that cause they have been most worthy to live . . .

*(Part 2,* Act IV, Scene vii)

There are genuine grievances here. We are reminded of how privilege and elitism look from outside the circle by those who are not part of that inner coterie. Culture and civilisation seem to be under attack here, but in a society where a man can be hanged merely for not being able to read, it is small wonder that those who are illiterate through no fault of their own revolt. History has not confined this apparent philistinism to the mass. Zahir Hadid's stunning design for the Cardiff Opera House was sunk by a virulent campaign against opera as an elitist pursuit by the current First Secretary of Wales and the then Lord Mayor. Cardiff got a rugby stadium instead.

We are reminded that Shakespeare may not often give voice to the commoner, but when he does, it is usually to articulate social injustice. The ludicrous interlude of the blind and crippled Simpcox, who is tricked by Gloucester into seeing and jumping, has a serious intent. As they are hustled off, Simpcox's wife cries out, 'Alas! sir, we did it for pure need' (Act II.i).

Cade at such moments becomes one of Shakespeare's most articulate social critics, but the problem with such a mixed-up philosophy – a cross between democratic utopianism and fascist dictatorship – is that it has no rules other than its own. The Clerk of Chatham is dragged off to be hanged with his pen and ink horn about his neck, merely for being able to read and keep accounts; Lord Say's head is severed and put on a pole so that he and his son-in-law may kiss. It is significant that Cade's most prominent sidekick and voluble supporter is Dick the Butcher, author of the most memorable line of the play: 'The first thing we do, let's kill all the lawyers'. Guaranteed to get a standing ovation.

As his sense of power grows, so Cade's targets progress from attacking the rich to attacking anyone who has something he desires:

The proudest peer in the realm shall not wear a head on his shoulders, unless he pay me tribute; there shall not a maid be married, but she shall pay to me her maidenhead, ere they have it.

It is ironic that the very era that Cade evokes as England's golden age, the reign of Henry V, is the very thing that undoes him. He says to the Staffords, also attempting to negotiate – I use the term loosely – 'Rebellious hinds, the filth and scum of Kent . . .':

**CADE: . . . Go to, sirrah, tell the King from me that for his father's sake, Henry the Fifth, in whose time boys went to span-counter for French crowns, I am content he shall reign; but I'll be Protector over him.**

**DICK: And furthermore we'll have the Lord Say's head for selling the dukedom of Maine.**

**CADE: . . . And more than that, he can speak French . . .**

*(Part 2*, Act IV, Scene ii)

At a third attempt, Clifford convinces the rabble to return to their homes by appealing to that same patriotic, xenophobic fear of foreigners. Contemptuously dismissing Cade, Clifford says,

**Will he conduct you through the heart of France,**
**And make the meanest of you earls and dukes?**

*(Part 2*, Act IV, Scene viii)

And home they go. Cade is left to ponder on the shifting sands of popular support. 'Was ever feather so lightly blown to and fro as this multitude? The name of Henry the Fifth hales them to an hundred mischiefs, and leaves me desolate'. The last we see of him he is eating grass. But with his disappearance, a light goes out of the play and his dying boast – 'Tell Kent from me, she hath lost her best man' – strikes a chord with audiences, left once again with the aristocratic mayhem of yet more battles for the hollow crown.

\* \* \*

Wakefield, Towton, Barnet and Tewkesbury. These are the battles at the heart of the action of the three plays. In real life, over 50,000 men died at Towton, more than had ever died on British soil before or since. In one simple, devastating scene, Shakespeare characterises the senseless slaughter, the inconsequential futility of these civil broils. Henry, seeking solitude and solace away from the battlefield, sits on a molehill and muses on the impotence of kingship. He longs for a simple existence away from the responsibility of the cares of state:

> O God! methinks it were a happy life
> To be no better than a homely swain;
> To sit upon a hill, as I do now,
> To carve out dials quaintly, point by point,
> Thereby to see the minutes how they run:
> How many makes the hour full complete,
> How many hours brings about the day,
> How many days will finish up the year,
> How many years a mortal man may live.
> When this is known, then to divide the times:
> So many hours must I tend my flock,
> So many hours must I make my rest,
> So many hours must I contemplate,
> So many hours must I sport myself,
> So many days my ewes have been with young,
> So many weeks ere the poor fools will ean,
> So many years ere I shall shear the fleece.
> So minutes, hours, days, months, and years,
> Passed over to the end they were created,
> Would bring white hairs unto a quiet grave.
> Ah, what a life were this! How sweet! How lovely!
>
> (*Part 3*, Act II, Scene v)

A man enters lugging a body which he hopes to rob, but removing the helmet he makes a grim discovery. 'Who's this?' he cries:

> . . . O God! It is my father's face,
> Whom in this conflict I, unwares, have killed.
> O, heavy times, begetting such events!

As if this irony were not enough, from the other side of the stage another man enters, this time a father carrying the body of his son.

> O pity, God, this miserable age!
> What stratagems, how fell, how butcherly,

**Erroneous, mutinous, and unnatural,**
**This deadly quarrel daily doth beget!**

The folly and impossibility of Henry's fantasy is exposed as he witnesses the dead sons and fathers. He cries out:

**KING HENRY: Woe above woe! Grief more than common grief!**
**O that my death would stay these ruthful deeds!**
**O, pity, pity, gentle heaven, pity!**
**The red rose and the white are on his face,**
**The fatal colours of our striving houses . . .**

York, Lancaster, white rose, red – What did it mean? Where was God in all this? Divine right . . . the scene has a savage beauty. The breakdown of moral order. While Henry sits on a molehill and longs for the life of a simple shepherd, the reality of the chaos he has helped create surrounds him. It is a familiar royal lament. Richard II and Henry V both, at moments of extreme personal crisis, cry out for the balm of a simple existence. But the reality is other. For Richard II it is assassination, for Henry it is Agincourt.

* * *

At the heart of *Part 1* and the next three plays lies the scene in the Temple garden, one of the few scenes for which there does not appear to be any factual basis. The garden metaphor prevalent in Richard II is here taken up once again as flowers become the symbol of governance. In diverting the plot away from mangled history, Shakespeare finds a flight of poetic imagination conspicuously lacking in most of *Part 1*. The action is driven on by Richard Plantagenet, Richard of Gloucester, later Richard III. As early as Act II.iv, we see the emergence of the confrontational style that is to bewitch and bother the course of England in the next period of time:

**RICHARD: Great lords and gentlemen, what means this**
**silence?**
**Dare no man answer in a case of truth?**

**SUFFOLK: Within the Temple Hall we were too loud;**
**The garden here is more convenient.**

RICHARD: Then say at once if I maintained the truth;
Or else was wrangling in Somerset in th'error?

SUFFOLK: Faith, I have been a truant in the law
And never yet could frame my will to it;
And therefore frame the law unto my will.

SOMERSET: Judge you, my lord of Warwick, then between us.

Warwick produces the ultimate in fence-sitting –

WARWICK: Between two hawks, which flies the higher pitch;
Between two dogs, which hath the deeper mouth;
Between two blades, which bears the better temper;
Between two horses, which doth bear him best;
Between two girls, which hath the merriest eye,
I have perhaps some shallow spirit of judgement;
But in these nice sharp quillets of the law,
Good faith, I am no wiser than a daw . . .

– But Richard is having none of it. He's feeling punchy.

RICHARD: Since you are tongue-tied and so loath to speak,
In dumb significants proclaim your thoughts.
Let him that is a true-born gentleman
And stands upon the honour of his birth,
If he suppose that I have pleaded truth,
From off this briar pluck a white rose with me.

SOMERSET: Let him that is no coward nor no flatterer,
But dare maintain the party of the truth,
Pluck a red rose from off this thorn with me.

Somerset calls him a liar. Warwick immediately jumps off the fence:

WARWICK: I love no colours; and, without all colour
Of base insinuating flattery,
I pluck this white rose with Plantagenet.

SUFFOLK: I pluck this red rose with young Somerset,
And say withal I think he held the right.

(Act II, Scene iv)

Two all.

And so they're off and running. The lawyer comes down on Richard's side, giving him the legal nod. It's a moot point as to whether it would have made any difference had the lawyer opted for Somerset – the die is cast; red and white roses merely an excuse for prosecuting the argument. Thus far, Richard is seen only as a younger son upholding the honour of his family. The monster is yet to come.

The way is paved by Suffolk. At the conclusion of *Part 1* he discloses his motives, Richard-like.

> SUFFOLK: Thus Suffolk hath prevailed; and thus he goes,
> As did the youthful Paris once to Greece,
> With hope to find the event in love
> But prosper better than the Trojan did.
> Margaret shall now be Queen, and rule the King;
> But I will rule both her, the King, and realm.

*(Part 1*, Act V, Scene v)

In *Part 2* Suffolk emerges as a man devoid of all sense of political responsibility, a fitting companion for Margaret, the two of them hell-bent on ruthlessly manipulating the course of England's destiny from behind the weak throne, partners in amorous amorality. Henry's sexual inadequacy propels Margaret into Suffolk's bed, the place she believes will lead to the power she craves. It was a huge disappointment to find that, far from ruling England, she is surrounded by feuding noblemen, each with an ambitious agenda to fulfil. They are obstacles in her path, none more so than the king's Protector, Gloucester, and his wife:

> QUEEN: . . . As that proud dame, the Lord Protector's wife.
> She sweeps it through the court with troops of ladies,
> More like an empress than Duke Humphrey's wife.
> Strangers in court do take her for the queen.
> She bears a duke's revenues on her back,
> And in her heart she scorns our poverty.
> Shall I not live to be avenged on her?

*(Part 2*, Act I, Scene iii)

The sharks, scenting blood, have gathered:

> GLOUCESTER: . . . A heart unspotted is not easily daunted.

> The purest spring is not so free from mud
> As I am clear from treason to my sovereign.
>
> (Act III, Scene i)

Gloucester was a naïve, an innocent; the guiltless need fear no danger. He just didn't get it. But Margaret backed the wrong horse. Suffolk's duplicity and his bid for ultimate power was always going to end in disaster, and it was only a matter of time before the efforts of the fighting factions, once they had got rid of the Gloucesters, turned their attention his way. Do we feel any sympathy for Margaret as she cradles the severed head of Suffolk?

> QUEEN: Here may his head lie on my throbbing breast;
> But where's the body that I should embrace?
>
> (Act IV, Scene iv)

I don't think so.

*Parts 2* and *3* show once again the dangers of hiding behind dodgy legal advice as an excuse for going to war, and the consequences of such duplicity. Attempting to apply a moral wash to actions that are plainly illegal leads only to the breakdown of moral order. The repercussions of the war in Iraq have led to the excesses of Guantanamo Bay, Abu Graib and the slaughter of thousands of innocent Iraqi civilians. When big men fight it is the little who get caught in the crossfire. The disintegration of society into chaos is a consequence of politicians eager to hide duplicitous actions behind a veil of self-justification. Thus in *Part 2*, Gloucester's enemies are eager to convince themselves and the world of the righteousness of their behaviour. By *Part 3*, moral order has broken down and trust is nowhere to be found. Characters continually lie for their own ends and go back on their word; oaths are broken right, left and centre, and loyalty lasts only as long as a player is on the way up. A new breed of power broker is on the scene. Richard of Gloucester defines existential *real politik* thus –

> But for a kingdom any oath may be broken;
> I will break a thousand oaths to reign one year.

This ethical vacuum was made for Richard, much as political and civil chaos, throughout history, have bred other such tyrants. 'Order', it seems, can only be restored by strong measures, the people subdued and brought into line by brute force and the elimination of dissent. And in Richard's case, his mental distortion is mirrored by his physical; indeed, he patently revels in his indigested and deformed shape.

It comes as a surprise to discover that Richard was not always the captivating monster who has thrilled and delighted audiences for four hundred years. Your starter for ten – who said the following?

> See how the morning opes her golden gates,
> And takes her farewell of the glorious sun!
> How well resembles it the prime of youth,
> Trimmed like a younker prancing to his love!

Wrong. It was the young Richard (*Part 3*, Act II.i). In the beginning, there is no hint of the tyrant to come and it is not until Act III.ii, that we get the first suggestion that it is a psychological reaction to his deformity that drives his ruthless quest for the crown:

> RICHARD: . . . Then, since this earth affords no joy to me
> But to command, to check, to o'erbear such
> As are of better person than myself,
> I'll make my heaven to dream upon the crown . . .
>
> *(Part 3*, Act III, Scene ii)

Just as Johnny Depp distorts Willy Wonka's callousness in the film of *Charlie and the Chocolate Factory* by attributing his heartlessness to a loveless childhood, so Shakespeare distorts Richard's motives by making his handicap an amoral virtue:

> Why, love forswore me in my mother's womb;
> And, for I should not deal in her soft laws,
> She did corrupt frail nature with some bribe
> To shrink mine arm up like a withered shrub;
> To make an envious mountain on my back,
> Where sits deformity to mock my body . . .

Mae Rose Cottage says in *Under Milk Wood*[3], 'I'll sin till I blow up'. Richard, too, is concerned with sin on an inhuman scale of myth-making proportions:

I'll drown more sailors than the mermaid shall;
I'll slay more gazers than the basilisk;
I'll play the orator as well as Nestor,
Deceive more slily than Ulysses could,
And, like a Sinon, take another Troy.
I can add colours to chameleon,
Change shapes with Protheus for advantages,
And set the murderous Machiavel to school.

*(Part 3*, Act III, Scene ii)

However, it is Henry VI who gives the myth substance, accurately fingering the dark future that England is about to face:

And thus I prophesy, that many a thousand,
Which now mistrust no parcel of my fear,
And many an old man's sigh, and many a widow's,
And many an orphan's water-standing eye –
Men for their sons', wives for their husbands',
And orphans for their parents' timeless death –
Shall rue the hour that ever thou wast born.
The owl shrieked at thy birth, aboding luckless time;
Dogs howled, and hideous tempest shook down trees . . .

(Act V, Scene vi)

Henry's prophesy gives Richard a new apocalyptic dimension. Richard has only one aim – to get the crown – and to do that he will kill as many people as he needs to kill. The crown matters and mattered little to Henry, and in death as in life his piety as a Christian shines through. As far as he is concerned, Richard has come 'to bite the world'. And at that moment, Richard kills him.

RICHARD: I'll hear not more; die, prophet; in thy speech!
*He Stabs him.*
For this, amongst the rest, was I ordained.

KING HENRY: Aye, and for much more slaughter after this.
O, God, forgive my sins, and pardon thee!
*He dies.*

Metaphorically sitting on the body of the dead king, Richard muses on the truth of his predictions:

The midwife wondered; and the women cried
'O, Jesus bless us, he is born with teeth!'
And so I was, which plainly signified
That I should snarl and bite and play the dog.
Then, since the heavens have shap'd my body so,
Let hell make crooked my mind to answer it.
I have no brother, I am like no brother;
And this word 'love', which greybeards call divine,
Be resident in men like one another
And not in me; I am myself alone.

I am myself alone. I kill therefore I am. Echoes of Franz Moor in Schiller's *Die Raüber* – 'God forgive me, I am no ordinary murderer.' Richard isolates himself from the conflicts around him. He even distances himself from his father, whose sole ambition it was to restore the House of York to the throne. But Richard is interested in power simply for its own sake, and the action is now no longer about the struggle of the two great Houses of York and Lancaster; it is about the complete breakdown of moral order, where the man of no belief tears up the rule book and rips apart the bonds of blood. The *frisson* of excitement will be rewarded for us in the next play.

**Notes**

1. *Green's Groatsworth of Wit, Bought with a Million of Repentance,* Pamphlet 1592.
2. *Shakepeare's Political Drama,* Alexander Legatt, Routledge, London 1988.
3. By Dylan Thomas.

# Richard III

## God say Amen

For a play that contains one of the world's great charismatic, quintessential villains, *Richard III* is pretty impenetrable. If you don't know what's gone on in the previous seven plays, haven't read it, had it explained to you, are seeing it for the first time, then a good third is unintelligible.

> RICHARD: Now is the winter of our discontent
> Made glorious summer by this sun of York,
> And all the clouds that loured upon our house
> In the deep bosom of the ocean buried.
> Now are our brows bound with victorious wreaths,
> Our bruisèd arms hung up for monuments,
> Our stern alarums changed to merry meetings,
> Our dreadful marches to delightful measures.
> Grim-visaged war hath smoothed his wrinkled front,
> And now, instead of mounting barbèd steeds
> To fright the souls of fearful adversaries,
> He capers nimbly in a lady's chamber
> To the lascivious pleasing of a lute.
>
> (Act I, Scene i)

What on earth does all that mean? No use looking in your Arden notes to see that the winter of discontent has nothing to do with Callaghan's misery, or that the sun of York is a dynastical pun. Sure, you can get the general gist of it, but without knowledge (and concentration in the very first minute of the play) the nuance and subtlety are lost. And who on earth is that batty old bag Margaret? What's she on?

QUEEN MARGARET: . . . Hear me, you wrangling pirates, that fall out
In sharing that which you have pilled from me!
Which of you trembles not that looks on me?
If not, that I am Queen you bow like subjects,
Yet that, by you deposed, you quake like rebels? . . .
. . . I do find more pain in banishment
Than death can yield me here by my abode.
A husband and a son thou ow'st to me –
And thou a kingdom – all of you allegiance.
This sorrow that I have, by right is yours,
And all the pleasure you usurp are mine. . . .
Did York's dread curse prevail so much with heaven
. . . That Henry's death, my lovely Edward's death,
Their kingdom's loss, my woeful banishment,
Should all but answer for that peevish brat?
Can curses pierce the clouds and enter heaven?
Why then, give way, dull clouds, to my quick curses!

(Act I, Scene iii)

Were Elizabethan audiences more knowledgeable about their own history than we are today? Richard III was defeated at Bosworth some seventy odd years before Shakespeare was born. Going back to tell the story of Richard II is the equivalent for us of going back to about 1750. In a world where today 25% of young people can't even name the current Prime Minister, it's a pretty safe bet that Wellington's legacy is simply a load of old boots. Is a folk memory and an oral tradition stronger than an electronic one? I believe an audience's knowledge of anything other than their recent history has always been pretty patchy and four hundred years ago, with no mass media to inform and literacy confined to a very few, the chances of anything other than a wholly inaccurate version of the past were pretty slim. What must have made the difference in the theatre, then, was a fascination with the Elizabethan equivalent of a soap opera. For *Eastenders* and the Windsors, read *Shakespeare's Serial History Plays* – The Plantaganets Versus the Tudors. At a time when the population of London was not much more that 150,000, compared with today an extraordinarily high percentage could be found at any one time inside a theatre, hungry for the next episode in the ongoing dynastical saga of England's war crimes. When James

Burbage, Theatre Manager, elder brother of Richard Burbage, the leading actor in Shakespeare's company, invented the box office, bringing bystanders off the streets and corralling them in the wooden Os of the newly-invented theatres, he created an unprecedented demand. And what you couldn't see for free you were determined to pay for, in case you missed anything. Similar to Sky, really, buying up world rights for sporting events. If you want to see it, pay for it. The Elizabethans did, in their thousands. Mind you, it must have been pretty confusing getting the histories out of order – the *Henry VI*s and *Richard III* preceding the *Henry IV*s and *Henry V*, and then *Richard II* tagged onto the end of *Richard III* – 5, 6, 7, 8, 1, 2, 3, 4. It certainly accounts, when played in chronological order, for the disjointed style of the language and the odd story-telling technique. Shakespeare's mastery of the material reaches a psychological depth by the time he reaches 'the skipping king' that was almost non-existent in the *Henry VI*s. But at least the figure of Richard Crookback followed on sequentially, allowing us to enjoy the full flavour of his ascent to the throne.

Despite coming out of order, *Richard III* is the natural culmination of two tetralogies, spanning the 100 years from Richard II, of bloody slaughter in the name of divine right. Brother kills brother, mother betrays son, cousin fights cousin, father slaughters son, all in the name of 'the golden round', 'the hollow crown', 'a little brief authority', proving – if it ever needed proving – that blood is not thicker than water when it comes to the exercise and possession of raw, naked power:

> **DUCHESS OF YORK:** Accursèd and unquiet wrangling days,
> How many of you have mine eyes beheld!
> My husband lost his life to get the crown,
> And often up and down my sons were tossed
> For me to joy and weep their gain and loss;
> And being seated, and domestic broils
> Clean overblown, themselves the conquerors
> Make war upon themselves, brother to brother,
> Blood to blood, self against self. O preposterous
> And frantic outrage, end thy damnèd spleen,
> Or let me die, to look on earth no more!

> (Act II, Scene iv)

Is this slaughter divine? Henry V attributes the carnage at Agincourt of ten thousand French dead to twenty-nine English to an act of God. Richmond, at the end of *Richard III*, prays to the Almighty to give him the strength in his right arm to kill as many of his enemies as possible. Once again, it takes a butcher to beat a butcher – a Churchill to overcome a Hitler, a Bush to beat a Hussein. (Don't mention Bin Laden). Ruthless pragmatism, superior numbers, inferior tactics or more sophisticated fire power? If God is around, so much the better, but don't bank on it. Better get out the Bullworker, practise your place kicks. Won't do to have God standing by helplessly as you miss a penalty. Richard understands this. He is the quintessential man of action. The one who says, 'This is what I'm going to do', and does it.

> RICHARD: . . . He cannot live, I hope, and must not die
> Till George be packed with post-horse up to heaven.
> I'll in, to urge his hatred more to Clarence
> With lies well steeled with weighty arguments;
> And, if I fail not in my deep intent,
> Clarence hath not another day to live;
> Which done, God take King Edward to His mercy
> And leave the world for me to bustle in!
> For then I'll marry Warwick's youngest daughter.
> What though I killed her husband and her father?
> The readiest way to make the wench amends
> Is to become her husband and her father,
> The which I will – not all so much for love
> As for another secret close intent
> By marrying her which I must reach unto.
> But yet I run before my horse to market:
> Clarence still breathes; Edward still lives and reigns;
> When they are gone, then must I count my gains.

(Act I, Scene i)

At a time when the authority of the Church held the world in awe of its power, where fear of retribution in this life and after held sway, and superstition bred terror in ready minds, the man of no belief in anything other than existential action is a killer. And if he has a smile on his face at the same time, we love him. Until we, too, succumb to his savagery. Sharing knowledge and insight with Richard, even sympathising with him against our better judgement, we are not just detached spectators: Richard enlists us as his accomplices and, like the character of Vice in the old morality plays, presents himself as a friend to the audience. But, as the play develops, we discover that this friend is not to be trusted. Appalled, we realise that we have let him get away with murder – literally. ('One person can make a difference and every person must try' – JFK.) It is easier to stand by, do nothing, appease, rather than stick one's neck out and risk having it cut off.

Life has mirrored art in giving us a distorted historical view of Richard, our knowledge almost entirely governed by Shakespeare's play. Will the real *Richard III* please stand up? Is it the one with the hump and the withered arm, denounced by successive centuries as a child murderer and a ruthless butcher of wife and family? Or the 'good king', a propaganda victim of the over-arching ambitions and political skullduggery of the Tudors whose patronage, Shakespeare recognised, must butter his bread? The view of others – not mine.

Acres of paper have been covered in rationalising Richard's behaviour as a result of the debit in his psychological makeup caused by Shakespeare's depiction of his deformity. Not helped of course by Richard's own admission of his personal problem in coming to grips with his physical defects. We gather as much as early as *Henry VI, Part 3*, Act III.ii, when he declares 'love foreswore me in my mother's womb' and resolving,

> . . . since this earth affords no joy to me
> But to command, to check, to o'erbear such
> As are of better person than myself,
> I'll make my heaven to dream upon the crown . . .

We are thus totally prepared for the amplification of this when immediately as part of his opening soliloquy in *Richard III* he turns and fixes us with his engaging grin and declares:

> . . . But I, that am not shaped for sportive tricks
> Nor made to court an amorous looking-glass;
> I, that am rudely stamped, and want love's majesty
> To strut before a wanton ambling nymph;

> I, that am curtailed of this fair proportion,
> Cheated of feature by dissembling Nature,
> Deformed, unfinished, sent before my time
> Into this breathing world, scarce half made up,
> And that so lamely and unfashionable
> That dogs bark at me as I halt by them –
> Why I, in this weak piping time of peace,
> Have no delight to pass away the time,
> Unless to spy my shadow in the sun
> And descant on mine own deformity.
> And therefore, since I cannot prove a lover
> To entertain these fair well-spoken days,
> I am determined to prove a villain
> And hate the idle pleasures of these days.

Do we go Freud's route of the twisted adult bruised by childhood experience – bullying at school, jeering in the shower – and now hell-bent on revenge? Or is it hatred of his mother?

> **DUCHESS OF YORK:** God bless thee, and put meekness in
> thy breast,
> Love, charity obedience and true duty!
>
> **RICHARD:** Amen! (*Aside*) And make me die a good old man!
> That is the butt-end of a mother's blessing;
> I marvel that her grace did leave it out.
>
> (Act II, Scene ii)

Envy of his brother? ('Simple, plain Clarence, I do love thee so / That I will shortly send thy soul to heaven.) Of the world? Whatever the cause, Richard's descant on his own deformity is a mocking self-cynicism that invites us to agree with him about how ugly he is, and therefore complicitly involves us in his deeds. Are the monstrous aspects of his appearance a reason or a pretext – merely an excuse in order to use them as a source of malevolent power?

As with other existential figures in Shakespeare, Richard is going along fine until doubt sets in. As long as the mind is moving forward, for men of action there is no problem. As soon as you start looking over your shoulder, that's the danger sign. The great poker player always plays the odds – is never tempted into a rash bet because of a hunch. That isn't to say that risks aren't taken, but along with that taken risk goes calculation. No leader ever lasted long merely by betting on certainties, but the better ones (notice I don't say 'good' – I'm not altogether sure what constitutes a 'good leader') know that nine times out of ten the risk that they take will pay off. Because the world believes that people are inherently 'good', it trusts the tiger with the wide grin, not recognising that the spread of the jaw is a prelude to devouring the onlooker. The Richard of action travels an almost obstacle-free path to the throne, the fox among the chickens. The Woodvilles and Greys make an awful lot of clucking, rushing around headless until the farmer arrives to sort it all out with his shotgun.

But the seed of Richard's downfall has already been planted in his own head. 'I could be bounded in a nutshell and count myself a king of infinite space were it not that I have bad dreams' (*Hamlet*, Act II.ii). Richard has bad dreams (the play is notable for containing more references to dreams than any other of Shakespeare's plays. Apart from *The Tempest* – itself a dream). His infinite space disappears. He turns inward. Instead of setting about cementing his relationship with the country, outflanking his enemies by turning domestic politician, paranoia sets in. Like Macbeth before (or, rather, after) him, he is

> . . . in blood
> Stepped in so far, that, should I wade no more,
> Returning were as tedious as go o'er.

> (*Macbeth*, Act III, Scene iv)

and like Lady Macbeth, Buckingham can no longer follow where Richard leads. Both Lady Macbeth and Buckingham fail to understand the nature of the beast to which they are yoked. Neither sees beyond the point of achieving the throne. To stay there at the top demands the purge, the elimination, the Night of the Long Knives, of all possible challengers. The uneasy head is prey to his own imagination. 'In the night imagining some fear / How easy is a Bush supposed a Blair' – A Midsummer Nightmare.[1]

KING RICHARD: Stand all apart. Cousin of Buckingham –

BUCKINGHAM: My gracious sovereign?

KING RICHARD: Give me thy hand.
*Sound*
*Here he ascendeth the throne*
Thus high, by thy advice
And thy assistance, is King Richard seated.
But shall we wear these glories for a day?
Or shall they last, and we rejoice in them?

BUCKINGHAM: Still live they, and for ever let them last!

KING RICHARD: Ah, Buckingham, now do I play the touch,
To try if thou be current gold indeed.
Young Edward lives. Think now what I would speak.

BUCKINGHAM: Say on, my loving lord.

KING RICHARD: Why, Buckingham, I say I would be king.

BUCKINGHAM: Why, so you are, my thrice-renownèd lord.

KING RICHARD: Ha! Am I king? 'Tis so. But Edward lives.

BUCKINGHAM: True, noble prince.

KING RICHARD: O bitter consequence
That Edward still should live true noble prince!
Cousin, thou wast not wont to be so dull.
Shall I be plain? I wish the bastards dead,
And I would have it suddenly performed.
What sayst thou now? Speak suddenly, be brief.

BUCKINGHAM: Your grace may do your pleasure.

KING RICHARD: Tut, tut, thou art all ice; thy kindness freezes.
Say, have I thy consent that they shall die?

BUCKINGHAM: Give me some little breath, some pause,
                        dear lord,
Before I positively speak in this.
I will resolve you herein presently.

                        (Act IV, Scene ii)

The 'deep-revolving, witty Buckingham', the Mandelson of his day, so skilled and adept at manipulating, suddenly fails to spot the strategically-placed banana skin, not only failing to step over it but hypnotised into placing his foot slap bang in the middle. The fickle, chameleon mind of the serial killer knows no rest, owes no loyalty:

> KING RICHARD: I will converse with iron-witted fools
> And unrespective boys. None are for me
> That look into me with considerate eyes.
> High-reaching Buckingham grows circumspect.
>
> (Act IV, Scene ii)

Richard is on the way down. Every move now will be an attempt to defend his position. The Macbethian bear chained to the stake. The retention of the crown now becomes the imperative, all thought of governing abandoned. It is inevitable that he will look for omens where he once gave the finger to fate. Claudius too becomes politically paralysed in the face of Hamlet's idiosyncrasy. The man who murdered his brother in order to take over the defence of the country – setting it on a war footing, initiating an immediate twenty-four-hour round-the-clock arms race – is strategically enfeebled by fear. Brutus on the eve of Philippi conjures up a vision of the murdered Caesar. Richard, on the eve of the Battle of Bosworth, summons up the lot – Anne, Clarence, the Princes, Rivers, Vaughan, Grey, Buckingham all those he's done away with. We know he's going to lose; it's not just a question of the sun not shining, in his head he's already blown it. Funny how ghosts always appear at the right psychological moment. They never turn up when we're having a good time – always seem to know when we're on a downer.

> KING RICHARD: Give me another horse! Bind up my wounds!
> Have mercy, Jesu! – Soft! I did but dream.
> O coward conscience, how dost thou afflict me!
> The lights burn blue. It is now dead midnight.
> Cold fearful drops stand on my trembling flesh.
> What do I fear? Myself? There's none else by.
> Richard loves Richard: that is, I am I.
> Is there a murderer here? No. Yes, I am.
> Then fly. What, from myself? Great reason why –
> Lest I revenge. Myself upon myself?
> Alack, I love myself. Wherefore? For any good
> That I myself have done unto myself?
> O no! Alas, I rather hate myself

> For hateful deeds committed by myself.
> I am a villain. Yet I lie, I am not.
> Fool, of thyself speak well. Fool, do not flatter.
> My conscience hath a thousand several tongues,
> And every tongue brings in a several tale,
> And every tale condemns me for a villain.
> Perjury, perjury, in the highest degree.
> Murder, stern murder, in the direst degree,
> All several sins, all used in each degree,
> Throng to the bar, crying all 'Guilty! Guilty!
> I shall despair. There is no creature loves me;
> And if I die, no soul will pity me.
> Nay, wherefore should they, since that I myself
> Find in myself no pity to myself?
> Methought the souls of all that I had murdered
> Came to my tent, and every one did threat
> Tomorrow's vengeance on the head of Richard.

(Act V, Scene iii)

Fear of retribution in the next life? A crisis of identity? Throughout history the greatest tyrants and dictators have ultimately fallen prey to over-weaning megalomania to be found finally cowering in a hole – either real or imagined. But not before they have wreaked havoc. And once again, like Macbeth, Romeo, Hamlet, Richard reaches that moment of existential clarity where 'the readiness is all':

> March on, join bravely, let us to't pell-mell,
> If not to heaven, then hand in hand to hell.

Richard, in his action mode, prefigures modern western nihilism, a forerunner of Nietzsche's *Übermensch*, a man for whom morality is a word used to describe cowards, appeasers and religious rabbits. He is an early Eastwood, Schwarzenegger, Stallone, Cruise in *The Collector*, sending a *frisson* of excitement coursing through our veins. We wait for the villain to get his comeuppance, yet will him on to more and more outrageous deeds. He carries a public health warning, the Elizabethan equivalent of an over-18 certificate – at least he would, had we not become desensitised by the gratuitous violence that is now the staple diet on the small and large screen. Were the Elizabethans as sanguine about blood-letting as we are today? Casual slaughter, brutality, disease, inhumanity – the chances of survival into old age were slim. The opiate of religion or existential amorality? An unequal choice, really. Give me life in the here-and-now any day. For if history is no more than an unending, unbroken chain of gigantic slaughter, what remains except a leap into darkness, a world where no laws exist, a choice between death and pleasure, hedonism and pain? Richard III is Shakespeare's homage to Machiavelli. Politics for Richard is the art of acquiring power. Politics is amoral, something practical, akin to engineering, the skill that of the dazzling footwork of a Thiery Henry. Human emotions, people, are clay to be shaped at will. The whole world is there to be thrown on a wheel, producing a pot into which Richard will pour his ambition with a terrifying, ugly, cruel grin on his face. But Richard himself will in time become a lump of clay that another butcher will shape. As Jan Kott says, 'He who thought he was making history becomes himself the object of that history'.[2]

Power, for Shakespeare, is the crown. It is land. It is territory. It is people. But the value goes beyond the pecuniary worth. It is priceless. The crown may be made of gold and heavy but it can be torn off a dying king's head and put on one's own. Then, merely by that one act, you're king. But either you wait until the king is dead or you do it for him (if Macbeth had waited he'd probably have been king anyway). Usurpation of the crown, fratricide, patricide, is a recurring Shakespearean theme. The history of slaughter is seemingly endless.

QUEEN MARGARET: . . . I had an Edward, till a Richard
killed him;
I had a Harry, till a Richard killed him;
Thou hadst an Edward, till a Richard killed him;
Thou hadst a Richard, till a Richard killed him.

DUCHESS OF YORK: I had a Richard too, and thou didst
kill him;
I had a Rutland too, thou holp'st to kill him.

QUEEN MARGARET: Thou hadst a Clarence too, and Richard
killed him.

From forth the kennel of thy womb hath crept
A hellhound that doth hunt us all to death . . .
. . . Thy Edward he is dead, that killed my Edward;
Thy other Edward dead, to quit my Edward;
Young York he is but boot, because both they
Matched not the high perfection of my loss.
Thy Clarence he is dead that stabbed my Edward,
And the beholders of this frantic play,
Th'adulterate Hastings, Rivers, Vaughan, Grey,
Untimely smothered in their dusky graves.
Richard yet lives, hell's black intelligencer;
Only reserved their factor to buy souls
And send them thither . . .

(Act IV, Scene iv)

Shakespearean tragedy, unlike Greek, is not a theatre of moral attitudes in the face of immortal gods. There are no fates, furies, supernatural forces that decide the hero's destiny. In the final analysis, this bare, forked animal is responsible for his own fate. The subject, object, result of the consequences of his own actions. The kings climb the Jan Kott staircase, his Grand Mechanism, pause briefly at the top to brandish a tarnished sword and then topple off, giving way to the next pretender, shuttling and shuffling his way up the moving staircase of history.

. . . There are no innocents . . . evil stems not from Richard but from a history he shares with others.[3]

That history began at the dawn of English dynasty. Save for the princes in the Tower – guilty only by the association of the fact of their birth – all those eliminated by Richard bear the mark of present or earlier crimes. If Clarence and Edward are torn by remorse and guilt, they have reason to be. And if Margaret appears to be an instrument of fate, gloating over the downfall of others as one by one her prophesies come true, this is only a playwright's device for demonstrating the predictability of human greed when power is at stake. What is remarkable is the exactness of the fate assigned by Margaret to each one of Richard's victims:

. . . Can curses pierce the clouds and enter heaven?
Why then, give way, dull clouds, to my quick curses!
Though not by war, by surfeit die your king,
As ours by murder, to make him a king!
Edward thy son, that now is Prince of Wales,
For Edward our son, that was Prince of Wales,
Die in his youth by like untimely violence!
Thyself a queen, for me that was a queen,
Outlive thy glory, like my wretched self!
Long mayst thou live to wail thy children's death
And see another, as I see thee now,
Decked in thy rights as thou art stalled in mine!
Long die thy happy days before thy death,
And after many lengthened hours of grief,
Die neither mother, wife, nor England's queen!
Rivers and Dorset, you were standers-by,
And so wast thou, Lord Hastings, when my son
Was stabbed with bloody daggers. God, I pray Him,
That none of you may live his natural age,
But by some unlooked accident cut off!

(Act I, Scene iii)

Her predictions go off like time-bombs throughout the play. The escalating picture of horror that she paints seems to drive all sense of morality down a never-ending tunnel of darkness, a nightmare world of unending slaughter. Not much sign of God around, then. And having lived to see the cycle of violence eventually broken by Richmond, she returns from whence she came – to France, a catalyst yet a survivor of the bloodiest episode in Britain's civil history. Strange that she didn't spot Buckingham's downfall, though:

O Princely Buckingham, I'll kiss thy hand
In sign of league and amity with thee.
Now fair befall thee and thy noble house!
Thy garments are not spotted with our blood,
Nor thou within the compass of my curse.

(Act I, Scene iii)

Just shows that clairvoyance is an inexact science.

And what about Anne? Of what was she guilty? Marrying Richard in the first place. Much has been made of the fate of a young, defenceless girl, cast adrift in a world of sharks. What alternative had she to the offer of the hand of a powerful, charismatic figure? Well, she could have said no. In Shakespeare, girls do. But in one of the most remarkable seduction scenes in world drama, Richard literally woos her over the dead body of her father in law, seducing her at the very moment of her deepest hate.

> . . . What though I killed her husband and her father?
> The readiest way to make the wench amends
> Is to become her husband and her father,
> The which will I – not all so much for love
> As for another secret close intent
> By marrying her which I must reach unto . . .
>
> (Act I, Scene i)

What dark subterranean sexual emotions did he awaken in her as his hand encompassed her breast? What black art of lust was unleashed in her young body to divert her so utterly from grieving? True, at moments of extreme emotion we are not always responsible for our responses but the awakening of desire in her at such a moment tells us more about Shakespeare's understanding of how sex drives our passions than all the acres of paper spent on Bill and Monica. 'Take up the sword again, or take up me' (Act I.ii) Maybe she does have no choice. Unable to kill him in cold blood, Anne surrenders. But going off without a backward glance, his ring on her finger? And what is the 'secret close intent' to which Richard alludes? Having taken us completely into his confidence, sharing every thought and plan with us, why does he now withhold something from us in his relationship with Anne? Some political pimping afoot, with Anne as the sexual bait? A predilection for S and M? Maybe humping for Richard has a different connotation. Curious.

The two scenes involving the seduction of Anne and the attempted seduction of Elizabeth are the most remarkable in the play. In the latter, Richard attempts his tried and trusted technique on the young Elizabeth's mother. Another Plantagenet queen for his bed to bring forth yet more Plantagenets. Even Richard has one eye on his own mortality.

Shakespeare often throws in a long verbal scene as in Act IV, ostensibly to give the protagonist a cigarette break in the dressing room before the big fight in Act V: *Hamlet, Macbeth, Coriolanus*. But here Richard is still in action, doing verbal battle with a strong woman more than his equal:

QUEEN ELIZABETH: How canst thou woo her?

KING RICHARD: That would I learn of you,
As one being best acquainted with her humour.

QUEEN ELIZABETH: And wilt thou learn of me?

KING RICHARD: Madam, with all my heart.

QUEEN ELIZABETH: Send to her by the man that slew her brothers
A pair of bleeding hearts; thereon engrave
'Edward' and 'York'; then haply will she weep.
Therefore present to her – as sometimes Margaret
Did to thy father, steeped in Rutland's blood –
A handkerchief, which say to her did drain
The purple sap from her sweet brother's body,
And bid her wipe her weeping eyes withal.
If this inducement move her not to love,
Send her a letter of thy noble deeds:
Tell her thou mad'st away her uncle Clarence,
Her uncle Rivers; yea, and for her sake,
Mad'st quick conveyance with her good aunt Anne!

KING RICHARD: You mock me, madam; this is not the way
To win your daughter.

(Act IV, Scene iv)

Act IV.iv has ostensibly the same structure as Act I.ii. Both follow the grieving for husbands, sons, daughters lost to Richard's death machine. Immediately prior to his entrance, Elizabeth has lamented the death of her two young sons. But where the scene with Anne was a striking demonstration of his powers, this is Richard's first big failure. The verbal thrust and parry is reminiscent of many a Shakespeare scene where the exchanges echo the dexterity of Elizabethan sword-play. Every attempt at forcing an opening is met with a reminder for Richard (and for us) of the litany of crimes he has committed. Mind you, it's a bit of a long shot trying to woo the mother of two young boys you've just done away with.

QUEEN ELIZABETH: What were I best to say? Her father's brother
Would be her lord? Or shall I say her uncle?
Or he that slew her brothers and her uncles?
Under what title shall I woo for thee
That God, the law, my honour, and her love
Can make seem pleasing to her tender years?

KING RICHARD: Infer fair England's peace by this alliance.

QUEEN ELIZABETH: Which she shall purchase with still-
lasting war.

KING RICHARD: Tell her the King, that may command, entreats.

QUEEN ELIZABETH: That at her hands which the King's
king forbids.

KING RICHARD: Say she shall be a high and mighty queen.

QUEEN ELIZABETH: To vail the title, as her mother doth.

KING RICHARD: Say I will love her everlastingly.

QUEEN ELIZABETH: But how long shall that title 'ever' last?

KING RICHARD: Sweetly in force unto her fair life's end.

QUEEN ELIZABETH: But how long fairly shall her sweet life last?

KING RICHARD: As long as heaven and nature lengthens it.

QUEEN ELIZABETH: As long as hell and Richard likes of it.

KING RICHARD: Say I, her sovereign, am her subject love.

QUEEN ELIZABETH: But she, your subject, loathes such
sovereignty.

KING RICHARD: Be eloquent in my behalf to her.

QUEEN ELIZABETH: An honest tale speeds best being
plainly told.

KING RICHARD: Then plainly to her tell my loving tale.

QUEEN ELIZABETH: Plain and honest is too harsh a style.

KING RICHARD: Your reasons are too shallow and too quick.

QUEEN ELIZABETH: O no, my reasons are too deep and dead –
Too deep and dead, poor infants, in their graves.

KING RICHARD: Harp not on that string, madam; that is past.

QUEEN ELIZABETH: Harp on it still shall I till heartstrings break.

Off she goes,

**QUEEN ELIZABETH: I go. Write to me very shortly,
And you shall understand from me her mind.**
**KING RICHARD: Bear her my true love's kiss; and so farewell –**
*Exit Queen Elizabeth.*
**Relenting fool, and shallow, changing woman!**

How should we be left? Does Elizabeth let him kiss her? If she does, is it a ploy to lure him into a false sense of security? 'Relenting fool and shallow changing woman'. Do we believe him? Is it necessary for the dramatic tension to believe he had a chance? We've already seen Anne succumb to his flattery. Is it tenable a second time so late in the play? I think not. And seeing Richard not believing it himself, even as he utters the words of contempt for her apparent reversal, leaves us tingling with anticipation as to how his final demise will be achieved. In the very next scene we learn that Elizabeth has offered her daughter to Richmond, thus cementing the Plantagenets and the Tudors, bringing a temporary pause in the hundred years of civil mayhem in the name of Divine Right. The Wars of the Roses are at an end. Not for another hundred and fifty years would Briton fight Briton, and then it was yet again to break the stranglehold of the royal family on the ruling of the country. But this time the cause was Republicanism. Oliver Cromwell. What a pity he failed. Maybe it was an act of God . . .

## Notes

1. Misquote from A Midsummer Nights Dream, 'In the night imagining some fear / How easy is a bush supposed a bear', Act V.1
2. *Shakespeare Our Contemporary,* Jan Kott, Methuen, 1964.
3. *The Dark Generations of Richard III, Criticism, Issue 1, Vol. 1, Article 3,* Murray Krieger, University of Illinois, 1959.

# Bibliography

**Tragedies and Comedies Introduction**
*Political Shakespeare,* ed. Jonathan Dolimore and Alan Sinfield, MUP 1985

**Hamlet**
*Short Organum for the Theatre,* Bertolt Brecht form the Introduction to *Die Dreigroschenoper (The Threepenny Opera)*

**Romeo and Juliet**
*The Family, Sex and Marriage in England, 1500–1800,* Lawrence Stone, London 1977

**The Tempest**
*Napoleon Immortal,* James Kemble, John Murray, 1959
*Selected Poems,* W.H. Auden, Faber and Faber, 1979
*Dreams and Nightmares,* J.A. Hadfield, Penguin, 1954

**A Midsummer Night's Dream**
*Shakespeare and the Welsh,* Frederick Harries, Unwin, 1919

**Twelfth Night**
*The Illusion of Power,* Stephen Orgel, UCP, 1975

**Macbeth**
*Die Rauber* Franz Schiller, Mannheim, 1782
*William Shakespeare,* Terry Eagleton, Basil Blackwell, 1986

**King Lear**
*Lear, Tolstoy and the Fool,* George Orwell, Polemic Magazine No 7, 1947
*King Lear: Writers and their Work,* Terence Hawkes, Northcote House, 1995

## Histories Introduction

*The English Shakespeare Company, The Story of 'The War of the Roses'*, 1986–1989 by Michael Bogdanov and Michael Pennington, Nick Hern Books, 1989

## Henry IVs

*Theory and Practice,* ed. Nigel Wood, OUP, 1995

*The Elizabethan World Picture,* E.M.W. Tillyard, Chatto & Windsor, 1943

*Sources of Shakespeare* Vol. IV, Geoffrey Bullough, Columbia UP, 1962

## Henry V

*Characters of Shakespeare's Plays,* Hazlitt, Wiley & Puttnam, 1945

*Shakespeare: A Critical Study of His Mind and Art,* Edward Dowden. A course of lectures at Trinity College Dublin, 1875

*Chronicles of England, Scotland and Ireland,* Holinshed

## Henry VIs

*Green's Groatsworth of Wit, Bought with a Million of Repentance,* Pamphlet 1592

*Shakepeare's Political Drama,* Alexander Legatt, Routledge, London 1988

## Richard III

*Shakespeare Our Contemporary,* Jan Kott, Methuen, 1964

*The Dark Generations of Richard III, Criticism, Issue 1, Vol. 1, Article 3,* Murray Krieger, University of Illinois, 1959

# Appendices

# Appendix I

**LADY MORTIMER:** (*weeping*)
**Pied mynd I ryfela, f'anwylyd,**
(Go not to these wars, my love)
**Pied mynd I gyflafan ddisynnwyr a ladd gariad ieuanc**
(Go not to the senseless slaughter of a love that is young)
**sym or ddi rodres a ieuenctid ei hunan.**
(And green as youth itself)
**Pied mynd I refela!**
(Go not to these wars!)

**MORTIMER:** This is the deadly spite that angers me;
My wife can speak no English, I no Welsh.

**GLENDOWER:** My daughter weeps: she will not part with you;
She'll be a soldier too, she'll to the wars.

**MORTIMER:** Good father, tell her that she and my aunt Percy
Shall follow in your conduct speedily.

**GLENDOWER:** Pied gofidio, fy merch, cei di a'th
(Do not worry girl, you and your)
**Chwaer-yng-nghyfraith ddilyn eich cariadon.**
(Sister-in-law can follow your loves)

**LADY MORTIMER:** Dilyn? I'r rhyfel?
(Follow? To the war?)

**GLENDOWER:** Cewch fod gyda nhw iw diddanu a'u.
(You may go with them to comfort them)
**hanog yng nghanol y frwydr.**
(And cheer them on in battle)

**LADY MORTIMER:** Cenedl ydym yn gwastraffu ein bywydau in meistri
(We are a nation wasting ourselves)

**Mewn rhyfeloedd ofer,**
(In fruitless battles for our masters)
**Mewn tiroedd nad oes gennym hawl arnynt**
(In lands to which we have no claim)
**Gyda dynion nad ydym yn eu casau**
(With men for whom we feel no hatred)
**Pied mynd I ryfela!**
(Go not to these wars!)

**GLENDOWER: She is desperate here; a peevish self-wind harlotry,**
**One that no persuasion can do good upon.**
**Fy merch, daw dim daioni o'r anfodlonrwydd yma!**
(My girl, no good will come of this reluctance!)

**LADY MORTIMER: Fy nhad, mae dyn un anferth dros fud bychan**
(Father, man is huge in a small world)
**Yn ei dywylly a'i falchder**
(Overshadowed by his pride)

**GLENDOWER: Dere 'ma, Catrin fach**
(Come here, Catrin bach)
**Rhoeddem yn genedl, acydym eto, pan**
(We are a nation still, and when)
**rhown heibio gweryla am friwsion o dan**
(we have finished grovelling for crumbs)
**fwrdd gnoi esgyrn diwilliant**
(under the table or gnawing)
**diflanedig. Ail atgyfodwn eto, wedi ein**
(on the bones of a dead culture, we will arise, armed)
**harfogi. Ond nid, dwi'n gobeithio, o dan yr hen drefn.**
(armed. But not in the old way)
**Cofia ddeall, Catrin Fach, 'na i gyd.**
(Try to understand, Catrin Bach, that's all)

**LADY MORTIMER: Annwylyd.**
(My love)
**Carcharwyd fi hyd nes y dathost ataf,**
(I was in prison until you came)
**Dy lais oedd yr allwedd a agorodd y**
(Your voice was a key turning)
**Clo anferth i anobaith. A agorodd y**
(in the enormous lock of hopelessness)

**drws i'm gollwng i neu dy adael**
(Did the door open to let me out)
**Di i mewn?**
(Or you in)

MORTIMER: I understand thy looks that pretty Welsh
Which thou pour'st down from these swelling heavens
I am too perfect in, and, but for shame,
In such a parley should I answer thee.

LADY MORTIMER: **Does dim amser i fwu a llai i farw, felly**
(No time there is for life and even less)
**Gyda'm holl ewllys ond yn erbyn**
(For death. So with my whole will)
**Dymuniad fy nghalon, ymwahanwn ein**
(But against the wishes of my heart)
**Dau yn awr,**
(We'll separate now)

MORTIMER: I understand thy kisses and thou mine,
And that's a feeling disputation:
But I will never be a truant, love,
Till I have learned thy language, for thy tongue
Makes Welsh as sweet as ditties highly penn'd,
Sung by a fair queen in a summer's bower,
With ravishing division, to her lute.

GLENDOWER: Nay, if you melt, then will she run mad.
**Dyna ddigion, fymerth cana, cana i mi**
(Enough, girl, daughter sing, sing for me)

LADY MORTIMER: **Rho dy ben, f'anwylyd, ar fy nghol a**
(Lay your head my love, in my lap)
**Chanaf gan i leddfu dy fryd anesmwyth.**
(And I'll sing to soothe your troubled mind)

MORTIMER: O, I am ignorance itself in this!

GLENDOWER: She bids you rest your gentle head upon her lap,
And she will sing the song that pleaseth you
And those musicians that shall play to you
Hang in the air a thousand leagues from hence,
And straight they shall be here: sit, and attend.

# Appendix II

## The Ballad Of Harry Le Roy

Come all you good people who would hear a song
Of men bold and men brave, of men weak and men strong;
Of a king who was mighty but wild as a boy,
And list to the ballad of Harry Le Roy.

*Of a King who was mighty but wild as a boy,*
*And list to the ballad of Harry Le Roy.*

Thirteen ninety and eight is the year we begin,
King Richard the Second the reign we are in;
Two Lords fought a duel one bright summer's day,
Henry Bolingbroke of Lancaster and Thomas Mowbray.

*Of a King who was mighty but wild as a boy,*
*And list to the ballad of Harry Le Roy.*

Both mounted with lances on fire for the fight
Their horses a-flame, brave knight against knight
'Stop the joust' called King Richard, at the very last breath,
'Henceforth you're both exiled upon pain of death.'

*Of a King who was mighty but wild as a boy,*
*And list to the ballad of Harry Le Roy.*

One year passes by, Henry Bolingbroke returns,
At the head of an army for vengeance he burns
Defeats and imprisons King Richard alone,
Then murders him shamefully, seizes the throne.

*Of a King who was mighty but wild as a boy,*
*And list to the ballad of Harry Le Roy.*

# Michael Bogdanov
# Shakespeare Productions

**1970/1**
Assistant Director Royal Shakespeare Company (RSC) to John Barton, Terry Hands, Trevor Nunn, David Jones, Robin Phillips, Peter Brook (*A Midsummer Nights Dream* – Associate Director on World Tour).

**1971**
*Two Gentleman of Verona* (Os Dos Cabelléros di Verona). Tearto Ruth Escobar, Sao Paulo Brazil.

**1972**
*The Tempest*, Newcastle Playhouse. Designer – Stephanie Howard. Prospero – Bill Wallis.

**1974**
*Twelfth Night*, The Phoenix Theatre, Leicester. Designer – Mike Bearwish. Olivia – Heather Sears. Orsino – Darryl Forbes-Dawson.

**1974**
*Romeo and Juliet*, Haymarket Theatre, Leicester. Designer – Adrian Vaux. Romeo – Jonathan Kent. Juliet – Mary Rutherford. Mercutio – Bill Wallis. Paris – Alan Rickman.

**1975**
*Hamlet*, The Phoenix Theatre, Leicester. Designer – Paul Bannister. Hamlet – Hugh Thomas. Claudius – Bill Wallis.

**1975**
'He That Plays the King' Trilogy; *Richard III, Hamlet, The Tempest*. The Phoenix Theatre, Leicester. Designer – Paul Bannister. Hamlet, Prospero & Richard III – Bill Wallis.

**1978**
*The Taming of the Shrew*, RSC, Stratford. Designer – Chris Dyer. Petruchio – Jonathan Pryce. Katherina – Paula Dionissotti. Grumio – David Suchet. Tranio – Ian Charleson. Bianca – Zoe Wannamaker.

**1979**
*Hamlet, The Tempest, Richard III* – The 'Action Man' Trilogy, The Young Vic Theatre. Designer – Paul Bannister. Hamlet – Phil Bowen. Richard III and Prospero – Bill Wallis.

**1979**
*The Taming of the Shrew* – RSC, The Aldwych Theatre, London. Cast as before. Society of West End Theatres (SWET) Director of the Year Award.

**1980**
The 'Action Man' Trilogy, The Old Vic Theatre, London. Hamlet – Tony Milner. Richard III & Prospero – Bill Wallis.

**1982**
*Macbeth*, The National Theatre Educational Touring Production. Macbeth – Greg Hicks.

**1983**
*Romeo and Juliet*, The Imperial Theatre, Tokyo, Japan. Designer – Chris Dyer.

**1984**
*Hamlet*, The Abbey Theatre, Dublin. Designer – Juliet Watkinson. Hamlet – Stephen Brennan.

**1985**
*Measure for Measure*, The Stratford Memorial Theatre, Ontario, Canada. Designer – Chris Dyer. The Duke – Alan Scarfe.

**1986**
*Julius Ceaser*, The Deutsches Shauspielhaus, Hamburg (The National Theatre). Designer – Chris Dyer. Brutus – Michel Degen. Cassius – Dietrich Mattausch. Antony – Uli Tukur.

**1986**
*The Henrys*, The English Shakespeare Company (ESC). Designers – Chris Dyer & Stephanie Howard. Hal, Henry V – Michael Pennington. Falstaff – John Woodvine.

# Michael Bogdanov Shakespeare Productions

**1986**
*Romeo & Juliet*, RSC. Designer – Chris Dyer. Romeo – Sean Bean. Juliet – Naimh Cusack. Mercutio – Michael Kitchen. Tybalt – Hugh Quarshie.

**1987**
*Romeo & Juliet*, The Barbican Theatre, London. Cast – as before.

**1987 – 1989**
*The Wars of the Roses*, English Shakespeare Company World Tour. Designers – Chris Dyer & Stephanie Howard. Richard II, Hal, Henry V – Michael Penningon. Henry VI – Paul Brennan. Richard III – Andrew Jarvis. Falstaff – Barry Stanton. Lawrence Olivier Award for Best Director.

**1989**
*Hamlet*, The Deutsches Schauspielhaus, Hamburg. Designer – Bill Dudley. Hamlet – Uli Tukur. Claudius – Christian Redl. Gertrude – Ilse Ritter.

**1990**
*Romeo & Juliet*, The Deutsches Shauspielhaus, Hamburg. Designer – Chris Dyer. Romeo – Marcus Bluum. Juliet – Caterin Striebeck. Tybalt – Hugh Quarshie. Lady Capulet – Monica Bleibtreu, Nurse – Christa Berndl.

**1990**
*Coriolanus* and *The Winter's Tale*, The ESC World Tour. Designers – Chris Dyer and Claire Lyth. Corialanus / Leontes – Michael Pennington (TMA Best touring Production).

**1991**
*The Tempest*, The Deutsches Schauspielhaus, Hamburg. Designer – Chris Dyer. Prospero – Uli Wildgruber.

**1992**
*Macbeth*, ESC. Designer – Claire Lyth. Macbeth – Michael Pennington. Lady Macbeth – Jenny Quayle.

**1992**
*Macbeth*, ESC; a landrover tour of Sierra Leone, Ghana, Namibia, Malawi – Africa. Designer – Claire Lyth. Macbeth – Don Warrington. Lady Macbeth – Lynne Farleigh.

**1992**
*Macbeth* and *The Tempest*, ESC World Tour. Macbeth – Tony Haygarth. Lady Macbeth – Lynne Farleigh. Prospero – John Woodvine.

**1994**
*Romeo & Juliet*, ESC. Designer – Chris Dyer. Romeo – Jo Dixon. Juliet – Joanna Roth.

**1997**
*Timon of Athens*, The Chicago Shakespeare Theatre, Chicago. Designer – Ralph Koltai. Timon – Larry Yando.

**1997**
*Macbeth*, Bayerisches Staatsschauspiel in Munich. Designer – Claire Lyth. Macbeth – Uli Tukur. Lady Macbeth – Julia Köhler.

**1998**
*Anthony & Cleopatra* and *As You Like It*, ESC, Bath Shakespeare Festival. Designers – Geraldine Bunzl & Yannis Thavoris. Anthony – Tim Woodward. Cleopatra – Cathy Tyson. Rosalind – Ivy Omere.

**2000**
*Troilus & Cressida*, The Bell Shakespeare Company for the Olympic Arts Festival, Sydney Opera House, Australia. Designer – Michael Scott-Mitchell and Ulrike Engelbrecht. Troilus – Toby Truslove, Cressida – Blazey Best, Pandarus – Billie Brown.

**2001**
*The Merry Wives of Windsor* Texas (Lone Star Love) a new musical for the great Lakes Festival, Cleveland, Ohio, Falstaff, Jim Belushi, Music – The Red Clay Ramblers.

**2002**
*The Merry Wives of Windsor*, Ludlow Festival. Designer – Chris Dyer. Falstaff – Philip Madoc.

**2003**
*The Winter's Tale*, Chicago Shakespeare Theatre, Chicago. Designers – Derek McClane and Claire Lyth. Leontes – John Reeger. Hermione – Barbara Robertson.

**2003**
*The Merchant of Venice* and *The Winter's Tale*, The Ludlow Festival. Designers – Chris Dyer & Mel Wing. Leontes – Russell Gomer. Hermione – Nickie Rainsford., Shylock – Philip Madoc. Portia – Heledd Baskerville.

**2004**

*Cymbeline* and *Twelfth Night* – The Ludlow Festival. Designers Ed Thomas and Sian Jenkins. Imogen – Nia Roberts, Cymbeline – John Labanowski, Malvolio – Paul Greenwood, Viola – Heledd Baskerville.

**2004**

*Twelfth Night*, Cymbeline, The Merchant of Venice – The Wales Theatre Company. Designers – Ed Thomas, Sean Crowley, Sian Jenkins. Malvolio – Paul Greenwood, Imogen – Lisa Zahra, Shylock – Philip Madoc. Feste – Bill Wallis, Viola – Heledd Baskerville, Cymbeline, John Lanowski.

**2005**

*Hamlet*, The Wales Theatre Company. Bi-lingual, back to back Welsh / English language production. Designers Ed Thomas & Sean Crowley. Hamlet (English) Wayne Cater – (Welsh) Gareth John Bale.

**2005**

*Lone Star Love* (The Merry Wives of Windsor Texas) off-Broadway New York. Designers – Derek Maclean, Joan Greenwood. Falstaff – J.O. Sanders.

**2008**

*Romeo & Juliet* – The Wales Theatre Company. Designer – Sean Crowley. Floats – Malcolm Ransom. Romeo – Jack Ryder. Juliet – Sara Lloyd Gregory.

**2010**

Invisible Bullets. Project devised with the students of the Schule Für Schauspiel, Hamburg. An investigation of Shakespeare the Subversive.

**2011**

*A Midsummer Night's Dream* (Sommernachts Droom). Plattdeutsch. The opening production of the new Ohnsorg Theater, Hamburg.

**2012**

Powerplay. A devised project based on 'The Taming of the Shrew' with the students of Gouler College, Swansea.

# TV & Film

**1982**

*Shakespeare Lives*, Channel 4. Twelve part series live from the Roundhouse, London.

**1987**

*Julius Ceaser*, ZDF, Germany.

**1990**

*The Wars of the Roses* – The English Shakespeare Company 7 play History cycle. Portman Films.

**1995**

*Shakespeare on the Estate*, BBC Bard on the Box series. (Royal Television Society Award Best Documentary. BAFTA Nomination, Banff Film Festival Award Best Documentary.

**1996**

*The Tempest in Butetown* – 90 minute feature film for BBC with the residents of Tiger Bay, Cardiff.

**1997**

*Macbeth*, Granada – Channel 4. Macbeth – Sean Pertwee. Lady Macbeth – Greta Scacci. Malcolm – Jack Davenport. Banquo – Michael Maloney.

**2004**

*The Welsh in Shakespeare*, BBC 60 minute drama documentary with Michael Sheen, Philip Madoc, Mark Lewis Jones.

**2010**

Invisible Bullets. 60 minutes exploring Shakespeare the Subversive.

# Theatre The Director's Cue
## by Michael Bogdanov

The theatre from the Director's perspective: this is a scintillating series of theatrical insights, autobiographical anecdotes and a response to critics. It touches on Peter Brook's production of *A Midsummer Night's Dream*, the history cycle, *The Wars of the Roses* and *The Romans in Britain* with its ensuing private prosecution on indecency brought by Mary Whitehouse. Comparisons are drawn between the British, German and Japanese approach to theatre and also the daily problems facing a director.

> **Michael Bogdanov is the Tyrone Guthrie of our day, and his signature is all over the work of many younger directors. He is at once scholar, provocateur, puritan and Lord of Misrule.**
> **Michael Pennington**

DOP:     08 August 2013

ISBN:    978-1-909305-34-2

Price:   £9.99

**www.capercailliebooks.co.uk**

Capercaillie Books